DIGITAL SLR HANDBOOK

JON SPARKS

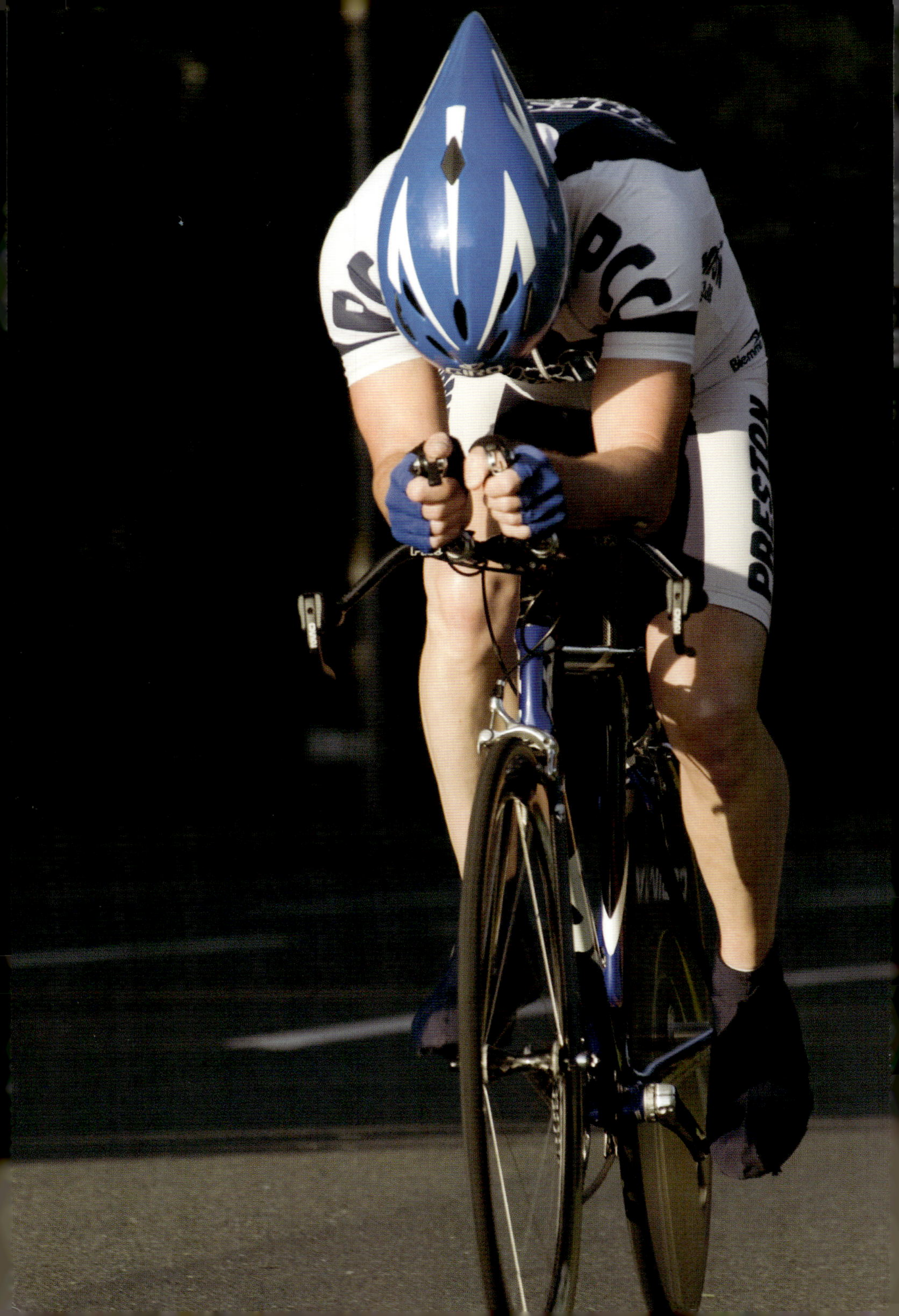
PCC
PRESTON

DIGITAL SLR HANDBOOK

JON SPARKS

AMMONITE
PRESS

First published 2009 by
Ammonite Press,
an imprint of AE Publications Ltd,
Castle Place, 166 High Street,
Lewes, East Sussex BN7 1XU

ISBN 978-1-906672-49-2

A catalogue record for this book is available from the British Library.

Editors Ailsa McWhinnie and Beth Wicks
Design Luke Herriott

Set in Trade Gothic
Colour origination by GMC Reprographics
Printed and bound by Hung Hing Printing Co. Ltd.

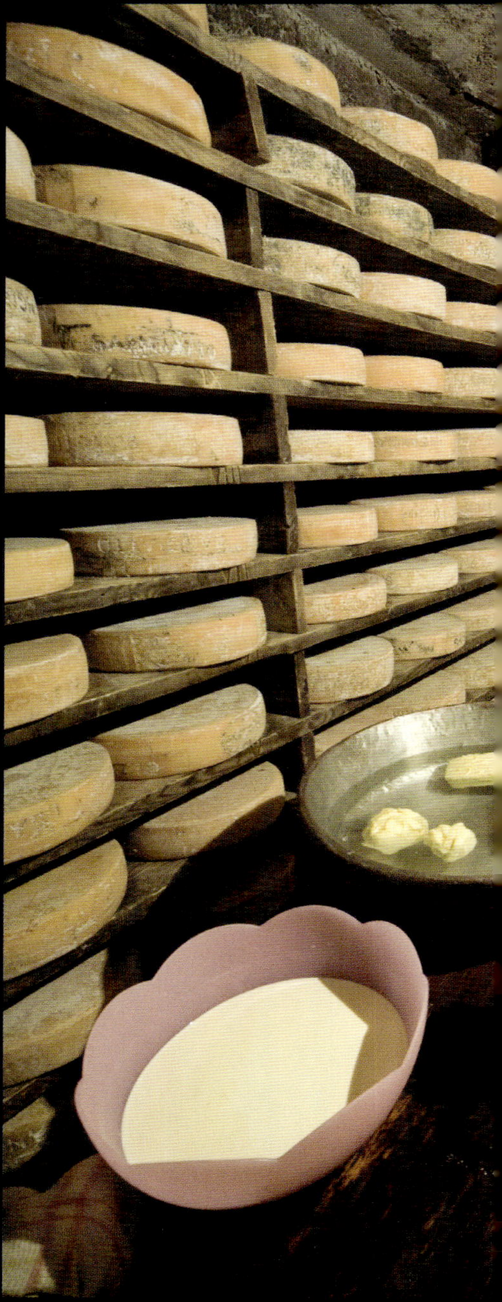

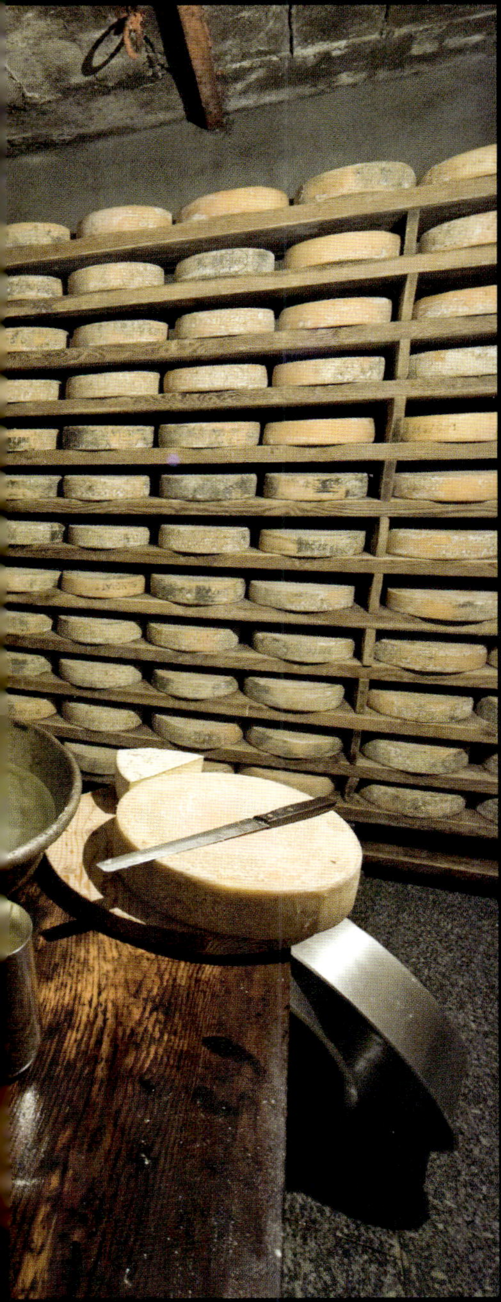

CONTENTS

Artisan cheese production at Crampiolo, Parco Naturale Veglia Devero, Italy
Nikon D700, focal length 16mm, ISO 6400, 1/10sec at f/7.1

Introduction

The other day I took a long hard look at the digital SLR in my hands. It happened to be a Nikon D90, a good mid-range camera and not by any means the most complex. Here's what I found: nine control buttons on the back; four buttons on the top, plus a mode dial (with 11 possible positions); four more buttons on the front, plus a focus mode selector (there are seven different focusing modes altogether, including Manual and Live View options). There's also a choice of 11 focus points. Then there are two command dials, main and sub, with various functions on their own and at least 11 when used in conjunction with other buttons.

Then there are the menus, six in all with more than 90 menu items, many of them boasting multiple options and in some cases sub-menus with yet more choices. The Custom Setting Menu alone has 41 items, each offering anything from two to 10 options.

By this point, calculating the total number of permutations of different settings and parameters was way beyond me. It certainly runs into thousands, more likely millions. And that's not counting the number of different lenses available – well over 50 from Nikon alone, plus many more from independent makers – not to mention the various flashguns and other accessories.

This is both bad and good news. It's easy to feel overwhelmed by all these choices, potentially to the point where you don't make any decisions at all and simply leave the camera on the default settings. This might be OK if you're an average photographer taking average photos of average subjects under average conditions. But it's my belief that none of us, and especially not readers of this book, are average.

That's why the feature-rich nature of a camera like the D90 is also good news. Any digital camera, even quite a modest model, offers a range of options that simply didn't exist with film. As for the digital SLR, it is arguably the most powerful, versatile and flexible camera yet developed. It can do just about everything that you could do with film, plus a great deal more. It can be exactly the camera you need it to be.

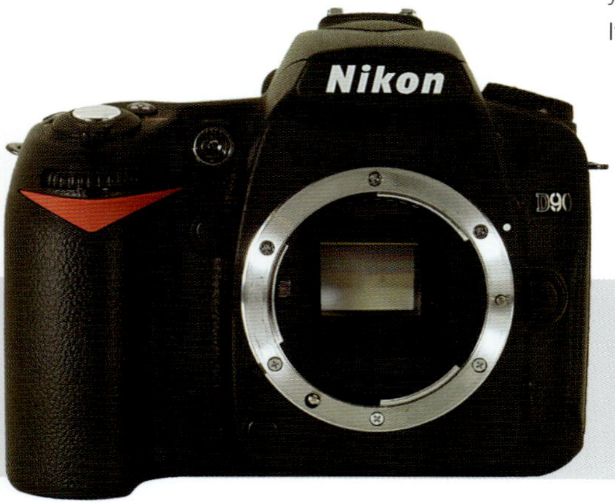

The Nikon D90
A fairly representative DSLR.

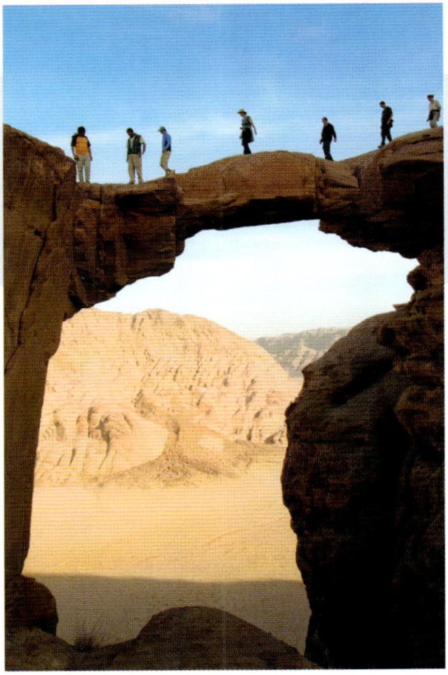

Trekkers on Rock Bridge, Jebel Burdah, Wadi Rum, Jordan
A DSLR has the potential to do justice to the most extraordinary experiences.
Nikon D70, focal length 21mm, ISO 200, 1/200sec at f/11

The even better news is that this book is specifically intended to help you find a clear path through it all. It should help you firstly, to make sure you have the right DSLR and, second, that you're in a position to make the most of all the imaging power and creative flexibility that lurks inside every DSLR, just waiting to be unleashed.

Yet there are some things this book can't tell you. Above all, only you can decide what kind of photographer you want to be. This refers not only to the type of pictures you want to take, but also how involved you want to be in the process. Are you happy to let the camera make lots of decisions for you or do you want to assert your independence at every stage, with all that implies? More input requires a bit more effort, but it also means a lot more control, more creative satisfaction and greater confidence that your pictures are going to look exactly the way you want.

Using your DSLR to its full potential means thinking about how you want to operate; the now-usual term for this is 'workflow'. This might sound highfalutin, but all of us already have a workflow and always did, whether we call it that or not. However digital offers greater choice, which means it's both necessary and slightly more challenging to establish a workflow that suits you.

Workflow covers the choices you make before you shoot (possibly even before you buy a camera!), while you're shooting, and after shooting. This book does not primarily focus on the post-shoot side of things, but this is such an integral part of the digital process that there's no way we can ignore it, especially as what you want to do after shooting will have a bearing on what you do before and during. If you're aiming to spend the minimum amount of time at the computer afterwards, it's doubly important to get the camera set up right beforehand and vice versa.

If the term 'workflow' sounds too much like, well, work, and you simply want to shoot for pleasure, take a lead from the *The Hitch Hiker's Guide to the Galaxy*: 'Don't Panic'. Establishing a workflow that's right for you doesn't have to be hard. It should also make the whole business of shooting with your DSLR both more rewarding and ultimately more enjoyable.

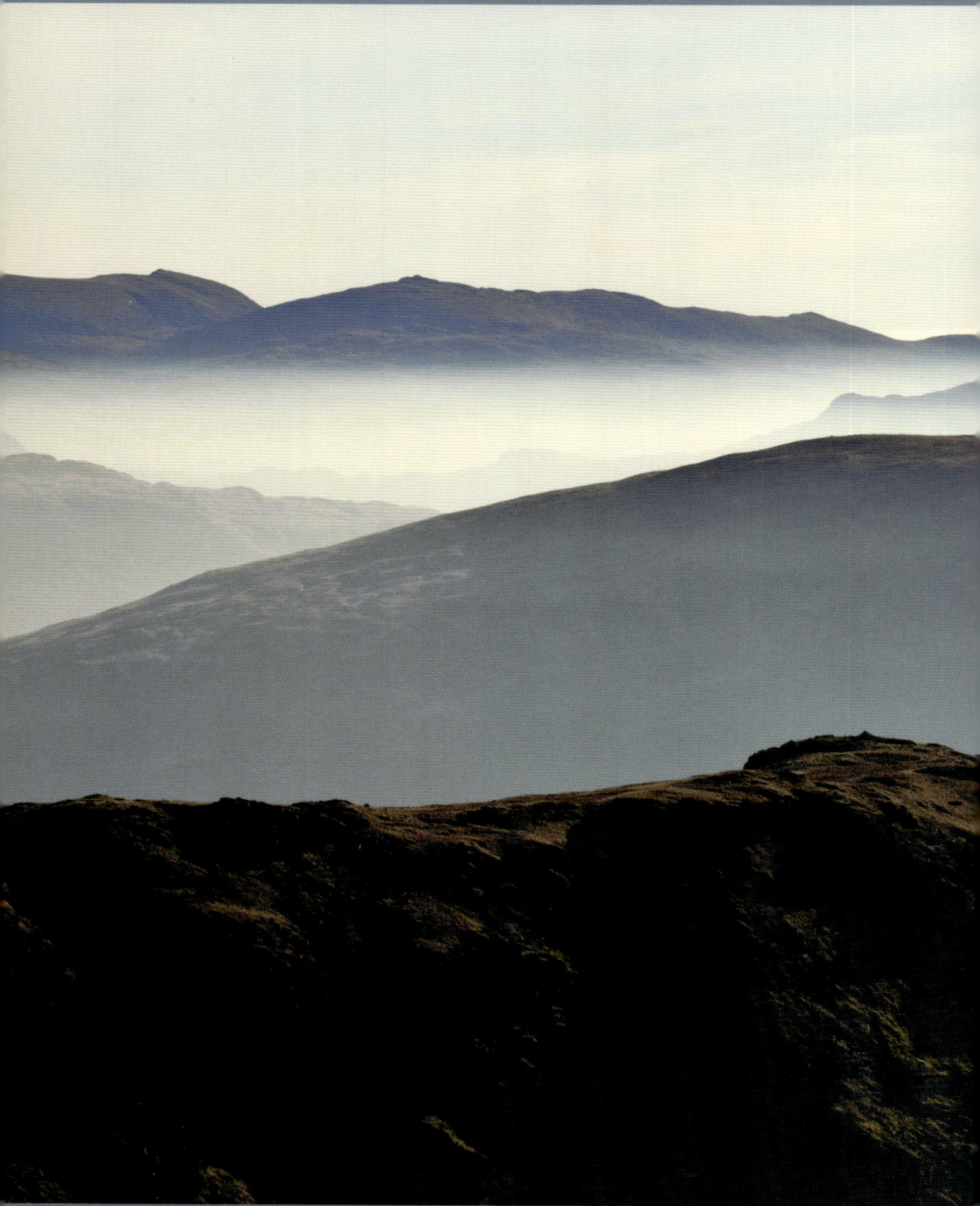

01: THE DSLR ADVANTAGE

The world of photography is now overwhelmingly digital. In the precursor to this book, only four years ago, it could be assumed that most readers would be new to digital and probably making the transition from a 35mm SLR. This is no longer true. In less time than most of us imagined, digital has become the mainstream. There are many reasons why this has change has happened, not all of them necessarily positive. Yet for the serious photographer – enthusiast or professional – digital photography offers many real advantages.

On Haycock, looking towards the Coniston Fells, Lake District, UK
Nikon D2x, focal length 80mm, ISO 160, 1/200 sec at f/14

Digital advantages

This may still seem controversial, but the facts – or rather the pictures – speak for themselves. The best digital cameras, by which I specifically mean DSLRs, can produce results equal to and often surpassing anything obtainable with film. Although few things can compare with the impact of a really good transparency displayed on a lightbox, at the real point of delivery, on screen or on the page, digital images can be just as good and sometimes better.

INSTANT REVIEW

Being able to review the image straight away on the back of the camera is no small advantage. With fast-moving subjects it's good to be assured that you've caught the moment, with landscapes it's useful to check focus and depth of field. Above all, I love having the image histogram (see p94). This provides more information than any exposure meter I ever came across.

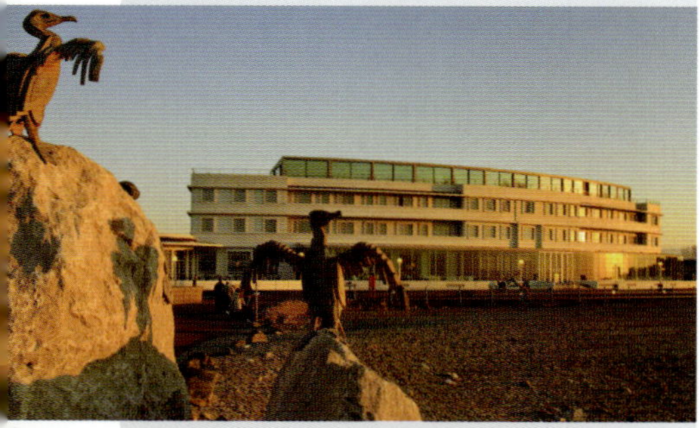

The Midland Hotel, Morecambe, UK
An image from my 2010 calendar; digital capture allowed careful tuning of white balance without fiddling with filters.
Nikon D2x, focal length 12mm, ISO 250, 1/100sec at f/10

EXPERIMENTATION

Digital cameras positively encourage you to try different things, both because you can see the results right away and because you no longer have to worry about wasting film.

However, don't confuse this with the myth that digital shooting is all about frantically snapping hundreds of images in the hope that one of them will be right. Shooting shed-loads of images condemns you to weary hours of editing at the computer afterwards. Besides, in real-world photography there are so many variables that you would have to shoot not hundreds but thousands or even millions of images to have any real chance of getting 'the' shot. It's akin to the notion that if an infinite number of monkeys are given an infinite number of typewriters one of them is certain to produce Shakespeare's *Hamlet*.

This metaphor is not to demonstrate the pinpoint possibility of such an occurrence, but rather the extremely small probability of it actually happening. Furthermore, even if the monkeys did produce *Hamlet*, they wouldn't realize it and would also be completely unable to distinguish it from the infinite piles of gibberish they'd also produced.

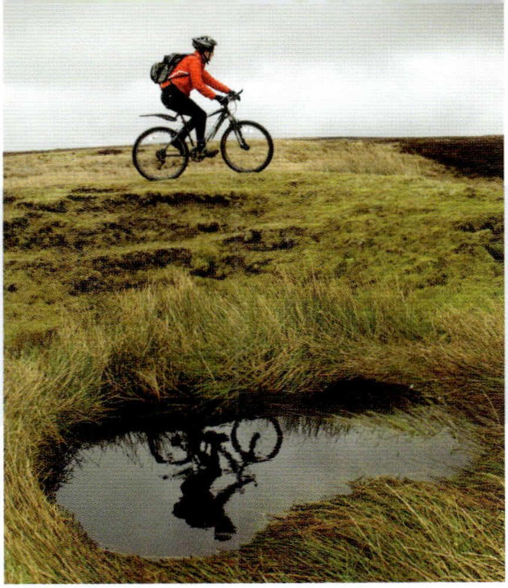

Mountain biker above Arkengarthdale, Yorkshire, UK
Timing was important to catch the reflection. Checking the camera screen confirmed that the shot had worked.
Nikon D700, focal length 26mm, ISO 640, 1/125sec at f/11

EASE OF IMAGE DISTRIBUTION

The digital age has brought many new ways of delivering and sharing photographs. Traditional formats like prints, books and greeting cards are still alive and well, with digital printing making them more accessible and affordable. Added to these are now all manner of new media, from the relatively familiar computer screen to the booming world of hand-held devices.

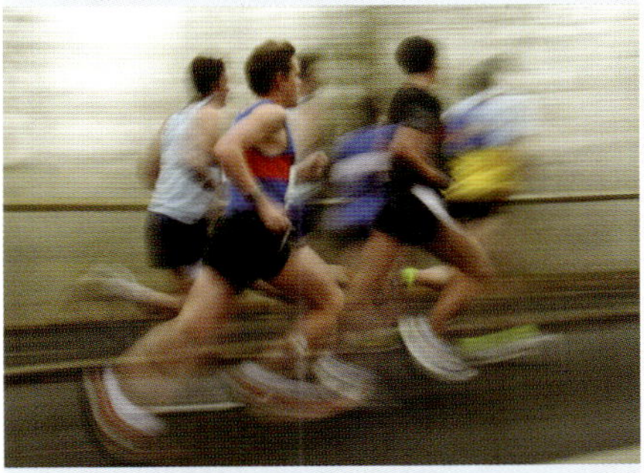

Runners in Wesham 10k, Lancashire, UK
The instant feedback of a DSLR has encouraged me to try different approaches to subjects where I might formerly have played safe.
Nikon D90, focal length 25mm, ISO 100, 1/10sec at f/16

ONGOING COST

Potentially, the daily running costs of digital photography account to almost nothing. A trickle of electricity to recharge camera batteries, a little more to run your computer and peripherals and that's about it.

However, this changes rapidly if you regularly print your photos. The cost of inkjet ink is extortianate. Then there's the capital outlay. The lifespan of a 35mm SLR could be 10 or 20 years, if not more. My Nikon FM2, which I acquired in 1990, is just as capable as it ever was. Digital cameras are much more complex and few boast anything like the same level of durability. The benchmarks of quality and performance also change rapidly in the digital world. Some of this is the result of pointless inflation, but there are also real and welcome improvements.

POINT OF VIEW

I've been involved in producing calendars in my local area for well over 10 years. When I started, everything was produced on film and until recently we were still using some legacy film images. However, I've gladly put this behind me for the 2010 calendar as the digital shots simply look so much better.

DSLR advantages

Your annoying friend is sure to ask, 'Why splash out on a DSLR when you could spend less and get something smaller, lighter and just as good?' To which I'd answer, 'What do you mean, just as good?' Yes, DSLRs are heavier and bulkier (although some are pretty svelte), but for very good reasons. If you're serious about photography a DSLR offers massive and often overwhelming benefits.

This section is not just about the advantages of DSLRs. It also aims to provide background information on the different makes and models. For example, why does one DSLR, complete with a lens, come in at a mid-range price, while another from the same manufacturer but without a lens have a high-end price? Or what are the differences between, say, a three-year-old DSLR and its current counterpart?

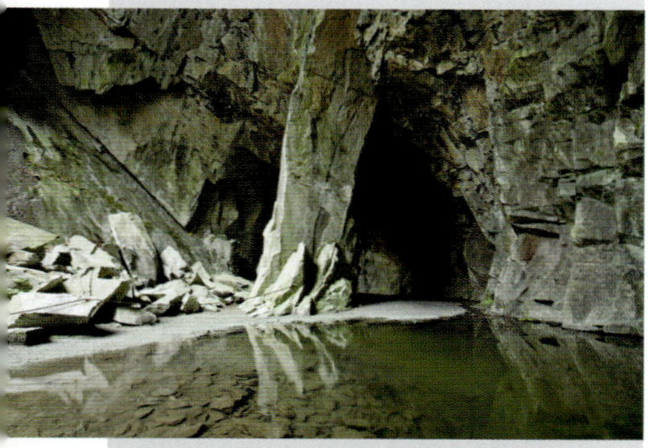

Cathedral Quarry, Tilberthwaite, Lake District, UK
This was shot on a Nikon D3x, which coped well with a massive dynamic range and delivered an image with the potential to make a huge print.
Nikon D3x, focal length 14mm, ISO 320, 15sec at f/11

IMAGE QUALITY

Image quality is what it's all about, but what does this actually mean? There's much more to it than just the number of pixels. Some are better than others; specifically, SLR pixels are better than compact camera pixels.

DSLRs have much larger sensors, which means that each individual photosite – the source of each pixel – is also much larger. For reasons we'll explore in Chapter Two, this means lower noise, better colour and the ability to capture more detail across a wide range of brightness. It may also deliver better practical resolution, i.e. crisp readable detail on screen, page or print.

DSLRs also invariably offer the option of shooting RAW files, with potential gains in quality (see p40); many compacts don't. If you shoot JPEGs, the in-camera processing is typically more heavy-handed in compacts. This is due to the fact that their undersized sensor means that the image requires more work (e.g. noise reduction) and because it's assumed that the images are to be viewed on screen or as small prints. Images optimized to look good at these sizes don't fare as well when you make larger prints.

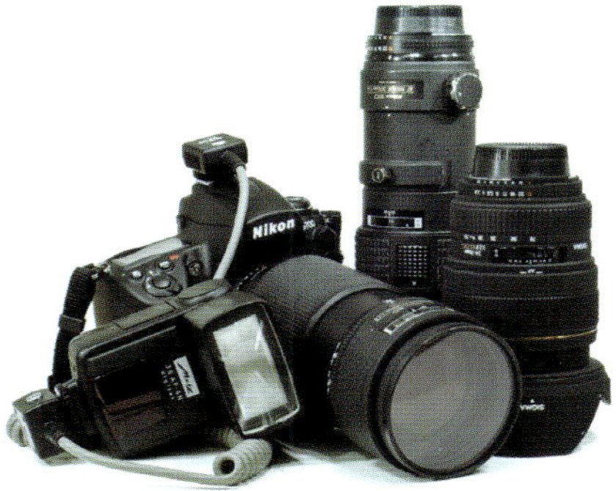

Nikon D700 with a range of lenses

SPEED

A few years ago, digital compact cameras were notorious for long shutter delays – sometimes half a second or more – and the inability to shoot more than a few images at a fast rate. From the start, the extra processing power in DSLRs meant that they performed faster; professional and serious amateur users would never have accepted them otherwise. Compacts have speeded up, but even entry-level DSLRs still start, focus, shoot, and record images significantly quicker.

FLEXIBILITY

A DSLR, whether a hulking professional model or an entry-level bantamweight, is a system camera with the ability to add a wide range of lenses and other accessories.

With rare exceptions, DSLRs also offer a much wider range of modes and functions. Higher-priced compacts may have wide-ranging functionality, but because of their small size and cramped control layout most of it is buried in the menu system, rather than being directly accessible with a flick of a dial.

HANDLING

Many people look at DSLRs and think they're too big. I look at compacts and think they're too small. On many compacts, virtually the entire back is occupied by the LCD screen. This may be great for image review, but leaves little room for other controls. The controls that are located there are often tiny and awkwardly placed, so most of the camera's functionality is only accessible by delving into menus. Even with a 3in (75mm) rear LCD (the current benchmark) a DSLR has a decent amount of space for the controls the photographer needs.

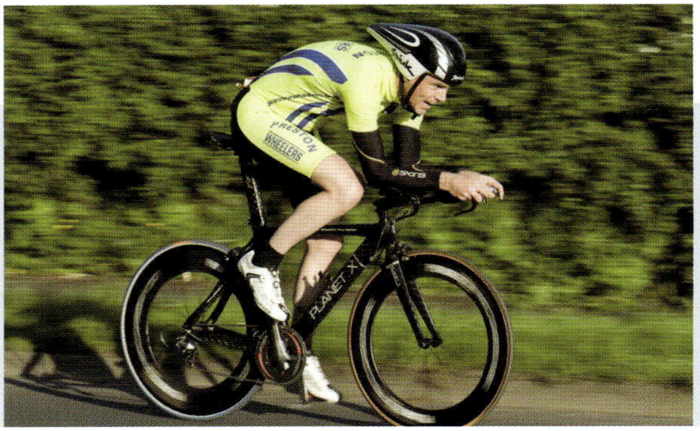

Rider in Preston Evening Time Trial Series, Lancashire, UK
The excellent handling and response speeds makes the DSLR the obvious choice for fast-moving action shots.
Nikon D3, focal length 125mm, ISO 400, 1/160sec at f/13

I also consider compacts to be too small in other ways. One concern I have is putting my fingers in front of the lens, and also the fact that I can hardly get both hands around the camera. An SLR is designed to be used two-handed. This is not a penalty, it's a very definite plus. The way you hold an SLR makes it much less susceptible to camera shake, and a bit of extra weight for ballast doesn't hurt either.

The basic SLR design has been around for more than 50 years. Its fundamentals have barely changed, so they were obviously sound from the start. However, the finer points of SLR ergonomics have evolved tremendously, driven by the most demanding and discerning of users, i.e. the vast majority of the world's professional and enthusiast photographers.

VIEWFINDER

SLR stands for Single Lens Reflex, which means you actually view through the lens. The reflex mirror diverts light to the viewfinder until the moment of shooting. With film, only an SLR or a very specialized view camera allows you to see what the lens sees. With digital cameras this is no longer the case and for compact users it has become the norm to use the rear LCD screen for framing pictures. Many compacts have no viewfinder at all, or a feeble token offering.

While the SLR viewfinder is brilliant, it's not as simple as 'what you see is what you get' for two reasons. First, most viewfinders don't show 100 per cent of the image area. Many have around 95 per cent linear coverage, meaning you only see 90 per cent of the picture area. This may be a hangover from the days of film, when commercial printing often cropped the edges of the image and slide mounts masked it slightly. Yet in DSLRs there's no good reason for it, except perhaps to save a little size, weight and production cost. Pro cameras should have 100 per cent viewfinder coverage.

The other limitation relates to depth of field (see p111). Only when the lens is wide open (at its maximum aperture) will the depth of field in the viewfinder match the final shot. This is why all decent SLRs have a depth of field preview button. Try and find a compact with one of those!

The SLR viewfinder is obviously not perfect, but neither are LCD screens, especially as even the best ones are hard to see in bright sunlight. The SLR viewfinder also provides a sense of direct connection with the subject, essentially turning the camera into an extension of your eye. Put simply, you look *through* the viewfinder; you look *at* the screen.

More and more DSLRs now offer Live View, giving the option to use the LCD screen to frame pictures. By offering the choice between the viewfinder and Live View, DSLRs are increasingly offering the best of both worlds.

DIGITAL ZOOM

Some compacts may boast astonishing zoom ranges, but beware of 'digital zoom', a misleading name which, in reality, refers to in-camera cropping. It simply enlarges part of the frame, in the process discarding most of the megapixels. If you have to do this, it's best done on the computer afterwards. Only 'optical zoom' is worth considering.

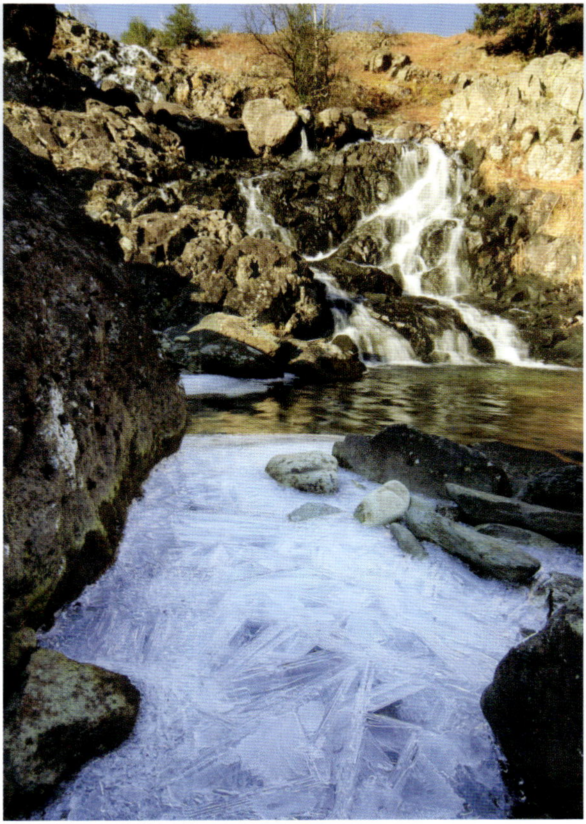

Sour Milk Gill, Easedale, Lake District, UK
A 12mm lens on an APS-C format body gave the angle of view necessary to include the all-important foreground detail.
Nikon D2x, focal length 12mm, ISO 100, 1/8sec at f/22

LENS RANGE

Interchangeable lenses are a defining feature of the SLR, exemplifying the flexibility of the basic design and allowing the SLR to 'grow' with the photographer.

There is a vast range available, especially for the major makes Nikon and Canon. Of course, many of these lenses are highly specialized and very costly, but it's possible to outstrip the lens range of any compact at just a modest cost.

For most users, the real gain is at the wide-angle end. Many compacts only stretch to about 35–38mm equivalent, although some go to 28mm and a few go a millimetre or two wider. A typical DSLR kit lens (e.g. an 18–55mm), easily matches this field of view with much wider lenses that are also available (e.g. 12–24mm or even 10–20mm).

Of course, there are downsides. Extra lenses mean extra cost, and extra weight to lug around. Additionally, changing lenses can allow dust into the camera. If the dust settles on the sensor, dark spots may appear in the picture. Having said that, there are ways to overcome this, especially as more and more DSLRs are now being equipped with an automated self-cleaning facility.

DSLR developments

Technology marches on, and the market lifespan of the average DSLR is now two years at most. Adding more megapixels is a dubious benefit for most users; there's a very strong argument that six megapixels is ample. Still, megapixel hype aside, the latest DSLRs show many real improvements over their predecessors.

STOP AND THINK

Do you need a new DSLR? Is your current camera holding you back? Can you point to real issues with its performance, for your photographic needs? If the answer is no, you may not need an upgrade at all. If it's yes, identifying the issues helps to establish your priorities when choosing between possible new cameras.

POINT OF VIEW

I didn't feel that my Nikon D2x was short of megapixels, so the fact that its replacement, the D3, had a similar number (12.1Mp) was immaterial. Nor did its blistering speed (9fps or more) really impact on most of my shooting. However, I was attracted by its improved dynamic range, colour depth and noise levels. When actually using the camera, I noticed many other improvements, from the bigger, brighter LCD screen to its simplified way of zooming into images during playback. Reading test reports and comparing sample images is only half the battle; you also need to get your hands on a camera and see how it feels. You can't do this on the Internet!

LARGER SENSORS

This change has so far only been evident at the top of the market, and it's likely to stay that way for the foreseeable future. Since early 2008, Nikon and Sony have joined Canon in producing 'full-frame' DSLRs, and prices have moderated to within the reach of many serious enthusiasts as well as professionals.

The differences between full-frame ('FX' in Nikon parlance) and the more common APS-C ('DX') sensors are exactly what you would expect; the bigger sensor means lower noise, better dynamic range, better colour rendition, and so on. Notably and commendably, when Nikon introduced its first FX-format DSLR, the D3, it had no more pixels than their best DX camera, the D300; in fact it had marginally fewer. Yet the D3 set new standards for noise, dynamic range and ability to shoot usable images at sky-high ISO ratings.

Additionally, larger sensors give a shallower depth of field. This is a bonus for certain kinds of shots – portraits, sports or wildlife for example – where the aim is to isolate the subject from the background. It's less advantageous when you want to maximize depth of field, as in traditional landscape shots.

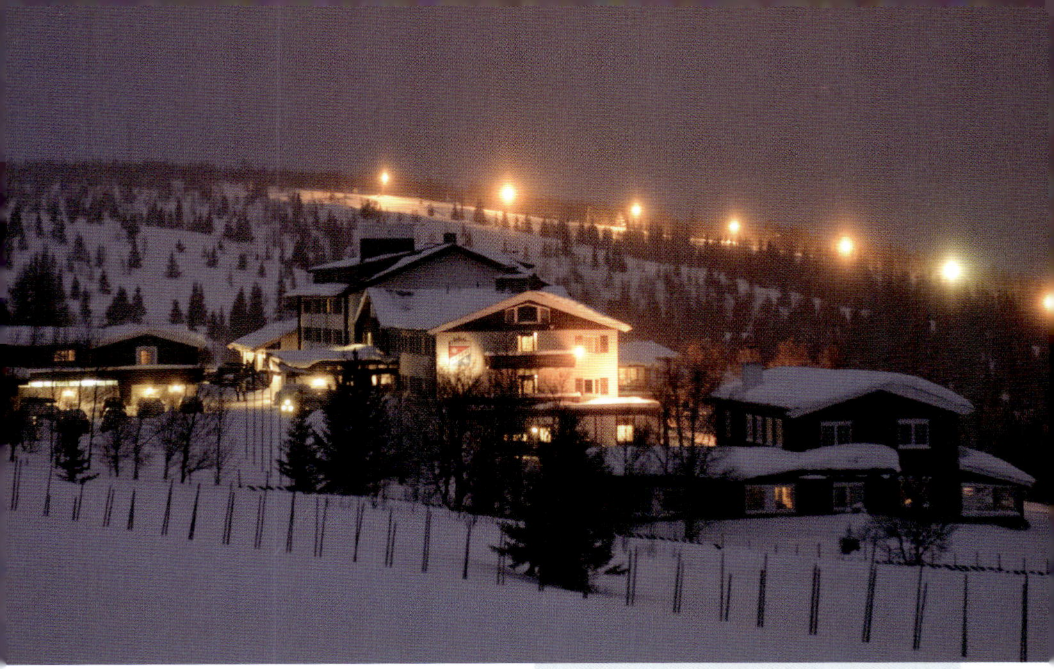

Wadahl Hotel, Gålå, Norway
Returning from a late ski lesson with no tripod, the Nikon D700 allowed me to set 6400 ISO for a hand-held shot remarkably free of noise.
Nikon D700, focal length 70mm, ISO 64000, 1/25sec at f/3.5

LOWER NOISE

Although bigger sensors have a clear advantage, especially when pixel numbers are similar, there have been technological improvements across the board. The smaller-sensor models also provide much cleaner images at any given ISO rating, and allow you to shoot at substantially higher ISO ratings than before.

POINT OF VIEW

It feels disloyal to say this, as the Nikon D2x was my main camera for several years and served me splendidly, but it was always noticeably noisy at anything above ISO 400 and I scarcely ever used it beyond 800. The FX-format D3 and D700 are streets ahead in this respect, but so are the newer DX-format cameras like the D300 and D90. The same is true for other manufacturers.

BETTER DYNAMIC RANGE

Again, although bigger sensors (specifically bigger, rather than more numerous in pixels) are best, there has also been a significant improvement in dynamic range within sensors of the same size. The ability to capture detail across a wide tonal range from highlights to shadows is vital for wedding photographers – thanks to the tradition of black suit and white dress. Yet, strongly lit landscapes, especially with white clouds in the sky, can be even more challenging. The Fujifilm Super CCD sensor has long had a reputation for extended dynamic range but the Nikon D3x (for those who can afford it) now seems to equal its ability.

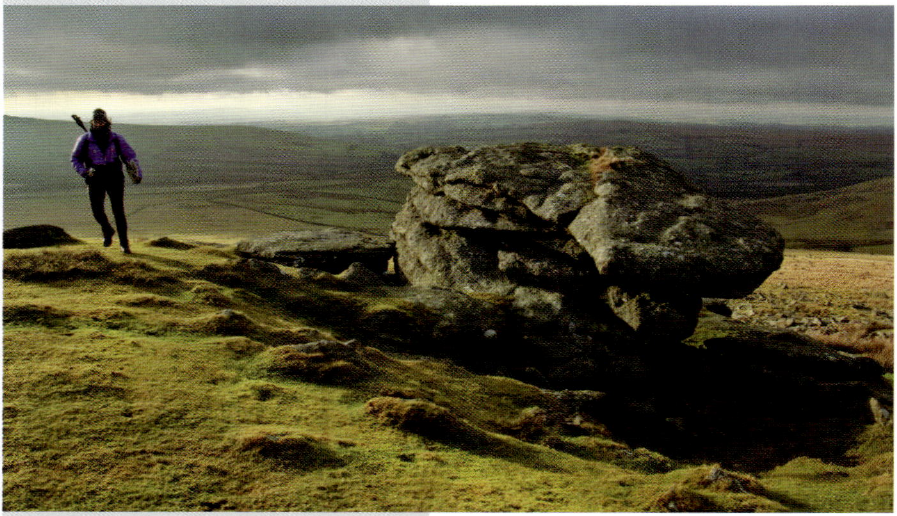

Walker near Lynch Tor, Dartmoor, UK
With bright sky in the distance and deep shadows close up, the dynamic range of this scene was immense. It also had the added difficulty of a moving figure in the frame, yet it was all captured in a single shot.
Nikon D2x, focal length 18mm, ISO 250, 1/125sec at f/14

SPEED

As I mentioned previously, DSLRs have always been much faster than compacts. However, problems can still occur when you are shooting sequences of images in rapid succession. This is caused primarily because the image data is stored temporarily in a memory called the buffer, before being written to the memory card. When the buffer is full the camera can take no more shots until some space is made available. This issue, known as lockout, was a major limitation of many DSLRs until quite recently. In 2003 Nikon's D2H achieved eight frames per second only by limiting image size to 4.1 megapixels – more than adequate for its target market of press photographers. Today, both buffer capacities and card-write speeds have improved enormously, and complete lockout is rarely experienced on modern cameras, despite the increase in image size. Anyone who uses single-frame release mode rather than continuous mode is unlikely ever to notice a problem; the camera can shoot faster than your finger can keep pressing the shutter button.

With entry-level to mid-range cameras, the stated maximum speed is still not always attainable, especially when shooting RAW images with their larger file sizes. However, you are now likely to experience a slowdown rather than a complete lockout. Shooting with a Nikon D90, for example, I found that the claimed top speed of 4.5fps was not always attainable, but the camera continued to operate at around 2fps even when shooting RAW. I never provoked it to complete lockout.

BETTER SCREENS

For most users, the rear LCD screen is an integral part of digital photography, so today's bigger, brighter and sharper screens are clearly a plus. But perhaps one should sound a cautionary note. Just because the screen image looks better does not necessarily mean that the photos themselves are any better, you only know for sure by comparing like for like. Secondly, the best new screens are really rather seductive, but time spent looking at the screen is time not spent looking at the subject or through the viewfinder. It also drains the battery! Finally, the most important aspect of image review, especially for judging exposure, is not the full-screen image, but the histogram (p94), for which a better screen makes very little difference.

Personally, I find a better screen makes the experience more pleasurable, and helps when you're showing others your shots. Yet the biggest practical benefit is that it's a lot easier to check focus, depth of field and general sharpness.

LIVE VIEW

Where DSLRs are concerned, Live View is not just an incremental improvement, but a whole new function. Some traditionalists have sneered at Live View, regarding it as another instance of 'digital dumbdown'. I was sceptical myself, until I tried it.

It's not going to replace the viewfinder for the majority of shooting: the ergonomics of the SLR are against it, for one thing. The viewfinder also gives that direct connection to the subject. However, some people find it helps framing by providing a different kind of view (see p122).

Live View really comes into its own when the camera is on a tripod (or another solid support) as the ergonomic disadvantage disappears. In very low light, when the viewfinder image may be too dim to be useful, the live image can be much clearer. More significantly, Live View on most DSLRs gives ultimate focusing accuracy. This is especially valuable when depth of field is at a minimum, i.e. when using very long lenses or shooting ultra-close-ups. This is enhanced by the ability to zoom in for an even closer view.

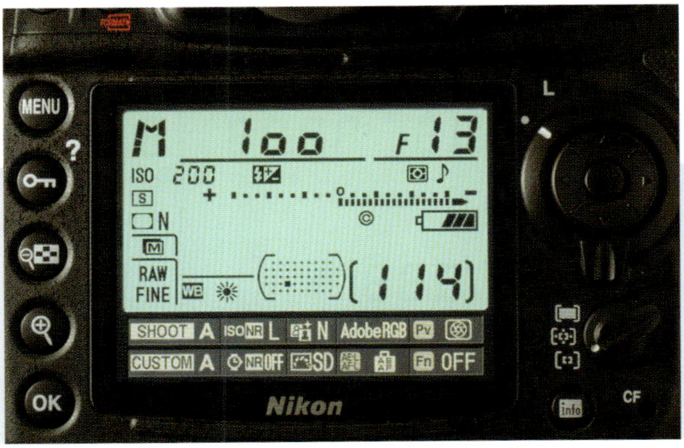

Information display
As well as providing image feedback, the screens on many modern DSLRs (such as this Nikon D700) offer a clear and detailed information display.

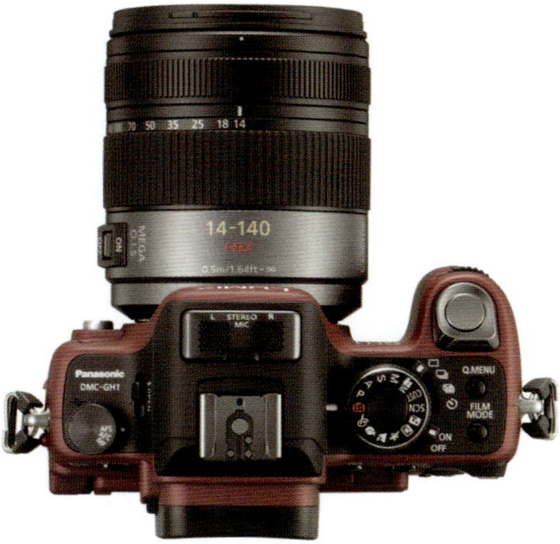

The Panasonic Lumix DMC-G1
With its mirrorless 'reflex' system, this camera may offer a foretaste of the future of the DSLR.

MOVIES

Nikon got there first, with the D90, but Canon was close behind with the EOS 5D Mk II, and it probably won't be long before video capture is standard on all DSLRs. Canon's video is full high definition 1080p standard, while Nikon's is a lower 780p standard. Yet it still looks good on a high-definition TV screen and is more than good enough to play back on most computer screens.

Shooting movies on these DSLRs means using the LCD screen, not the viewfinder, as it's an extension of Live View mode. This sacrifices the brilliant ergonomics of the SLR and is generally pretty hopeless without a tripod or a shoulder stock. The DSLR is not about to replace the dedicated video camera, but for those who may want to shoot an occasional holiday or 'event' video it's a bonus feature.

THE SHAPE OF THINGS TO COME?

Nothing betrays the DSLR's 35mm ancestry more than the reflex mirror. There was never really a viable alternative with film, but the mirror box creates a big empty space at the heart of the camera, and you need a bulky pentaprism on top to display the image the right way up and the right way round. The mirror action creates noise and vibration too. It also dictates a minimum distance between the sensor and the lens, imposing certain limitations on lens design.

If it's possible to feed image data from the sensor directly to the LCD screen (Live View), there's no reason why it can't also be fed straight to the viewfinder. Many compacts already have electronic viewfinders – early examples were pretty awful, but they have improved by leaps and bounds.

The Panasonic Lumix DMC-G1 is the first interchangeable-lens camera that does away with the reflex mirror (and therefore strictly isn't an SLR). The DMC-G1 uses the same Four Thirds sensor as the Olympus range but dispensing with the mirror gives it a smaller form factor; most noticeably, the body is much shallower, front to rear, than 'normal' DSLRs. Hence it is described as a Micro Four Thirds system. It has limitations – there aren't many lenses available and the electronic viewfinder reportedly performs poorly in low light – but already it's been followed by the Olympus EP-1 (also Micro Four Thirds) – and the Samsung NX system, which follows similar lines but with an APS-C size sensor.

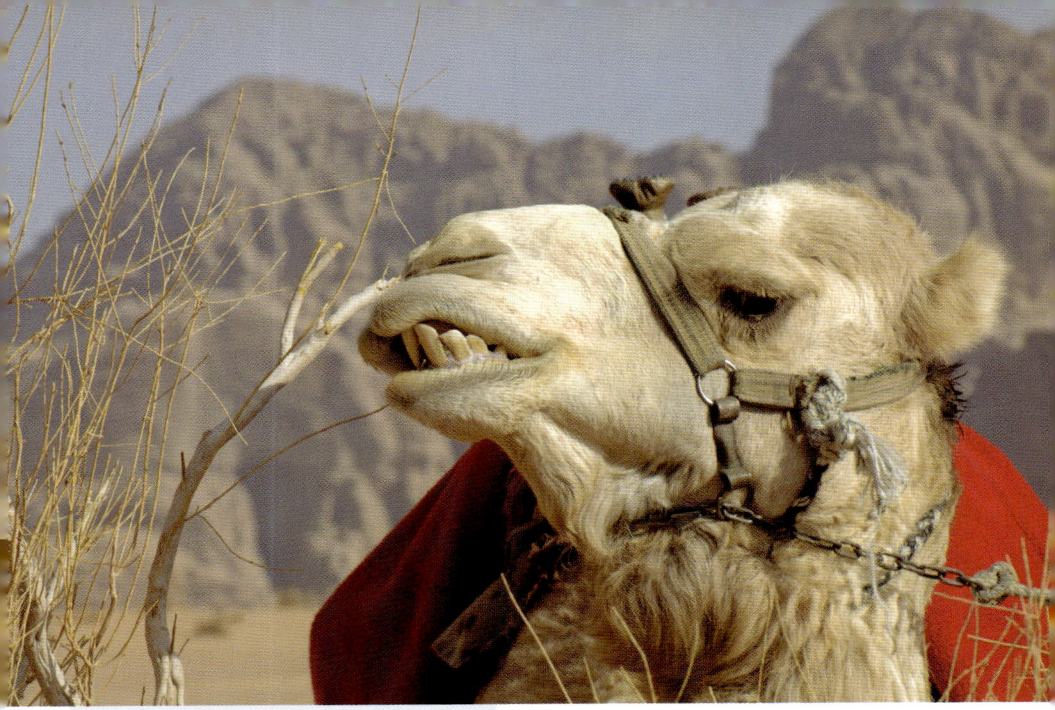

Camel, Wadi Rum, Jordan
A natural subject for video shooting as well as stills. With the latest DSLRs you can do both.
Nikon D2x, focal length 125mm, ISO 125, 1/160sec at f/11

There is a bit more to it. The larger sensor of the SLR, compared with most digital camcorders, means less image noise, especially in low light. It also allows shallower depth of field; this alone has been enough to attract some movie makers to DSLRs, for at least some of their work.

DUST REMOVAL

The one big problem with interchangeable lenses is dust and the resulting spots on the images. Prevention is better than cure, which is why most new DSLRs now have some system for automatic dust removal. This usually works by vibrating the sensor (strictly its covering filter) whenever the camera is switched on or off.

IMAGE STABILIZATION

Camera shake remains a major cause of unsharp pictures. While there's still no substitute for careful handling and the use of a tripod, camera makers have produced hardware solutions to the problem. In essence these aim to react instantaneously to camera movement and move something else in the system to counteract it. This may take place within the lens or in the camera body. Both Nikon and Canon have opted for a lens-based approach (Nikon calls it Vibration Reduction, so look for VR lenses), while Pentax, Sony and other manufacturers have camera-body image stabilization (IS). The obvious advantage of lens-based IS is that you can use VR/IS lenses on older camera bodies. Allied to the high-ISO and low-light abilities of the latest DSLRs, this means hand-held shooting is possible under a far wider range of conditions than could ever be tackled on film. But don't chuck away your tripod just yet!

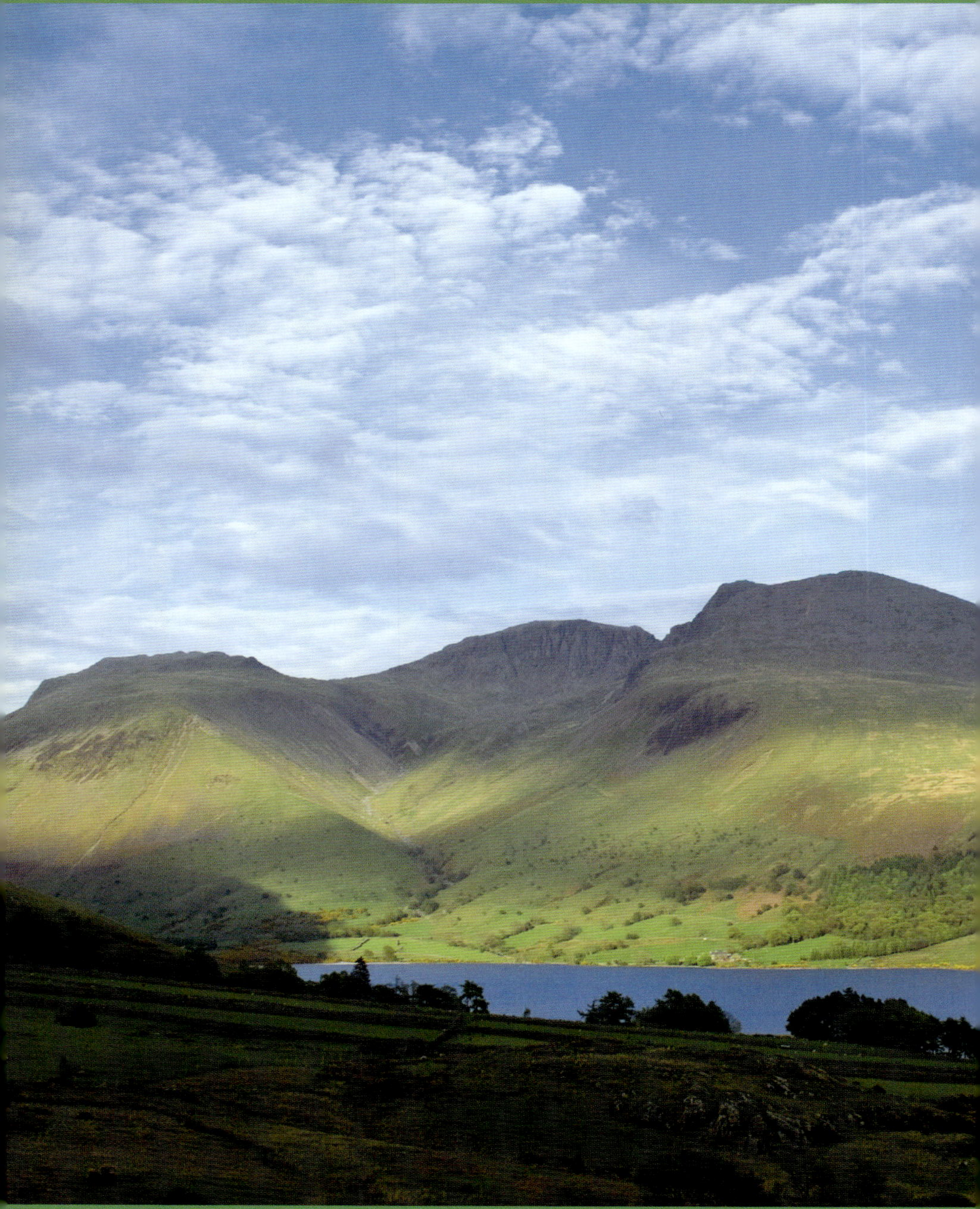

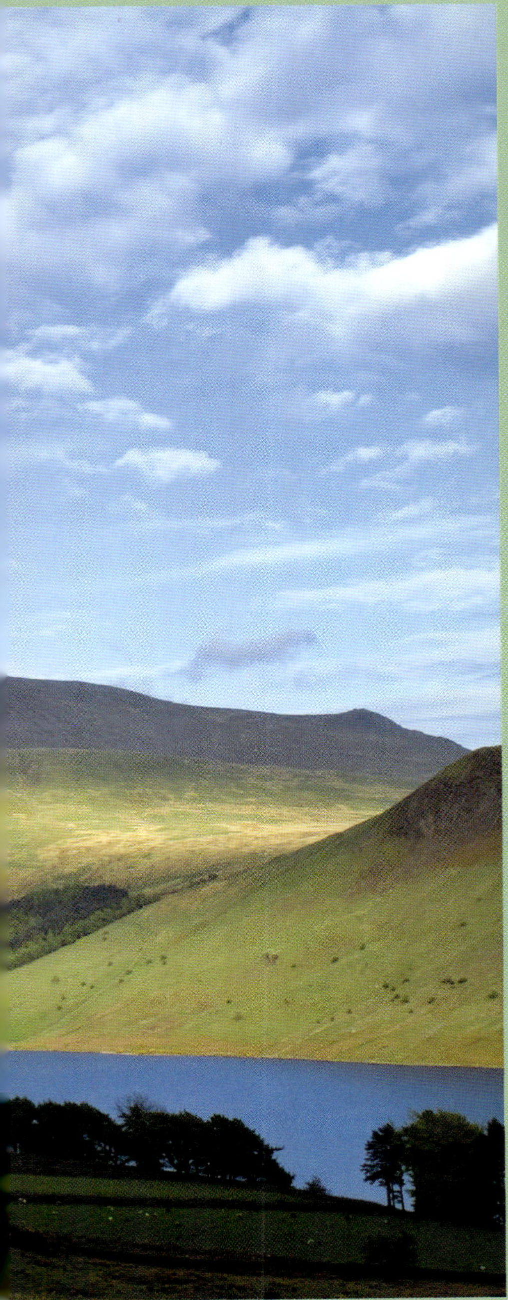

02: INSIDE THE IMAGE

There are still a few dinosaurs around who claim that digital photography is not 'real' photography. In reality it doesn't matter whether an image is captured chemically or electronically; the qualities that make a great photograph are exactly the same. However, getting the best from digital photography does sometimes demand a different approach. Understanding how digital images are produced is a vital foundation.

Wastwater and Scafell, Lake District, UK
Fujifilm FinePix S3Pro, focal length 24mm, ISO 100, 1/60sec at f/9.5

Unpicking image quality

The big issue is: how good are the pictures? Of course the answer depends on what we mean by 'good'. What is image quality anyway? First of all, let's dispose of the idea that the only thing that matters is 'resolution', by which people generally mean the number of megapixels (Mp) you have. This widespread fixation on megapixel numbers has got to run its course sometime, but it shows few signs of fading just yet. The four key points to remember are as follows:

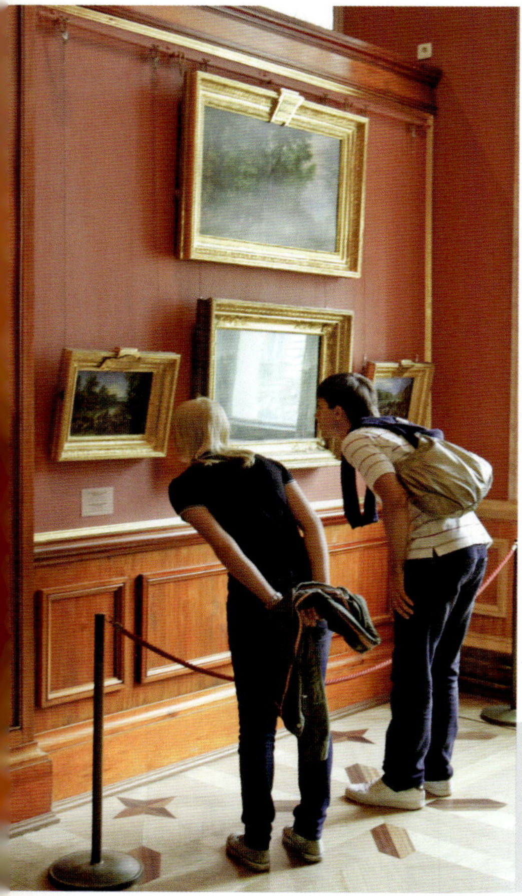

1. IMAGE QUALITY IS NOT JUST ABOUT RESOLUTION

When you buy a picture to hang on the wall, look solely at how sharp the detail is when you peer at it closely? Lots of additional factors come into play, such as the vibrancy and accuracy of colour, plus the ability to capture detail and texture over a wide tonal range.

2. RESOLUTION IS NOT JUST ABOUT MEGAPIXEL NUMBERS

Thinking in practical terms, rather than esoteric technical definitions, what we generally look for is the ability to record fine details and textures. A camera's ability to do this depends on many things; most importantly the quality of the lens, as well as the accuracy of its focusing and the photographer's ability to hold it steady!

The Hermitage Museum, St Petersburg, Russia
There's often a lot to be gained from looking closely at pictures – whether paintings or photographs.
Nikon D2x, focal length 30mm, ISO 640, 1/20sec at f/5

3. MOST CAMERAS ALREADY HAVE MORE THAN ENOUGH MEGAPIXELS

What do you actually do with your pictures? If you only show them on screen then you already have too many megapixels. Even a high definition TV screen is only equivalent to about a two (yes, two) Mp image. For hard copy, 6Mp is enough for a very good A4 (12x8in [297x210mm]) print. You can usually go considerably larger, for two reasons. Firstly, a good quality digital image can usually be scaled up considerably – referred to as up-rezzing or interpolation – and secondly, bigger prints are generally viewed from further away. In fact many experts reckon that 6Mp, when correctly handled, is ample for printing up to the maximum size of desktop inkjet printers (A3+ or approx. 13x19in [297x420mm]).

4. NOT ALL MEGAPIXELS ARE EQUAL

A DSLR will have a much larger sensor than a compact camera with the same number of pixels (see p36 for details). In essence this means that there's a much bigger light-collecting area for each pixel. This has lots of implications, including better dynamic range (p32), lower noise (p85), lower aberrations and probably better real-world resolution.

Pony at Old Holly Farm, Lancashire, UK
There's masses of fine detail in the pony's coat and mane, which will test the ability of the camera, lens and photographer to deliver a sharp result.
Nikon D700, focal length 70mm, ISO 1600, 1/100sec at f/5.6

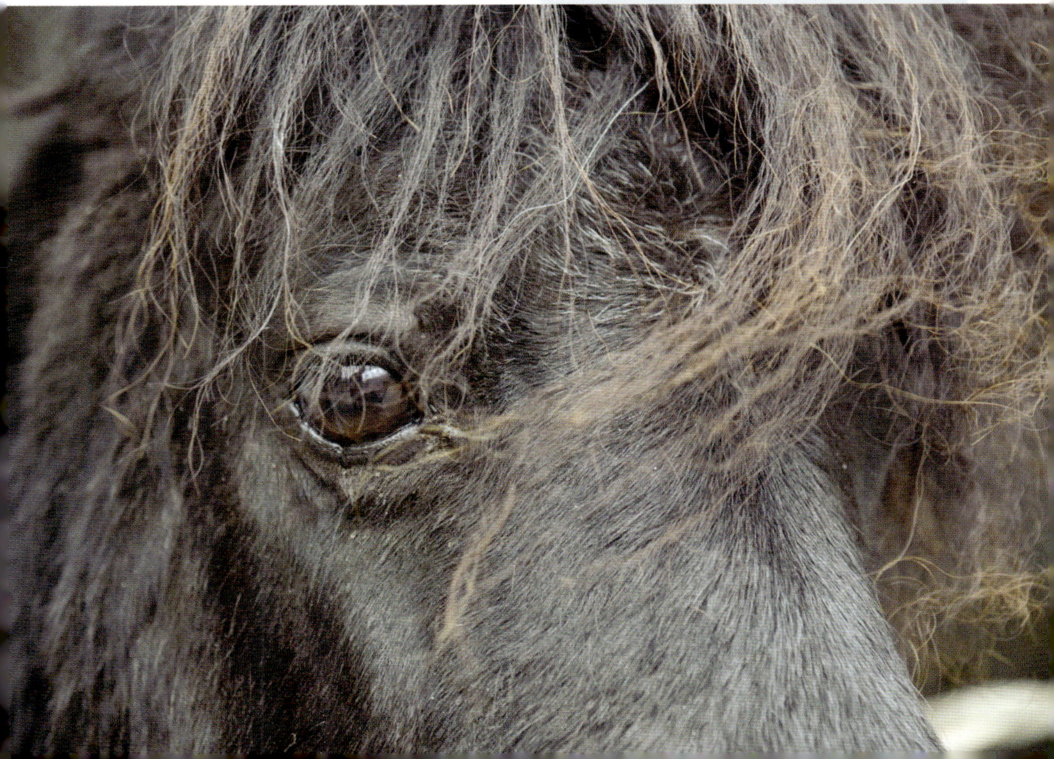

Resolution: beyond the megapixel myth

Despite arguments to the contrary, marketing hype still leans heavily on pixel numbers. A cynic might suggest that this is because numbers are easy to sell; 12Mp must be twice as good as six, and so on. But actually, even if everything else stayed the same, 12Mp still wouldn't be twice as good as 6Mp.

On a simple practical level, 12Mp doesn't let you make prints twice the size. The size difference is not x2, but x1.4. A 6Mp image could be 3000x2000 pixels, allowing you to make a 10in (25.4cm) long print at 300dpi. The 12Mp equivalent would be about 4250x2830 pixels, allowing a print of just over 14in (35.6cm) long.

BIGGER PIXELS ARE BETTER

To understand why some megapixels are more equal than others, it's worth thinking about what happens at the pixel level on the sensor itself. There are differences at the detail level between different types of sensor. More information is provided on pages 34–9, but a generalized overview will do for now.

The sensor is composed of a grid of photosites, each corresponding to one pixel. At each photosite there is a microscopic diode which reacts to light by generating an electrical charge. These diodes do not discriminate between different colours of light, so to generate a colour image they are overlayed with a grid of microlenses containing coloured filters. Each diode therefore receives light from only one part of the spectrum – red, green or blue. However, to compile a full-colour image we need RGB values for each pixel. The 'missing' values are deduced from those of adjacent pixels – a process called demosaicing. This can be done either in-camera to produce a JPEG file, or later on using RAW conversion software.

The key is the size of the individual diodes. On a typical 12Mp APS-C format DSLR, like a Nikon D300, they measure about 5.5 μm (nanometres: one nanometre is one millionth of a millimetre). On a full-frame SLR with a similar pixel count, like the Nikon D3, this pixel pitch is nearer 8.5 μm, which more than doubles the area of each pixel and therefore its light-gathering capacity.

Larger pixels harvest more light. If you think of light as being made up of individual photons, then larger pixels gather more photons. This has several effects. Firstly, it reduces image noise, partly because when larger numbers of photons are collected, random variations in the numbers are smoothed out. Also, there is always a base level of electrical activity within the sensor itself. As fewer photons are collected, this element becomes more prominent and the signal-to-noise ratio suffers. Consequently, larger pixels are better for shooting in lower light levels and at higher ISO speeds. The current record for production DSLRs is ISO 25600. One of the joint record-holders is the Nikon D3. Significantly, its close relation, the D3x, with twice as many pixels on the same size sensor, is limited to ISO 6400.

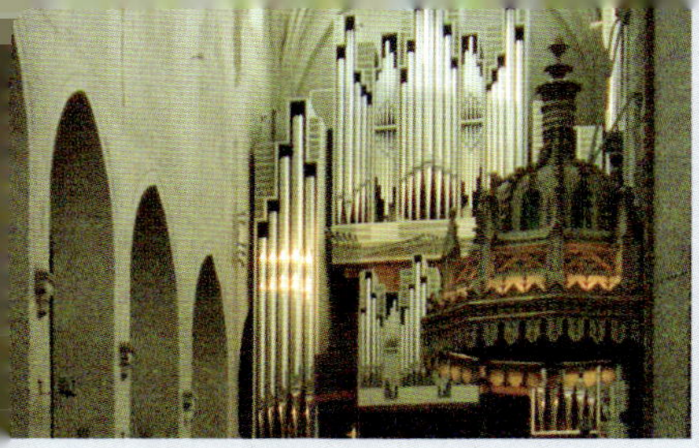

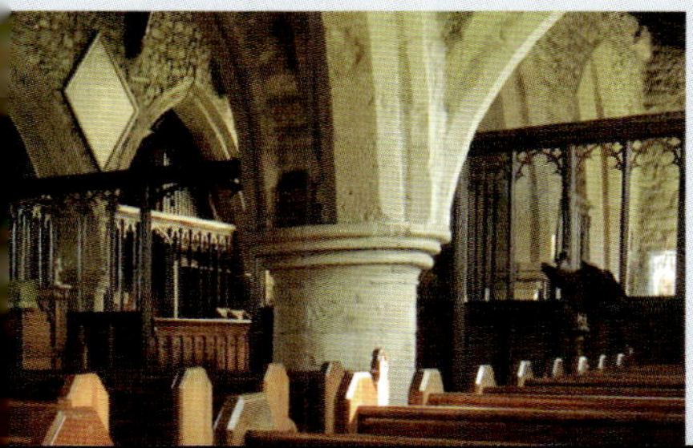

Turku Cathedral, Finland and St Mary the Virgin, Gisburn, Lancashire, UK
Two church interiors, two 12Mp cameras, but very different noise levels. The first picture was shot at ISO 800 on a Nikon D2x, and underexposure of the darker areas adds to the very obvious noise. The second image was shot on a Nikon D700 at ISO 6400, and while a little noise is still detectable, it's much less obvious.

Above: *Nikon D2x, focal length 12mm, ISO 800, 1/30sec at f/5*

Below: *Nikon D700, focal length 12mm, ISO 6400, 1/40sec at f/8*

DISPLAY OR PRINT TYPE	PIXEL DIMENSIONS	MEGAPIXEL EQUIVALENT *(approx.)*
15x10in print at 300dpi	4500x3000	13.5
12x8in print at 300dpi OR 15x10in print at 240dpi	3600x2400	8.6
10x7in print at 300dpi	3000x2100	6
6x4in print at 300dpi	1800x1200	2.1
High-end laptop, HD TV (Full HD (1080p))	1920x1080	1.9
Typical desktop computer monitor (XGA)	1024x768	0.8
SVGA	800x600	0.5
Handheld device e.g. iPhone	480x320	0.15

To deal with the higher noise levels intrinsic to their tiny sensors, compacts usually employ strong noise-reduction in JPEG processing. This may mask the noise, but also tends to mask fine detail, wiping out much of the benefit that extra megapixels supposedly bring.

For the same kinds of reasons, bigger pixels also contribute to better dynamic range and colour depth. In fact in just about every aspect of picture quality, a bigger pixel pitch is a definite advantage. The benefits in terms of noise reduction become more noticeable at higher ISO ratings; on better compact cameras noise may be acceptable at 100, 200 or even 400 ISO. However, a wider dynamic range is noticeable across the entire ISO range.

SHARPNESS

I've already hinted that sharpness is not the same thing as resolution or megapixel numbers. Sharpness is the delivery of crisp fine detail in the image itself, which is generally reckoned to be a positive. In the rare cases where we actually want a soft image for creative effect, it's relatively easy to soften a sharp image – much easier than attempting to sharpen one that starts out soft.

Other things being equal, more pixels will provide a sharper image. The first question is whether we can actually see the difference. We'll probably only do so when the image is examined really closely, on screen at 100 per cent view or when peering nosily at a really big print. The second question is whether other things really are equal. The full benefits of extra pixels can only be realized with top-notch lenses and excellent technique.

Final sharpness is also influenced by software sharpening (for more on this see p84).

Raindrops on Alchemilla foliage
Good sharpness does justice to fine detail.
Nikon D700, focal length 48mm, ISO 640, 1/60sec at f/9.0

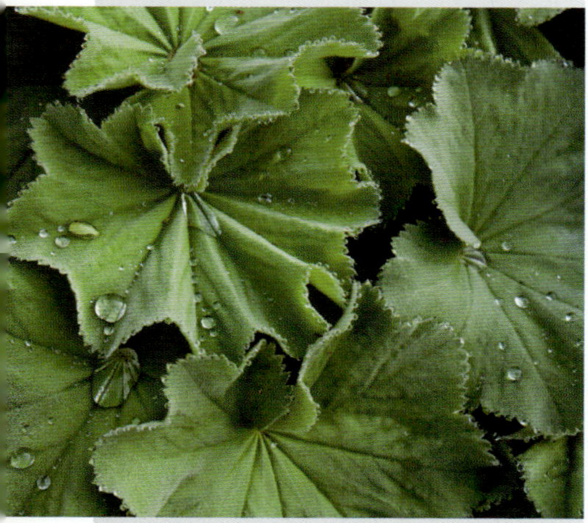

RESOLUTION

There's a strong argument that we shouldn't use phrases like '12-megapixel resolution' at all; it's better to refer to 'image size' or 'pixel count'. The potential confusion that arises with the word 'resolution' is easily illustrated when you consider that the same 12Mp image can be printed at many different sizes: small prints with high resolution and large ones with lower resolution. Equally, it could be argued that a small sensor has higher resolution than a large one with the same number of pixels.

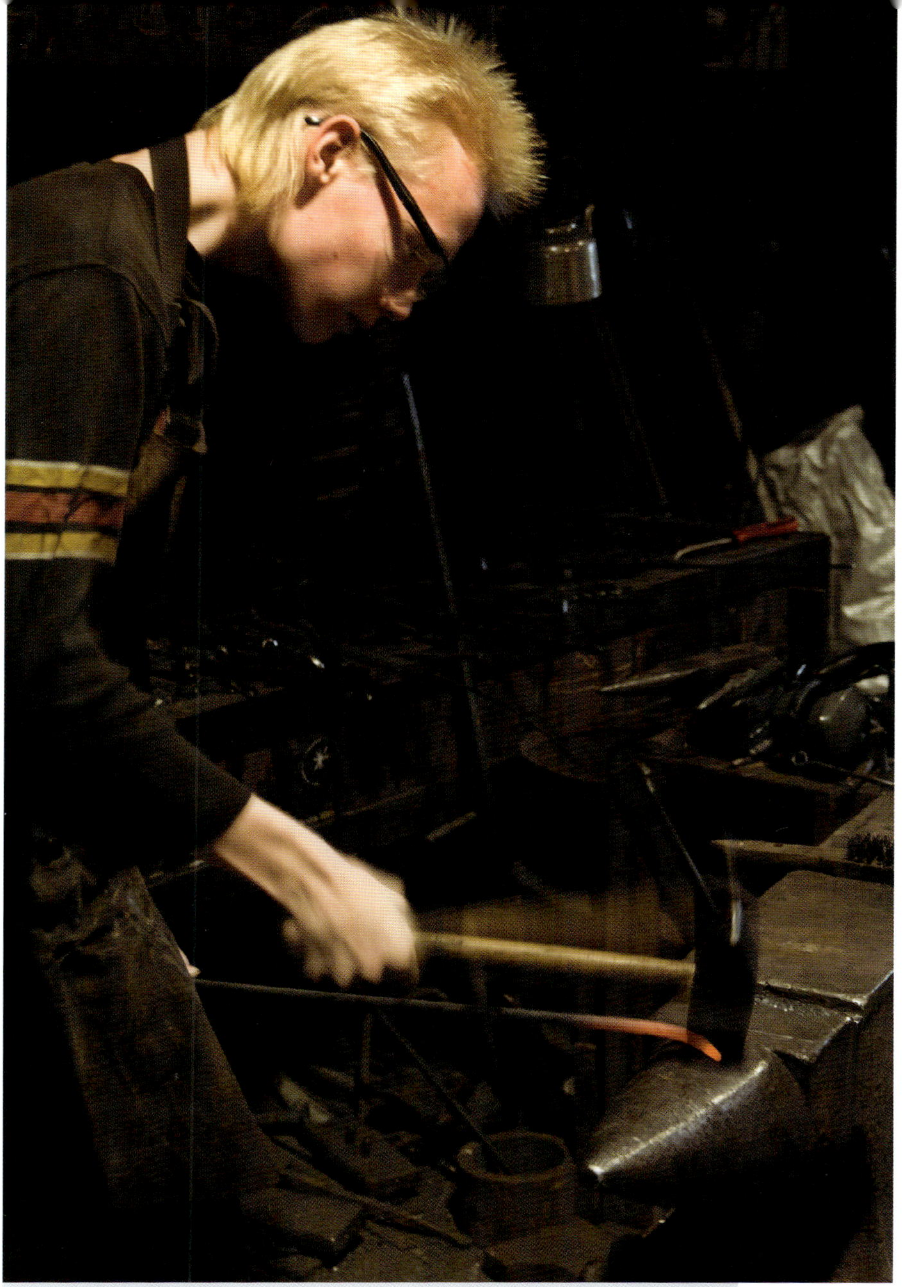

Blacksmith at Fiskars, Finland

Relying entirely on natural light from a skylight, this shot needed a high ISO and has deep shadows in the background; with the small photosites of most compacts, this would be a recipe for visible noise.

Nikon D2x, focal length 44mm, ISO 640, 1/50sec at f/4.5

Colour and tone

Colour and tone are the essence of every photograph. When we look at pictures we don't see pixels or RGB values, we see colour and tone. This is where the apparently exact science of digital imaging collides head-on with the subjective nature of human perception. We can measure image quality, but do we like the qualities of the image?

BLACK & WHITE vs COLOUR

Throughout the history of photography, many practitioners have preferred to work in black-and-white rather than colour. One reason, historically, was purely practical: the technology allowed much greater control than the relatively primitive colour processes then available. But there also were, and for some still are, aesthetic reasons. Colour gave the illusion of reality, as if a photograph were just a copy of a bit of the world. Black-and-white made it clear that all photographs are abstractions. Photographs do not show movement; they can only suggest it. Photographs do not show depth – the third dimension – they can only imply it. To paraphrase the great Alfred Stieglitz, a photograph is merely an equivalent to what the photographer saw.

No photograph can show us exactly what the human eye sees. We can't even be sure that my eye sees exactly what yours does. The eye and the brain work in a fundamentally different way to any camera. Specifically, the eye can see a wider range of colours, and a wider range of brightness, than the camera can record.

Asking whether a camera reproduces colours accurately is clearly not a simple question. And even if we can find an objective measurement to say that one camera reproduces colour more accurately than another, it does not mean that we will like the results any better. Ultimately, perception may trump science.

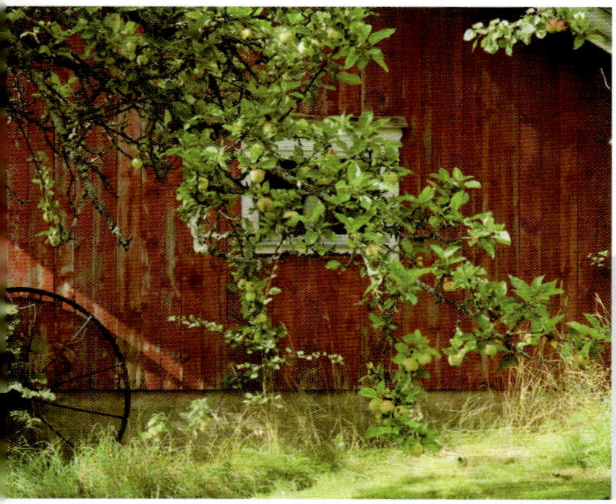

Faffas, Turku Archipelago, Finland
This photograph relies heavily on colour, specifically on the tension between red and green; if these colours are muddy or inaccurate it won't work.
Nikon D70, focal length 70mm, ISO 200, 1/125sec at f/10

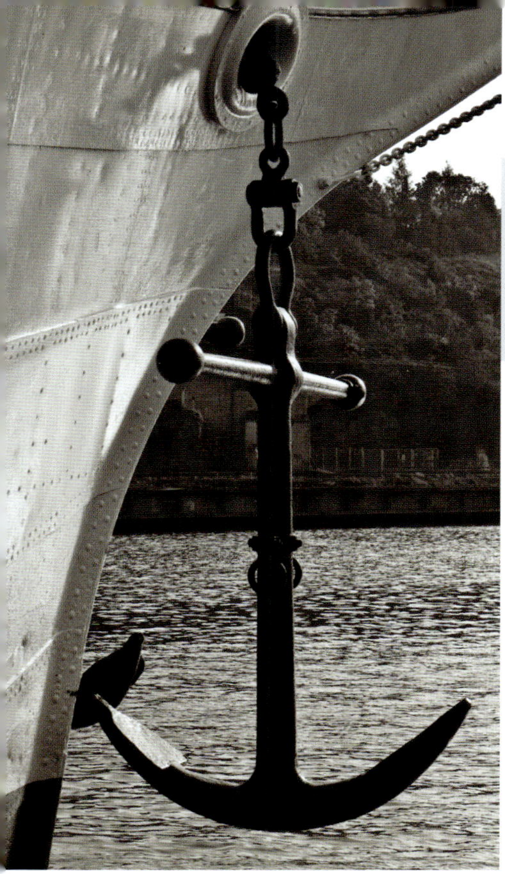

Anchor of Suomen Joutsen, Turku, Finland
This image is quite monochromatic anyway and loses little impact when converted to grayscale reproduction.
Nikon D2x, focal length 50mm, ISO 100, 1/125sec at f/14

LIKE FOR LIKE

Probably the worst possible way to compare the images produced by different cameras is to look at them on the respective cameras' rear screens. The problem should be obvious: are we actually comparing the images themselves, or the qualities of the different screens? To make a meaningful comparison it's essential to eliminate all other variables and to view the images on the same device, ideally a properly calibrated computer screen (see p62).

VARIABLES

Many aspects of the image, including the colour quality, are determined by more than which camera you use. Different lenses may give subtly different colours, but this is usually only a minor factor. More importantly, if you shoot JPEG the colour is radically affected by the White Balance setting and also by the way the camera processes the image. Modern cameras now provide the user with considerable scope to change the processing settings, which can make a big difference to the final results. Similarly, if you shoot RAW the results depend on which RAW conversion software you use and the settings you apply within that software.

Having said all of this, it does not mean that all cameras are equal or that science has nothing to tell us. One useful benchmark is colour sensitivity, the ability to distinguish between very similar colours. To derive this data cameras are tested under carefully controlled laboratory conditions. One of the systems used is the DxO Mark from DxO Labs (dxomark.com) which examines RAW data from each camera's sensor.

DYNAMIC RANGE

Dynamic range, in relation to light (it's used in sound and other media too), is simply the range between the lightest and darkest points. When referring to the scene in front of the camera, it's the range of brightness from the brightest point (which may include light sources) to the deepest shadow. The eye has a remarkable ability to adapt to an enormous dynamic range because it continuously scans the scene, adjusting nimbly to different brightness levels. Cameras and their sensors are less nimble. Even relatively recently, their limited dynamic range has been one of the biggest criticisms of digital capture. This limitation is more evident in digital images than with film as the cut-off at the ends of the range (known as 'clipping') tends to be more abrupt. This has always been an issue for wedding photographers, among others; it's simply not acceptable for the bride's dress to appear as a featureless pure white mass.

The latest cameras and sensors have been much improved. Dynamic range is still finite, but it's considerably extended. Where 10EV (Exposure Value) or so was pretty much the norm five years ago, many new cameras can now capture a range of 12EV or more – remember that each Exposure Value is a factor of 2, so this is a fourfold improvement. Nikon's relatively inexpensive D90 has a maximum dynamic range of 12.5EV and the very best current cameras (Fujifilm FinePix S5 Pro and Nikon D3x) clock up 13.5EV or more (figures from DxO Labs).

On-board processing (see p80) can help to overcome a high dynamic range, but can still only work with the information that the sensor can capture.

Dynamic range matters

Wedding photographers aren't the only ones for whom a camera's extended dynamic range may be a big benefit. Anyone who shoots scenes with a high dynamic range, probably all of us, can benefit. The exceptions might be studio-based photographers, who can control the lighting to keep the dynamic range within the camera's capabilities. For portraits and other close-up subjects it's possible to regulate the dynamic range using reflectors and/or flash.

F-stops and EVs

The use of the term 'stop' or 'f-stop' goes back to the early days of photography and initially referred to the stops controlling the aperture of a lens. You may still have some older lenses with a click-stopped aperture ring, but on modern DSLRs the aperture is normally set by the camera. 'Stop' is also used in a more general sense, more or less interchangeably with Exposure Value. A difference of one stop/EV represents a factor of 2 in brightness. A range of 10EV is a brightness ratio of 1024:1 (2^{10}=1024).

POINT OF VIEW

As someone who spends a lot of time shooting landscapes, dynamic range is really important. I'd rather shoot on a 6Mp camera with 15EV of dynamic range than a 20Mp camera with 10EV. (Neither of these cameras actually exists. I've just made up the numbers to make a point).

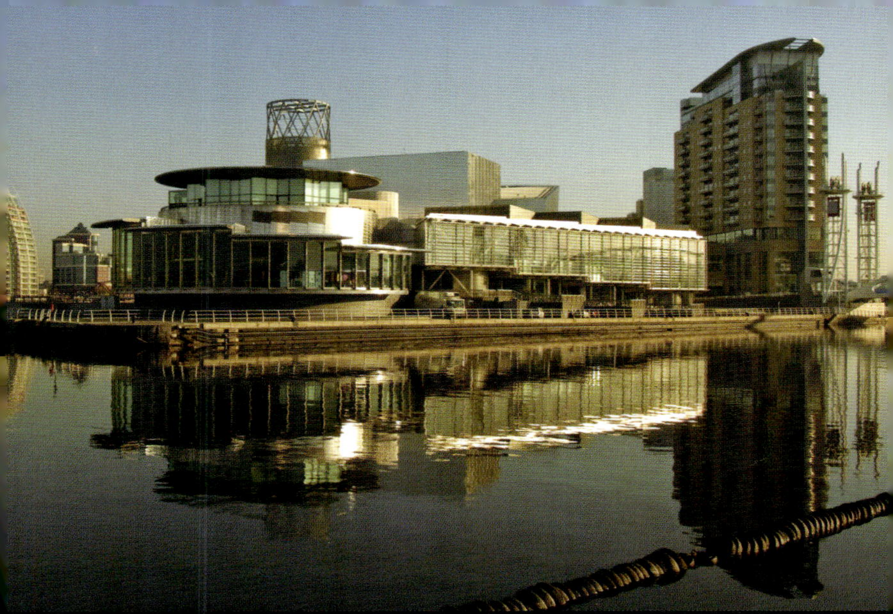

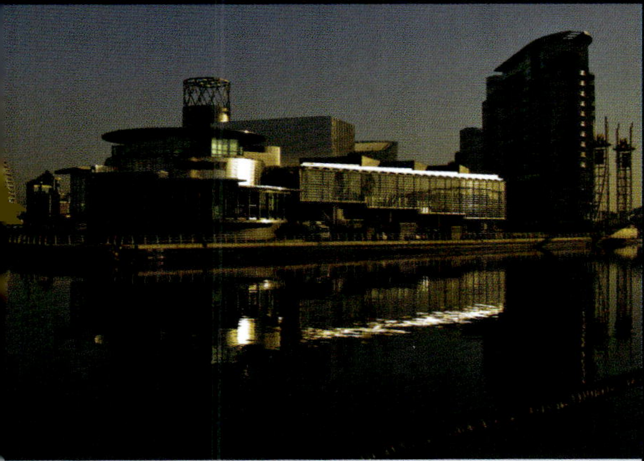

The Lowry, Salford Quays, UK
Strong morning light and highly reflective surfaces create serious dynamic range issues. The Nikon D2x failed to record any significant detail in the highlighted areas. Even a strong exposure reduction in RAW conversion could not rescue these areas (see inset). I need to return to this subject with the D700!
Nikon D2x, focal length 18mm, ISO 100, 1/80sec at f/10

The sensor

The sensor is the heart of any digital camera. It's where light turns into numbers, beginning the journey of the digital image. If the sensor is not up to the task, even the smartest software cannot rescue the image. On the other hand, two cameras can have identical sensors, yet produce significantly different results. Lenses have a great deal to do with it, as does the image-processing software, especially in relation to JPEG files. So the sensor is far from being the whole story, but it is an absolutely crucial element.

The quality of the sensor determines the camera's potential. The final results – our photographs – always depend on the processing of the RAW data. For the real photographer in the real world, the proof of the pudding is in the pictures we achieve. If the colours are disappointing, the camera may be at fault and may require a change in the White Balance settings, JPEG processing parameters or an alternative RAW conversion software. Another setting to look at is the Colour Space (see p78).

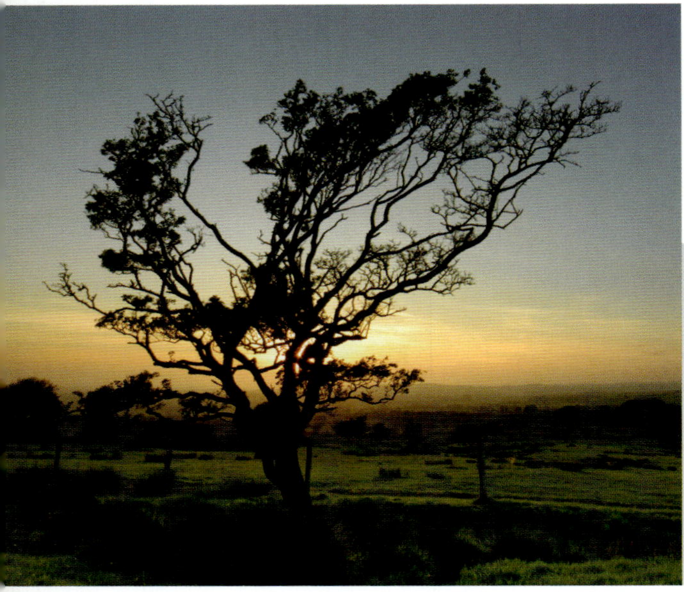

Wyresdale, Lancashire, UK
Even with the sun masked by the tree (always a good standby), the dynamic range is pretty wild here. The image has detail throughout, but needs a bit of work in RAW processing to balance the foreground and the sky.
Nikon D2x, focal length 12mm, ISO 100, 1/15sec at f/14

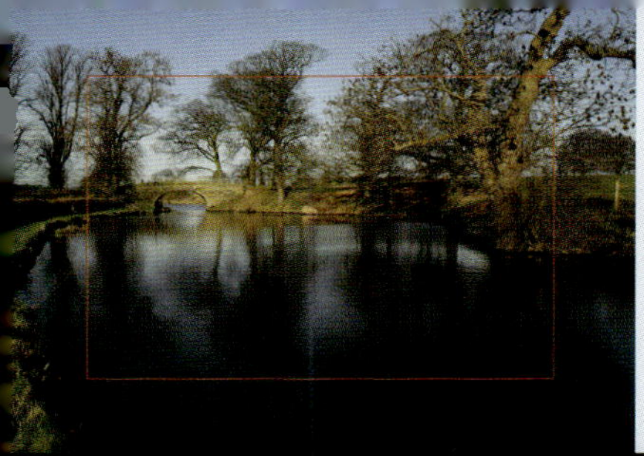

Lancaster Canal, Winmarleigh, Lancashire, UK
A direct comparison between full-frame and APS-C coverage. This image was taken with a Nikon D700 and a 24mm lens. I used the camera's DX-crop facility to simulate the coverage of an APS-format camera, shown by the red rectangle. The difference is obvious and explains why anyone who likes wide-angle views will be drawn to full-frame cameras.
Nikon D700, focal length 24mm, ISO 400, 1/320sec at f/11

SENSOR COMPARISON

	Full-frame	**APS-C**	**Foveon**	**Four Thirds**
Maker's designation	FX (Nikon); Full-frame (Canon, Sony)	DX (Nikon) APS-C	Foveon	Four Thirds
Cameras by	Nikon, Canon, Sony	Nikon, Canon, Sony, Pentax, Samsung, Fuji	Sigma	Oympus, Panasonic
Size (approx.); (there are some slight variations)	36x24mm	22x15 to 24x16mm	20.7x13.8mm	18x13.5mm
Aspect ratio (approx.)	3:2	3:2	3:2	4:3
Max megapixels (current)	24.6	15	14	12.3
Crop factor	1:1	1.5.1 to 1.6:1	1.7:1	2:1
Wide-angle coverage	As 35mm	>	>	Reduced
Telephoto magnification	As 35mm	>	>	Increased
Depth of field	Shallower	>	>	Deeper
Image noise	Less	>	>	More
Cameras are	Larger, heavier, more expensive	>	>	Smaller, lighter, (possibly cheaper)

SIZE MATTERS

DSLR sensors come in a significant range of sizes, although even the smallest are much larger than those that are used in the majority of compact cameras. As we've already seen, other things being equal, a larger sensor – more precisely, one with larger individual pixel sites – is likely to be superior in several critical respects, notably in relation to image noise and performance in low light.

Yet it may be more complex. In particular, sensor size relates directly to the angle of view obtainable with different lenses. The widest view is achieved with a full-frame sensor. With smaller sensors there is also a focal length multiplication factor to consider – more succinctly, a crop factor. An 18mm lens on a full-frame camera gives an angle of view of about 100 degrees. Put the same lens on an APS-C camera, like the majority of digital SLRs, and its effective coverage is reduced to about 75 degrees. On the larger sensor, this can be achieved with a 28mm lens. In other words, the effective focal length on the APS-C camera is increased by about 50 per cent, often described as a crop factor of 1.5. This is a definite handicap for landscape photographers and those who like to use really wide-angle lenses. Yet on the other hand, it's potentially a real benefit to sports and wildlife photographers who regularly use long lenses. It's all swings and roundabouts.

Smaller still...

Although the Four-Thirds sensor may seem small compared to some of the others, it's still huge compared to those in most compact cameras. The commonest size here, known as 1/2.5in, measures about 5.8x4.3mm, giving it an image gathering area around 35 times smaller than a full-frame sensor. Comparing a 12Mp camera with such a sensor against a 12Mp full-frame SLR of course means that each pixel site is also 35 times smaller. Some superior compacts feature a 1/1.8in sensor, a 'mere' 22 times smaller than full-frame.

And larger...

There are also, of course, cameras with larger sensors, which are usually developed from medium-format film cameras. Their image quality can be astounding, but they're also bulky, expensive and mostly designed for use on a tripod. The Leica S2 promises a body similar in size and weight to current DSLRs, yet with a 45x30mm sensor. Together with legendary Leica lenses, it should yield incredible image quality with agile handling.

SENSOR TYPES

Sensors are not only differentiated by the size and number of pixels. Today, the vast majority of DSLRs use a Bayer pattern sensor, with a couple of significant exceptions.

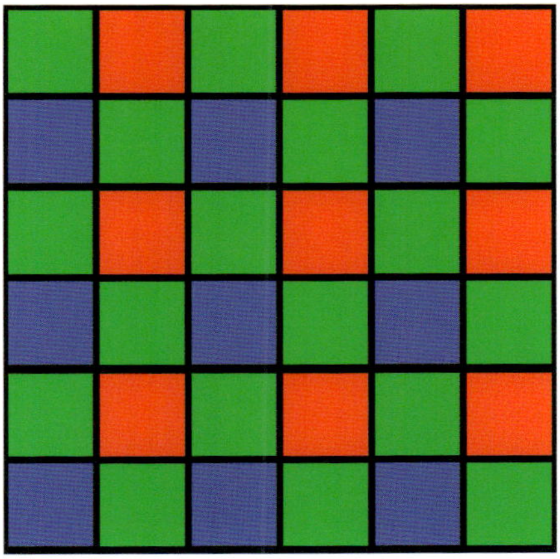

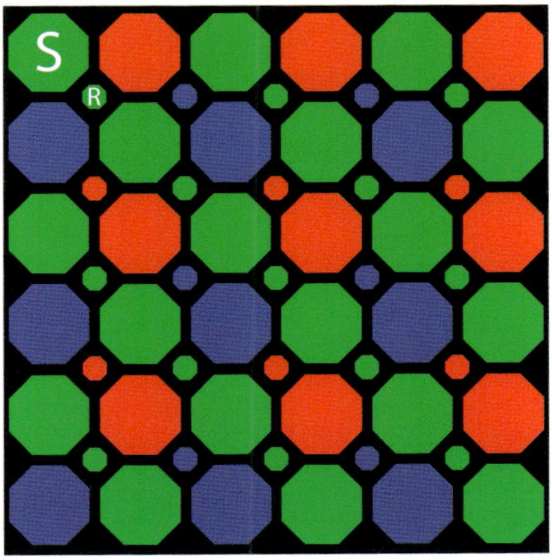

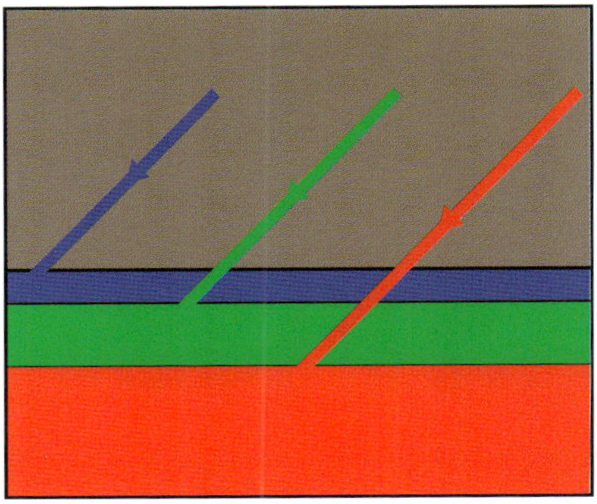

Bayer pattern sensor

The Bayer pattern uses a simple 'chessboard' mosaic of cells or diodes. It's distinguished by having two green cells for each red and blue one. This is achieved by placing a tiny filter over each diode. The reasoning is that the human eye is most sensitive to fine detail in the green region of the spectrum. The result is that the sensor actually only registers one colour of light at each pixel site. Extensive processing (demosaicing) is required to interpolate the missing colours to provide the RGB information for each site (processing takes place in-camera for JPEG files and in the computer for RAW files). This has been linked with a tendency to produce jagged edges and other 'artifacts', partly corrected by the use of a low-pass or anti-aliasing filter in front of the sensor. This also becomes less and less evident as the processing software gets better.

Top
A highly schematic plan view depicting the pattern of microlenses over a Bayer sensor.

Middle
A highly schematic plan view depicting the pattern of 'S' and 'R' pixels in the Fujifilm Super CCD sensor.

Bottom
A highly schematic cross-section depicting the layers of silicon and absorption of light in a Foveon sensor.

CCD and CMOS

Bayer-pattern sensors (and some others) are of two main types: CCD (Charge-coupled Device) and CMOS (Complementary Metal Oxide Semiconductor). It used to be reckoned that CCD sensors produced better image quality, but they were more costly to produce and consumed more power. A lot of research has been devoted to improving the performance of CMOS sensors and they are now used in DSLRs like the Canon EOS 1Ds Mark III, Sony 900 and Nikon D3x, which set current benchmarks for image quality.

The APS-C sized Fujifilm Super CCD sensor uses a unique layout which interweaves two different types of photodiode. Larger 'S' photodiodes capture the bulk of image information, while the smaller 'R' photodiodes capture extra detail in the brightest areas. With currently just over six million of each type, there's some dispute over whether this is a 6Mp or 12Mp sensor. JPEG images and RAW files, processed using Fuji's own software, produce 12Mp files, but the detail is probably not as crisp as it would be from a decent camera with a 12Mp Bayer sensor. Where the Super CCD undoubtedly scores highly, however, is in dynamic range, where its performance is exceptional. Independent tests show that it can capture a range of over 13EV in a single exposure, unequalled by any other DSLR until very recently – the Nikon D3x now edges ahead in some tests.

The sensor is currently available only in a single camera, the Fujifilm FinePix S5 Pro. Like its predecessor, the S3 Pro (there never was an S4), it is particularly popular with wedding and portrait specialists. It's based on a Nikon body (D200), giving compatibility with a huge range of lenses and other accessories.

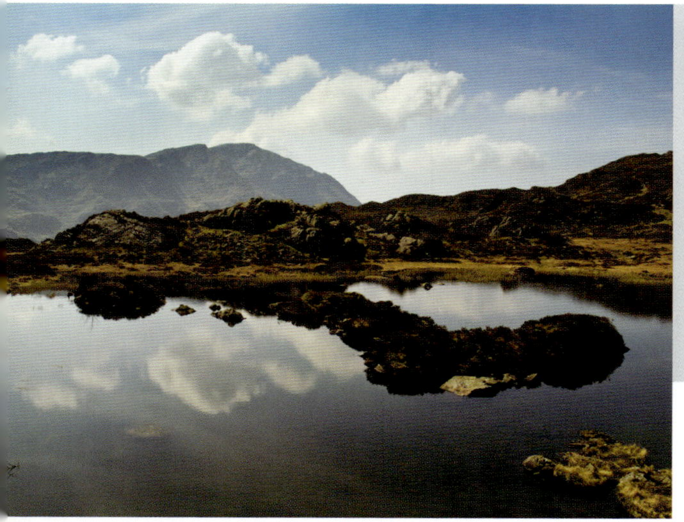

Innominate Tarn, Lake District, UK
The Fujifilm Super CCD sensor claims very good dynamic range and this does seem to be borne out here, with detail remaining even in the brightest clouds – many DSLRs would have struggled with this scene.
Fujifilm Finepix S3 Pro, focal length 18mm, ISO 100, 1/250sec at f/8

The Foveon sensor

The Foveon sensor is arguably an even more radical departure from the mainstream. Both the standard Bayer and the Super CCD use a single layer of sensors in a mosaic pattern. The Foveon, on the other hand, incorporates three stacked layers, using the silicon itself as a filter. It therefore claims to record all the colour data at each and every pixel location. Foveon protagonists argue that this means that images require less processing to interpolate missing colour data. They also claim that they need less sharpening in processing as Foveon sensors don't require a strong anti-aliasing filter. It's interesting that this multi-layer approach is more akin to the way that film works.

Independent tests give a mixed appraisal of the Foveon. Its resolution appears to be superior to Bayer for colour detail but weaker in monochrome detail. The overall performance of the current X3 version, with 14Mp, is usually rated comparable to a nine or 10Mp Bayer sensor. Noise levels appear to be similar, perhaps just losing out to the best Bayer-equipped cameras at high ISO ratings.

The sensor is only available in cameras from Sigma. There's the intriguing DP-1 compact and the SD-15 DSLR. This uses a unique lens mount, but as Sigma are one of the world's leading lens makers that is not too much of a massive handicap.

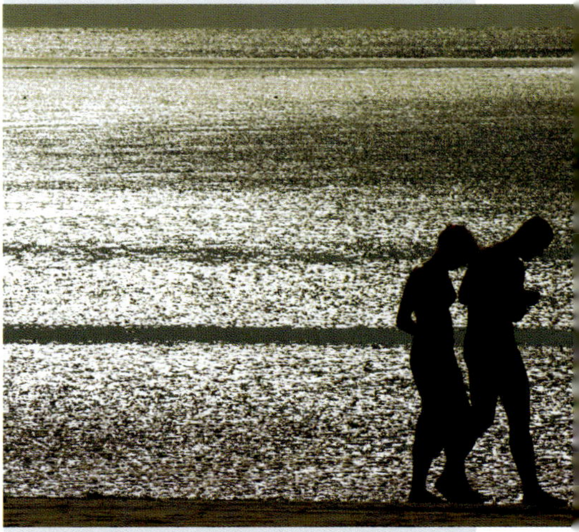

Morecambe, Lancashire, UK
Dynamic range was really high and I decided it was better to let the figures turn into silhouettes and make sure the highlights didn't blow out.
Nikon D2x, focal length 200mm, ISO 200, 1/400sec at f/13

POINT OF VIEW

My experience with the Fuji Super CCD sensor was not a happy one. I was attracted to the S3 Pro by its claims of high dynamic range capture – very appealing for landscape work – but I found it hard to reap any benefits. Fuji's own software for processing the RAW files was almost impossibly slow and clunky. Yet at that time, other RAW processors refused to recognize the files as 12Mp images and couldn't take full advantage of the improved highlight detail. The camera was also too slow for any serious action shooting.

By all accounts the S5 Pro is a vast improvement, although I've moved on to the latest full-frame Nikons which can equal its dynamic range anyway.

RAW vs JPEG

A key decision for any DSLR user is whether to shoot RAW or JPEG. Like many other aspects of digital photography, there is no one-size-fits-all solution. The right choice depends on the kind of photographer you are and the type of images you are shooting.

Both RAW and JPEG refer to digital image file formats. JPEG is a specific image format with image data being recorded in a specific way. The acronym stands for Joint Photographic Experts Group. JPEG is the most widely used image format in computing and photography, in fact many people will never need to use anything else.

RAW, on the other hand, is a generic term. Each camera maker has its own variety of RAW file and its own designation for them; Nikon's are NEF and Canon's are CR2 or CRW. File formats for each camera model are subtly different too. RAW is not an acronym, it simply means that the file contains raw, unprocessed data from the camera's sensor. It's purely a convention to write it in capitals.

All digital camera images start out as RAW data. The choice is whether this is processed in the camera to produce a JPEG file, or whether it's saved as RAW, to be processed later on the computer. This is a fundamental difference and a major factor in any workflow.

IMAGE QUALITY

It's often been claimed that shooting RAW produces better image quality than shooting JPEG. This may once have been true, but it's now regarded as a serious overstatement. The quality of JPEG files straight from the camera is now generally very good and will certainly be more than good enough for most people, most of the time. In many cases there can be little detectable difference between a JPEG straight from the camera and a processed RAW file.

More accurately, shooting RAW may not produce a better image (whatever 'better' actually means), but it does give you much more control over the final image. A RAW file that you have processed yourself might not be 'better' by any objective measurement, but it may be much closer to the exact aesthetic look and feel that you were after. In my book that's better.

FLEXIBILITY

Perhaps the key point, however, is that shooting RAW gives you extra room for manoeuvre, for several reasons.

First, JPEG files have 8-bit colour depth (see p44), yet RAW files have 12 bits per channel, or in some cases 14. That's either 16 or 64 times as much colour information to play with.

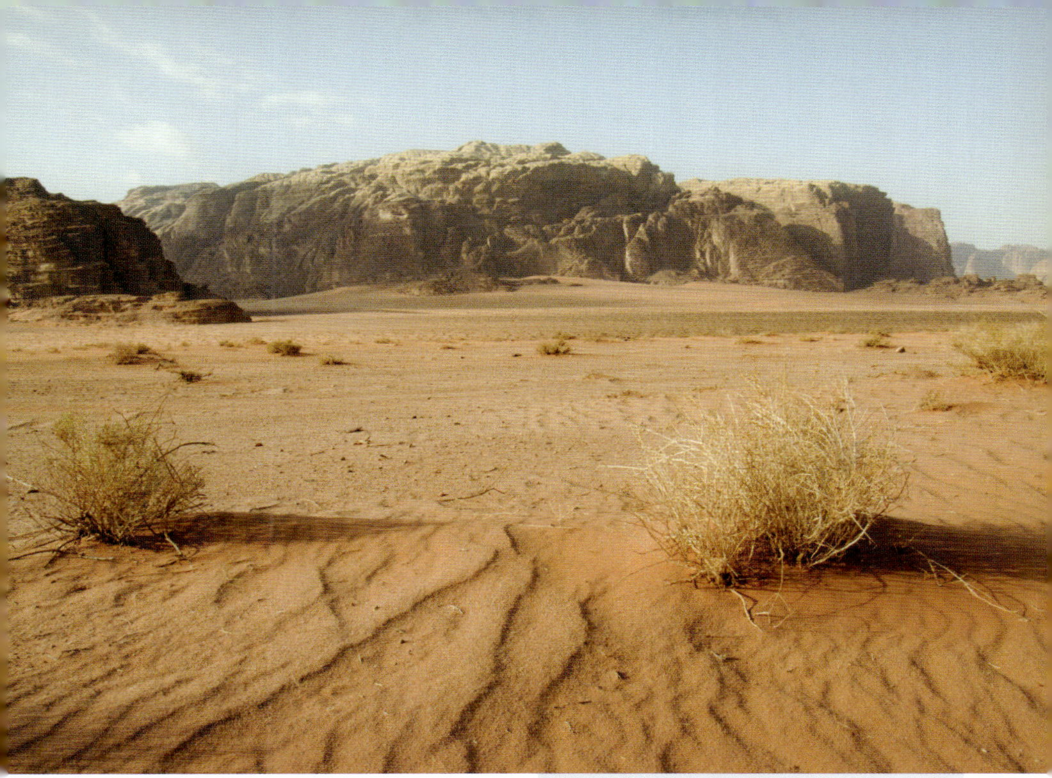

Wadi Rum, Jordan
To save card space and to minimize card changes in this dusty environment, I mostly shot JPEGs during my Wadi Rum trek. The quality is good, but I've had to accept that there is less scope for fine-tuning the images later.
Nikon D2x, focal length 18mm, ISO 125, 1/100sec at f/13

Second, JPEG files are compressed and that compression is 'lossy'. Compression discards data. As much as possible the compression algorithms aim to throw away only the least important data, but it is still irretrievable.

Third, JPEG files usually undergo other in-camera processes, such as noise reduction and sharpening. If you don't like the results, there are severe limits on what you can do to rescue the images. For example, if noise-reduction is too strong it can produce a smeary 'watercolour' effect that obscures detail and makes the images look highly artificial. Sharpening the image afterwards can't restore the lost detail and may even make the watercolour effect more obvious.

Fourth, RAW conversion is not a one-shot deal, therefore it's 'non-destructive'. The conversion software merely keeps a record of the editing parameters – Exposure, White Balance and so on – that you applied. You can revisit the original file at any time and change any of these parameters. Alternatively, you can make multiple versions for different readings of the same image.

The flexibility of RAW becomes crucial in demanding shooting situations, especially where contrast is high; the available dynamic range is greater and, above all, there's scope to recover highlight and shadow detail that may be lost in the JPEG.

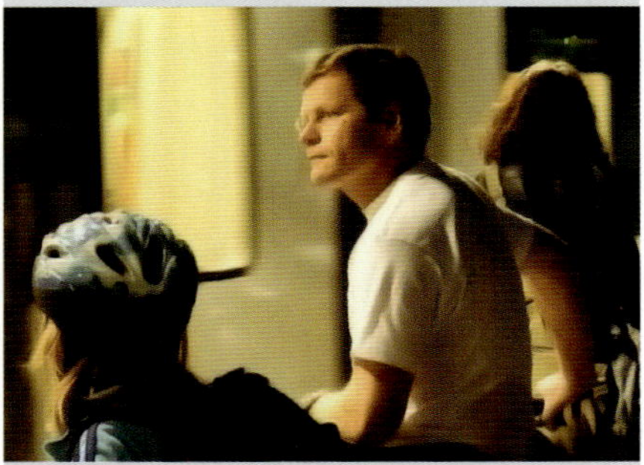

Metro station, Oslo, Norway
A blow-up from the full frame shows the over-smooth results of excessive noise reduction. Fortunately this shot originated as a RAW file and I can adjust the NR level.
Nikon D2x, focal length 18mm (cropped), ISO 800, 1/30sec at f/3.2

COMPRESSION

Compressing files means more images will fit onto a memory card and also speeds up shooting as smaller files take less time to record. However, not all compression is equal. JPEG compression is 'lossy', although at higher quality settings the losses may become unnoticeable. Other file formats, like TIFF, support 'lossless' compression. RAW files can also be compressed, Canon's sRAW format being one example. Nikon offers a choice between 'Compressed' (lossy) and 'Lossless Compressed'.

VARIABLES

If you shoot JPEG, the final image quality is dependent on the quality of in-camera processing. If you're weighing up possible new cameras, this can and should be assessed through independent review sites. However, bear in mind that most of the default settings for JPEG processing can be changed. For instance, the defaults may apply strong sharpening and noise reduction, which can be beneficial in small prints and Web images, but tend to look awful in larger prints.

When shooting RAW, the final results depend both on the camera itself and on the RAW-conversion software. Camera-makers' own software may be well tuned to their own RAW files but won't work with files from other brands. Third-party RAW converters may produce results that look significantly different, but you may of course prefer these. Like cameras, the software changes rapidly. Independent reviews are always a useful resource and, unlike cameras, you can usually give software a free trial.

SMART OR CASUAL

It's tempting to think of JPEG as a 'point and shoot' format for the casual snapper, while RAW is the vehicle of the involved, thoughtful photographer. But hold on; shooting RAW gives you more scope to err at the time of shooting and to have some chance of rescuing a usable image. Because JPEG shooting offers less of this flexibility, it actually involves greater commitment at the shooting stage.

This does not mean that I'm advocating a sloppy approach to shooting RAW. Far from it. You might get away with it sometimes, but

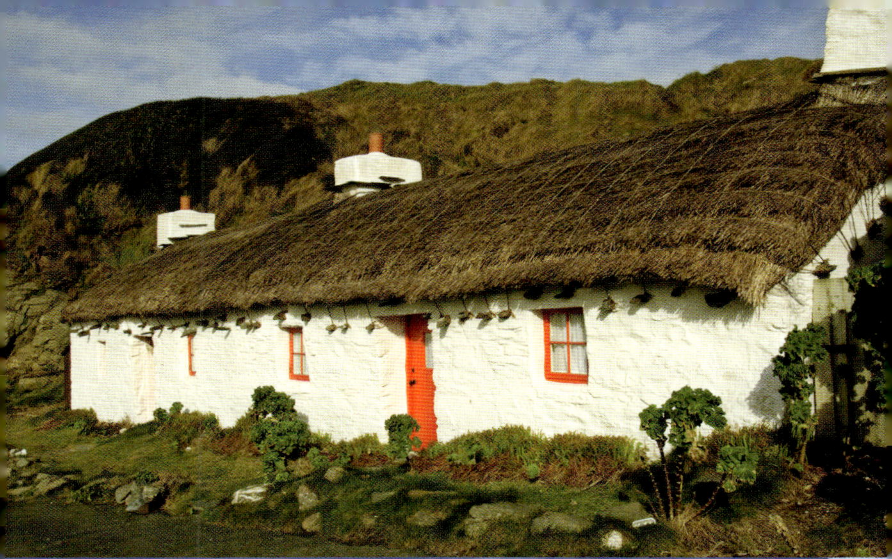

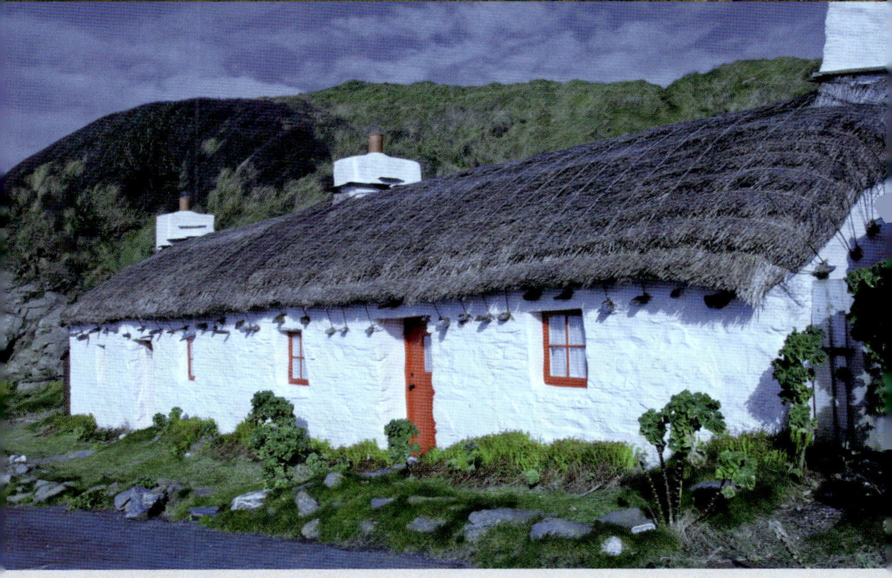

Ned's Cottage, Niarbyl, Isle of Man, UK

The white cottage will make an inappropriate White Balance all too obvious – and because it's white, all the information here is close to the end of the tonal scale, so there may be nothing to play with in the 'wrong' shot.

Nikon D2x, focal length 23mm, ISO 125, 1/125sec at f/14

not always. The point is that a casual approach to shooting JPEG often causes problems. You can get excellent results shooting JPEG with modern DSLRs, but you have to get the camera settings right.

Some camera settings are equally crucial for either format, yet many are most critical for JPEG shooting.

A perfect example is White Balance, as it affects image processing, not image capture. An inappropriate White Balance setting on a RAW shot is a trivial matter; you can fix it in a second at the processing stage. A JPEG shot with the wrong White Balance is a larger problem. You can adjust it in Photoshop later on, but it's more hassle and in the worst cases the necessary data is simply not there. (See p76 for reasons why Auto White Balance is no panacea.)

Generally, settings like sharpening and noise reduction also have no bearing on the RAW file. They are, however, locked in to the JPEG file. It's good to remember that you can't remove them, but you can add to them. Adding sharpening to a JPEG file is easy, but you can't subtract sharpening that's already there.

While processing settings only affect JPEG files, the same is not true of capture settings, such as aperture and shutter speed. A RAW file may provide some headroom for adjustments to exposure, such as the ability to recover highlight detail, but this is not limitless. In addition, shooting RAW does not make the slightest difference if the image is poorly focused, or an inappropriate shutter speed has caused camera shake or motion blur in the subject.

BIT DEPTH

Bit depth (or colour depth) is a measure of how much colour information an image contains. A monochrome image can be represented using 8-bit data, which gives 256 (2 multiplied by itself 8 times, or 2^8) possible levels of grey; 0 represents dead black and 255 pure white.

A digital camera image normally comprises of data from three colour channels – red, green and blue. An '8-bit colour' image has eight bits per channel, so can be described as '24-bit colour'. The total number of possible colours is 256x256x256, or about 16.7 million. JPEG images are 8-bit/24-bit images.

POINT OF VIEW

My approach is to shoot 14-bit RAW as much as possible. I may not always see a visible difference, but it probably does help in high-contrast situations. There's also the possibility that RAW conversion software is going to get better at extracting extra detail – I'm hedging my bets with that. However, when speed is all-important I switch to 12-bit RAW capture.

Not every DSLR gives the option for 14-bit capture, and I wouldn't get too hung up about it. There is a difference but most of the time it's pretty marginal.

16-bit colour

16.7 million seems a lot. It certainly represents finer distinctions than the human eye can easily see. However, it's not always enough! It's fine for image display, but gives limited room for manoeuvre when editing and manipulating images.

Consider a grayscale image, with 256 levels for each pixel. Image-editing changes these numbers and as you start shunting numerical values around they 'bunch up'; this becomes evident in smooth areas (e.g. clear skies), which start to show definite tone breaks or posterisation.

This may be less obvious in RGB images, because tone breaks may be in different places for each channel, but it still occurs. You can also see it in the histogram (p94), which acquires a 'toothcomb' appearance.

This is just part of the argument that image-editing should always be done in 16-bit colour. Sixteen bits per channel, therefore 48 bits in total, to give 65536 levels per channel, or about 280 trillion permutations. Needless to say, this does require hefty number-crunching power. Even just a few years ago handling 48-bit images was quite a stretch for most computers (for more on computer needs p60).

Most cameras capture RAW files in 12-bit colour depth. Only a few offer 14-bit RAW capture, which records four times as much colour information. There's some dispute as to how much real benefit this is, as all RAW files are expanded to 16-bit during the conversion process. Some tests suggest that 14-bit capture allows a small increase in the dynamic range, most obvious in shadow detail. However, the files are around 25 per cent larger and there's usually a noticeable slowdown in shooting speed. Even the mighty Nikon D3x slows from its normal 5fps to around 1.8fps.

APPROX. FILE SIZES FOR A 12-MEGAPIXEL IMAGE (4200 X 2800 PIXELS)

Image mode	**File size** *(approx.: file sizes vary when images are compressed)*
12-bit RAW (Nikon NEF, lossless compression)	30MB
16-bit TIFF, uncompressed	68.5MB
8-bit TIFF, uncompressed	34.3MB
8-bit TIFF, LZW compression	12.7MB
JPEG, maximum quality (12)	4.5MB
JPEG, medium quality (6)	1MB

FILE SIZE

JPEGs discard data, but this means they produce much smaller files. Big files naturally tend to fill up camera memory cards and computer hard drives. This is less of an issue than it used to be, as cards and hard disks have become relatively cheap. Yet when you are on long shoots, or if you're shooting massive numbers of images, it still counts.

ALTERNATIVES

Hedging your bets: RAW + JPEG

Most modern DSLRs permit simultaneous recording of RAW and JPEG versions of the same shot. This consumes more card space and may slow shooting down slightly, but ensures you cover all bases. This may fit into specific workflows. For instance, some professionals will use the JPEGs for client previews, yet rely on the RAW files for the final images. It's also a good strategy when you're new to the game or you're assessing a new camera. If, after shooting for a while over a range of subjects, you consistently find that JPEG files are good enough for your needs, then you might choose to shoot JPEG only. Conversely, if you regularly turn to the RAW file to get the images looking just right, you might turn off the +JPEG option.

TIFF

It may surprise some readers that we've barely mentioned TIFF files, which are traditionally regarded as offering better quality than JPEG. Many DSLRs still offer TIFF as a shooting option; yet, this is a legacy feature of debatable value. TIFF files are larger than JPEG, but unlike RAW they don't capture significantly more data. There is little to be gained therefore by shooting TIFF in-camera. However, editing in TIFF on the computer may be a different story (p56).

SPEED

File size also impacts on speed. Although JPEGs are processed by the camera, the time penalty is more than offset because they can be written to memory card more quickly. Again, it's a less crucial issue with modern cameras and cards because write speeds have improved so much. The landscape photographer will never notice the difference, but it's still significant for sports photographers, for example.

Using compressed RAW files also speeds up write times. While 14-bit RAW files contain four times more data and may extract extra dynamic range, the maximum shooting rates may slow noticeably.

INSTANT ACCESS

If you need instant access to your images, when taking the memory card straight to a printer, for example, then JPEG is the only choice.

CONVENIENCE

If you shoot RAW, you'll have to do a bit more work on the computer afterwards. However, the true impact is often exaggerated. With either format, you still have to download images, review them, discard duds and so on. The extra time spent processing individual images may be a minor addition, particularly with modern software which allows you to apply predetermined settings and to batch-process clusters of images.

DNG

We've already mentioned that RAW files are not a standard format, but unique to each camera. Nikon RAW files, for example, can't be edited using Canon software or vice versa. Neither can NEF files from newer Nikon cameras be processed using older conversion software. In an attempt to harmonize this confusion, Adobe, makers of Photoshop, have introduced the DNG (Digital Negative) format. You can use their free DNG Converter to convert any RAW file to DNG. Adobe Lightroom software can also convert proprietary RAW formats to DNG as it imports the files.

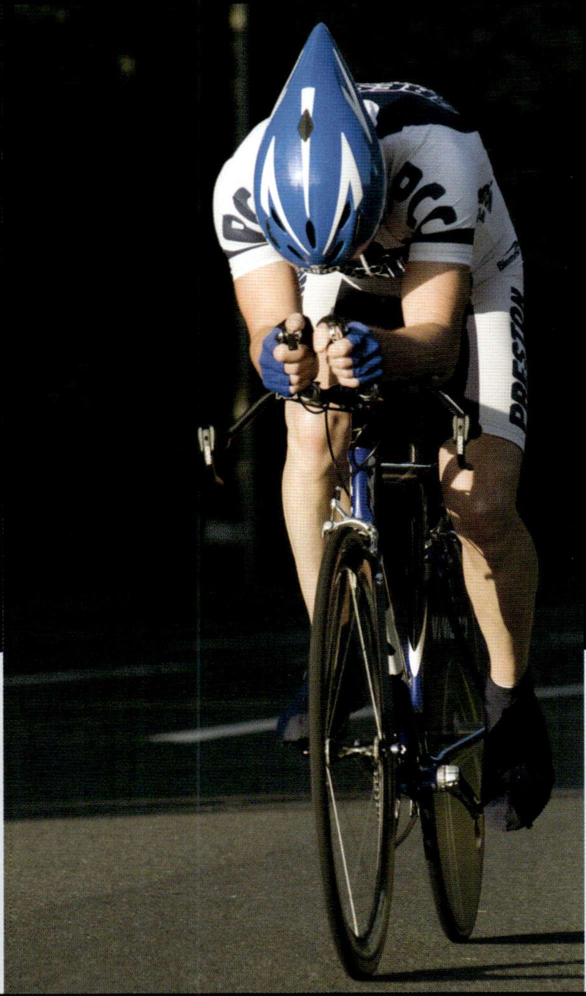

Rider in Preston Evening Time Trial Series, Lancashire, UK
Shooting 14-bit RAW should not make the camera any less responsive when capturing single frames, but may cause a noticeable slowdown in its maximum rate for continuous sequences.
Nikon D3, focal length 200mm, ISO 400, 1/500sec at f/8

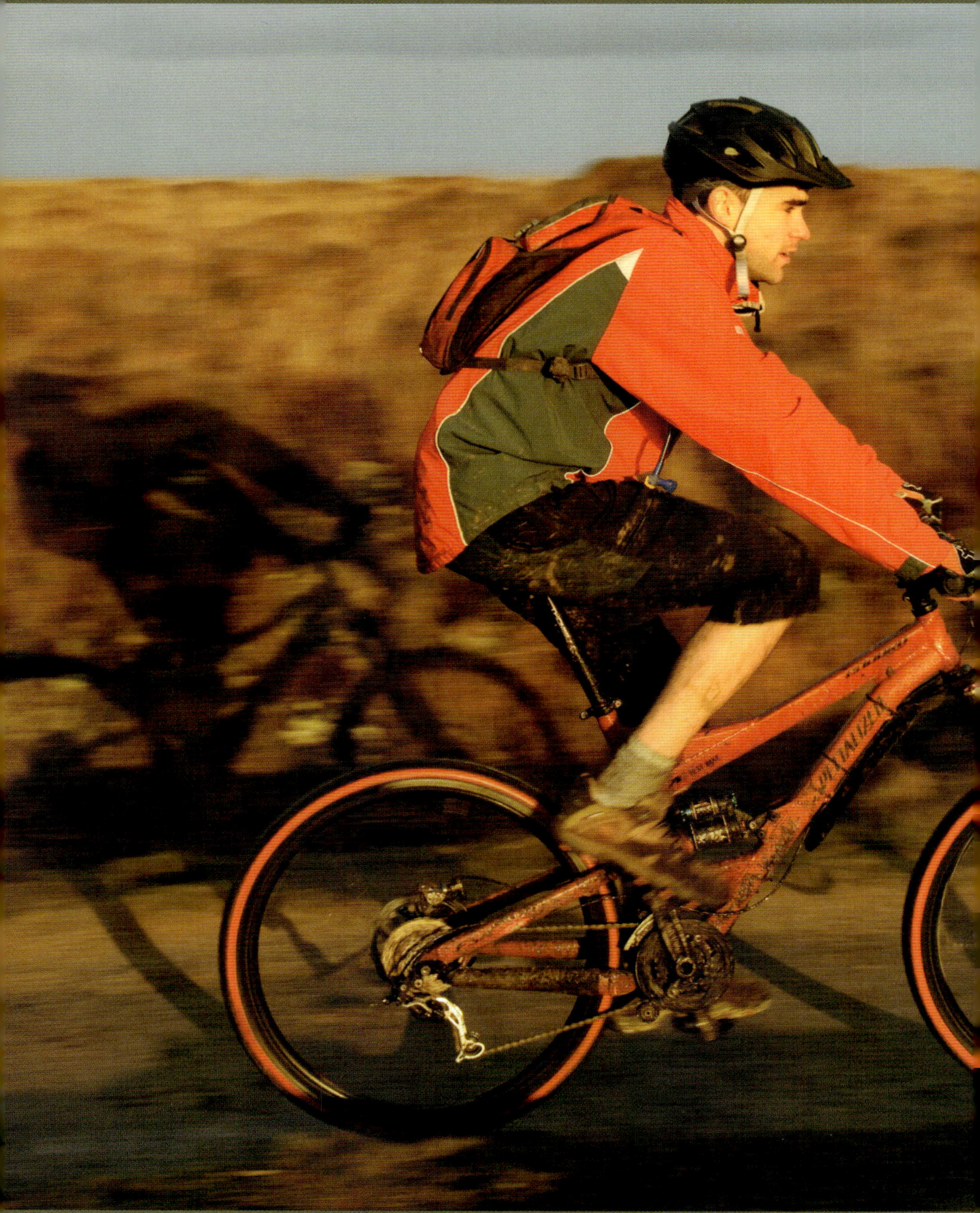

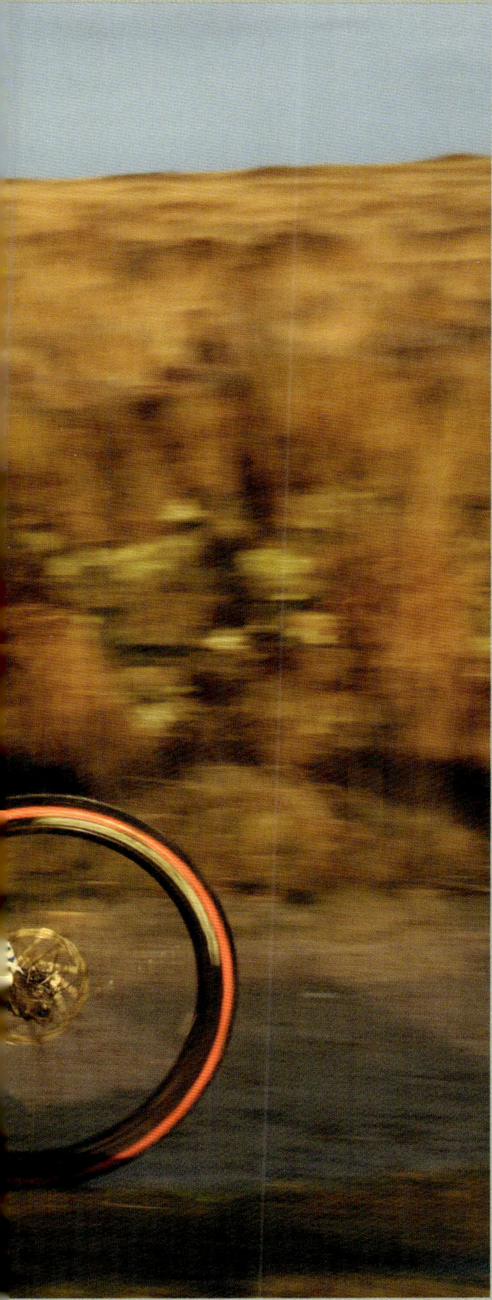

03: WORKFLOW

Workflow is essential to getting the best out of your DSLR. It may sound a bit dour and professional, but workflow is just the word that has come into general use. It doesn't mean shooting with a DSLR has to be hard work; in fact the right workflow is key to enjoying your shooting as well as getting the best results – fun as well as satisfaction.

Mountain biker near South Hessary Tor, Dartmoor, UK
Nikon D2x, focal length 38mm, ISO 250, 1/80sec at f/9.0

What is 'workflow'?

Workflow just means what you do with your photographs, and it pretty much boils down to five key aims.

- Shoot: capture good images to start with.
- Save: keep the images safe.
- Find: keep track of the images so you can find them again.
- Enhance: ensure images look as good as they possibly can.
- Enjoy: print, publish, enjoy and share them.

Every photographer has a workflow. We always have had; workflow wasn't born with digital. What digital, with its wider range of options, has done is make more people think about workflow, whether or not they use that term. Of course, in pre-digital days a common workflow looked something like this:

Buy film> Load camera> Take pictures> Rewind film> Take to chemist> Collect prints> Look at prints> Put in shoebox> Forget about prints.

One of the arguments for thinking about workflow is to ensure that your photos don't end up in the digital equivalent of the forgotten shoebox. And one thing that this example illustrates is that when you're thinking about workflow, one of the key questions is where you want to end up, because that has a bearing on where you start. Decisions like whether to shoot RAW or JPEG, whether to rely on adjusting images in camera or to do most of the work on the computer later, are fundamental.

In the film era, your end-point was either prints or slides. This immediately dictated what type of film you would use, as well as having a

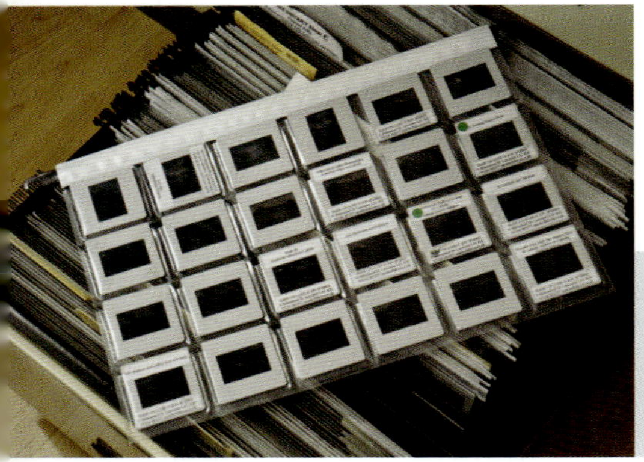

Organizing your slides
Without some sort of catalogue, hanging files are not much better than the proverbial shoebox.

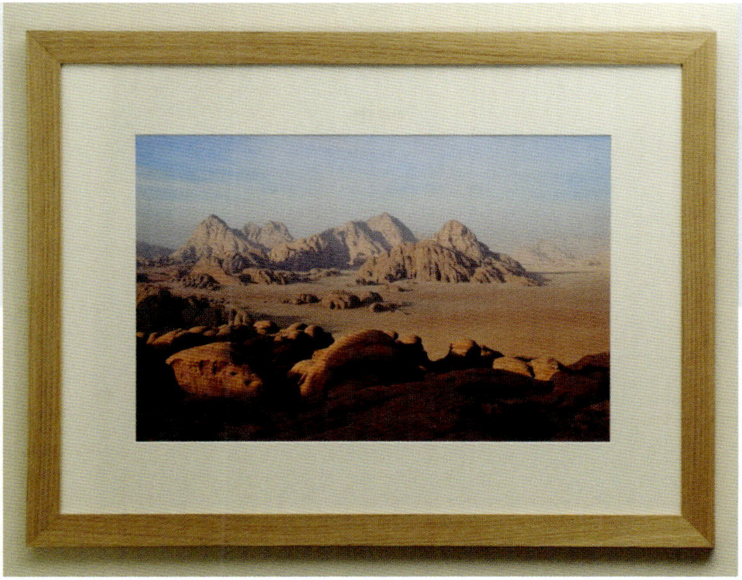

Display methods
The print on the wall is still a favourite way to display your best shots.

bearing on other aspects of the way you might shoot. In the digital age the number of possible end-points (delivery methods) has multiplied. It's true that these can be broadly divided into hard copy and virtual forms, but there are many varieties of each and also a lot of overlap; you email a photo to your aunt in Auckland but she then prints out a hard copy.

Thinking 'backwards' from the end-point is (or should be) second nature for the professional photographer; workflow needs to offer the most efficient and cost-effective way to deliver the required end product to the client. Time is money, and inefficient ways of handling, storing, editing or distributing images represent a real cost.

For the average family snapper, these things may not represent a monetary cost – though they can do. Printing out the same image repeatedly because the colours don't look quite right can work out quite costly. More usually, the various intermediate stages are simply seen as hassle that needs to be minimized. But simply not thinking about these things is not the answer: again, getting the workflow right is key to minimizing hassle and maximising satisfaction with the results.

For the enthusiast photographer, the picture may be more complex; it's quite possible that the journey may be just as important as the destination, if not more so. It's perfectly possible, and entirely commendable, to see the process itself, or certain stages of it, as the main attraction. For many it's the actual business of taking photos out in the field. Others may take equal pleasure in working on their images in Photoshop, just as many were and some still are, devoted to the craft of darkroom work.

Sample workflows

The best way to shed light on workflow is to look at some specific examples. I'll start with my own workflow, not because I think it's the best, but because I know it inside out.

Even if it is the best strategy for my own needs (I hope it is) my workflow definitely isn't appropriate for everyone; so we'll also look at a couple of other very different examples. One of these may be closer to your needs, but everyone is different and we can't possibly cover all the bases. The most we can do is illuminate the thought processes that go into developing a suitable workflow. Probably the most important consideration at this stage is that camera settings are an integral part of your workflow. We'll look at the whole business of camera setup in more detail in the next chapter and other stages of the workflow in later chapters.

WORKFLOW 1

My workflow does change subtly according to circumstances. For a shoot that lasts a few hours it looks something like the table on the right. Ready to Roll is a key point. It means all images I want to keep are backed up, have basic keywords and have been assigned to Collections so I can easily find them again. At this stage I've looked at images as previews and may have made a few quick adjustments, but probably no more than that. And I can do all this (and more) from within a single software application, Adobe Lightroom. Apple's Aperture covers a similar range of functions. See p156 for more detail.

What happens next? That depends. Many images may just sit there until I have a need for them. For example, as I write, I've had an enquiry from a newspaper for images covering a particular walk in the Lake District, and I've been able to find them within minutes. When I've shot for more immediate use – e.g. example images for this book – I can do further adjustment work if needed (cropping, checking for dust spots, fine-tuning colour and tonal values) before exporting as max-quality JPEG. If I think some images need further work in Photoshop, however, I'll export them as 16-bit TIFF.

Longer shoots may include some extra steps. For instance if I'm out all day there may be some downtime (lunch break or when sitting on a train or bus) where I can do a Field Review on the camera screen, delete obvious duds and perhaps decide whether there are some shots I ought to go back to.

The longer the trip, the more anxious I'll be to include a backup stage earlier in the workflow; otherwise I'm amassing ever more images which only exist in one place – on the memory card(s). If possible (e.g. I'm overnighting in hotel or B&B accommodation) I'll backup daily to my laptop, but unless I can do a second backup I won't delete the images from the card(s); the principle is to ensure that images always exist in at least two locations.

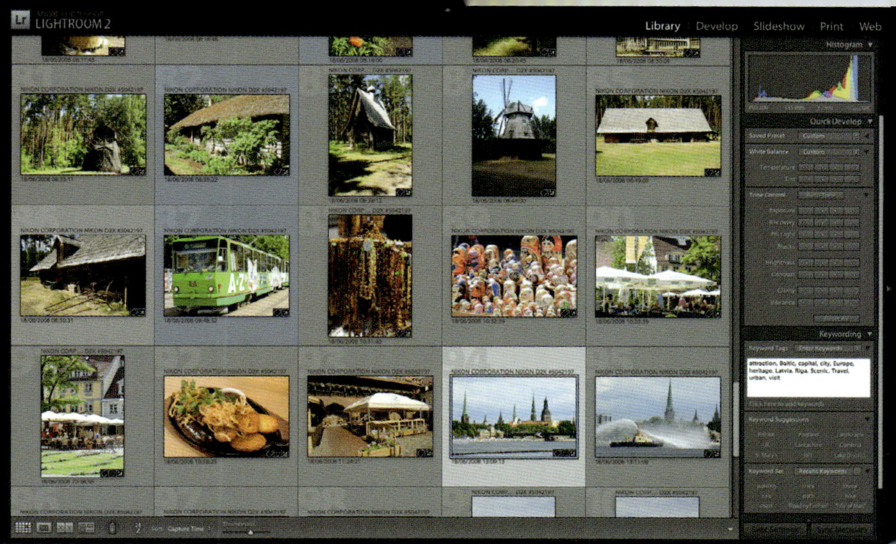

Adobe Lightroom screenshot
This shows preliminary keywords and Quick Develop settings being applied to a batch of images.

WORKFLOW 1

SHOOT	DOWNLOAD & TAG 1	REVIEW	TAG 2	BACKUP & SELECT	READY TO ROLL	EXPORT *(immediate or later)*
Shoot RAW	Adobe Lightroom			Manual or automated system backup copies all files to external hard drive	Format memory card in camera ready for next shoot	Images exported as required; some may need further editing work either in Lightroom or in Photoshop
Shooting settings, e.g. 14-bit RAW, White Balance	Basic keywords added at import	Mark 'picks'; delete rejects; use quick edit controls for preview adjustments	Images assigned to appropriate collection(s): e.g. Lancashire and/or Walking and/or Winter and/or Digital SLR Handbook			
Exposure settings, e.g. aperture and shutter speed						

WORKFLOW 2

This photographer loves her DSLR, and wants to spend as much time as possible out shooting with it, with the minimum necessary time back home on the computer. She wants good quality images; the best will be turned into handsome prints and she'll also upload selected shots to a personal website or a community like Flickr.

WORKFLOW 3

This photographer has a very different approach. A few years ago he'd probably have spent half his time in the darkroom producing fine prints. He's still interested in fine prints but recognizes that digital can do this without sloshing noxious chemicals around. He shoots relatively few images, taking time to ensure that composition and lighting are just right.

This photographer uses the camera-maker's own RAW conversion software on the principle that it has been specifically developed to get the most out of that maker's RAW files.

Note that backup happens twice in his workflow. The first backup protects the original RAW files, as he may want to revisit them in the future (perhaps because of improvements in RAW conversion software). The second protects the carefully crafted TIFF file in which he has invested considerable Photoshop time.

Nikon Transfer, a basic download manager
One of Nikon Transfer's key features is the ability to backup files automatically as they are downloaded. Most camera makers provide something similar.

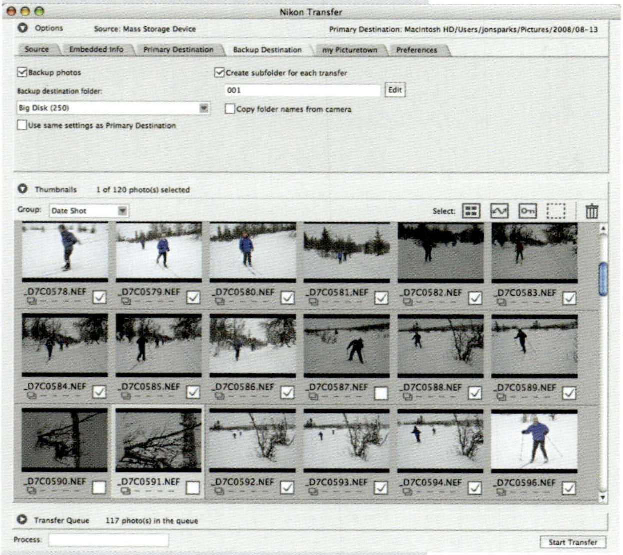

WORKFLOW 2

SHOOT	FIELD REVIEW	IN-CAMERA RETOUCHING	DOWNLOAD & BACKUP	REVIEW SELECT, TAG	EDITING AND ENHANCEMENT	PRINT/ SHARE
Shoot JPEG Fine, sRGB	One or both of these stages may be omitted if short of time		Download manager software automatically creates backup copies on external hard drive; tags may also be added here	Some images may be deleted at download stage (i.e. don't select for import)	Where necessary, images may receive enhancements in iPhoto or Photoshop Elements	Images for web use may need to be downsized and sharpened
Shooting settings, Picture Styles						Format memory card in camera ready for next shoot
Exposure mode, e.g. Aperture Priority						

WORKFLOW 3

SHOOT	FIELD REVIEW	DOWNLOAD, REVIEW, SELECT, BACKUP	RAW CONVERSION	FINE ADJUSTMENT	SAVE AND BACKUP	PRINT
Shoot RAW (14-bit if camera supports it)	Each image is carefully assessed, looking at the histogram to judge exposure and zooming in to check sharpness. If not perfect, the shot is repeated with adjusted settings	Download manager software automatically creates backup copies on external hard drive; tags may also be added at this stage	Initial adjustments to tonal values, extracting full range from RAW file	Using Photoshop or other full-featured image-editing software. Adjustments may include work on specific areas of the image	Image saved as 8-bit TIFF or Max-quality JPEG	Print at home or send to bureau
Shooting settings, e.g. White Balance			Export as 16-bit TIFF		Manual or automated system backup copies all files to external hard drive	Format memory card in camera ready for next shoot
Exposure settings, e.g. aperture and shutter speed						

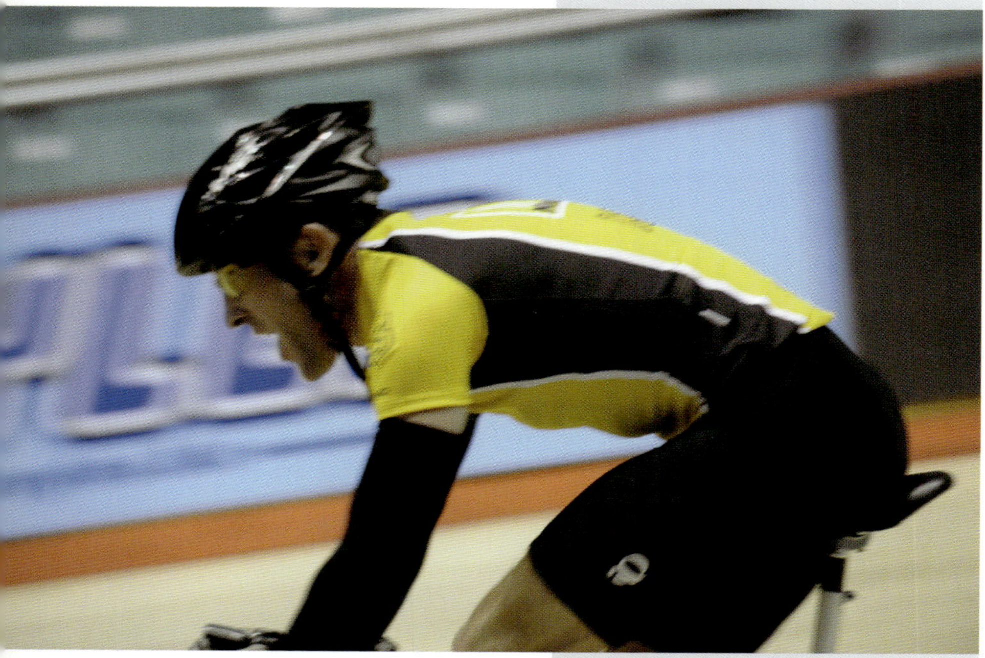

Rider at National Cycling Centre, Manchester, UK
I don't usually shoot 'stadium' sports but on this occasion I was able to transfer files as they were shot to a computer on the far side of the building.
Nikon D3, focal length 200mm, ISO 1800, 1/200sec at f/4.5

Tip of the iceberg

These examples on pages 52–55 are just that; three possible workflows from a huge range of possibilities. There could be many more. Consider the pro photographer shooting a major sporting event. She'll shoot JPEG because there's no time to play with RAW files, but will be absolutely on top of every single camera setting to ensure those JPEGs are as good as they can be. Images will be transferred by WiFi to her MacBookPro as she shoots and at any break in the action she'll add quick tags (who, what, when) and send them to the Picture Desk. In some cases she'll have an assistant managing this side of things and/or a field office at the venue. In any case, once they're uploaded, the pictures essentially become someone else's responsibility.

Futureproofing

In the example on p55, the photographer is careful to preserve his original RAW files as well as the edited versions. He's implicitly aware that what you can do with your images now may not be the final word. In a few years' time you may discover whole new ways to enjoy or deliver them: some may not even have been invented yet!

Even for the professional this can be true. Not, perhaps, if you work on commission and your interest in a job ends once you've delivered the images to a satisfied client (and been paid, of course!). On the other hand, if you're like me and much of your photography is for stock images, then there's a strong possibility that you'll want to return to images some time after shooting, perhaps several years later.

In addition, the value and significance of any given image can change unexpectedly. A casual snapshot of a pub singer might suddenly become valuable a few years later when she wins a TV talent contest.

Futureproofing has two main implications. One is that it's vital to store images safely. This means keeping at least one backup of everything. Let the mantra be: if it's worth keeping at all, it's worth backing up.

However, it's not much use keeping images safe unless you can find them again. The digital 'shoebox' can quickly fill up with thousands, even tens of thousands, of images. How do you find that shot of the pub singer? It might be worth your while to open every image folder on your hard drive to look for her, but it would be a lot better to be able to locate those shots within a few mouse clicks.

The other implication is that RAW (or DNG) is a much more futureproof format than JPEG. It's not that JPEG images are more susceptible to data corruption or similar problems. However, image-editing software continues to improve; if that pub singer shot is a tad dark and noisy, future software has a better chance of extracting a better image from a RAW file than a JPEG that has already been heavily processed.

Sty Head Tarn, Lake District, UK
This shot was taken in 2005, but never used until I had a specific enquiry for images of this tarn in 2009.
Fujifilm Finepix S3 Pro, focal length 12mm, ISO 100, 1/125sec at f/9.5

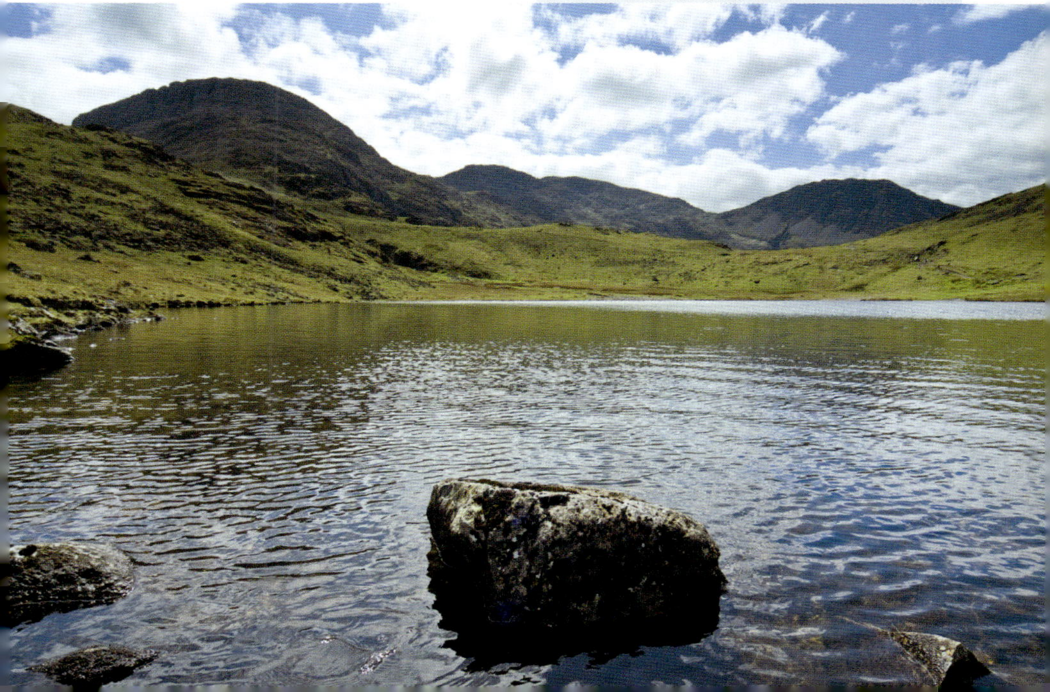

Working with images

There's much more about working with images in later chapters, but as this is such an integral part of the workflow, it is worth sketching some outlines here.

SAVING IMAGES

I hope this doesn't seem like a daft heading. After all, your images are already saved on the memory card. However, this is only short-term storage; you will want to format the card and reuse it.

There are several ways to get images from the camera/card into the computer, including 'tethered shooting' where the camera is connected directly, either with a cable or over a wireless network; images may bypass the memory card entirely or also be saved to it. This usually requires extra software. Tethered shooting with a cable severely limits your mobility but is feasible for studio type work; wireless shooting requires an adapter attached to the camera.

It's much more common to transfer images to the computer after shooting. You can connect directly with a USB or FireWire cable, normally supplied with the camera, or use a card reader. These are very inexpensive and most people find this method most convenient. Some 'media centre' PCs have built-in card slots.

It might seem natural to copy the images across to your computer as you would do when copying other files, but for various reasons it's nearly always better to manage the process using some dedicated software. Managing the download helps to ensure that all your photos are stored together and in a logical way: see p143 for the lowdown.

STORING IMAGES

Two of the five workflow goals identified at the start of this chapter were Save and Find. In other words, store images securely and in a way that makes it easy to find them again. Your collection of photos can quickly come to number in the thousands. This represents a lot of time, creative effort and unique memories. If it's not secure, you can lose it all without warning. And if you can't find particular images when you need them, you might as well have lost them anyway.

The key to security is backing up. Any data that exists in only one place is vulnerable, and digital images are just a special form of data.

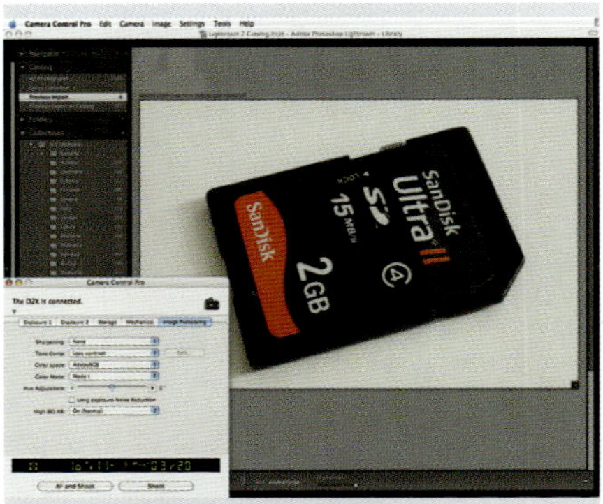

Tethered shooting
Nikon Camera Capture Control Pro can be set up to transfer images directly to Adobe Lightroom.

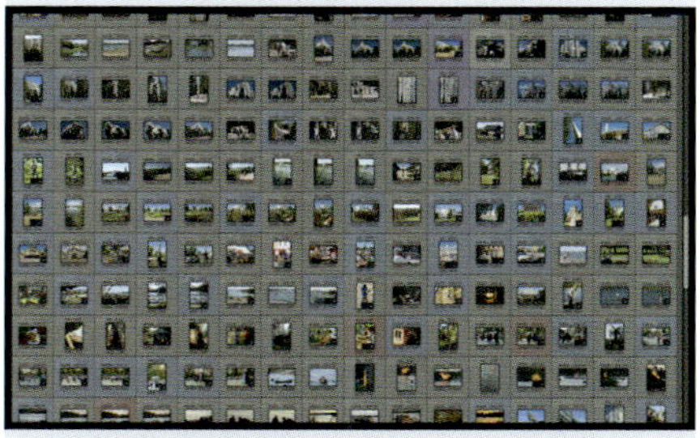

Image management
160 images on this screen, and these are just a fraction of my images of one city (Helsinki) in one country (Finland). Images need to be managed!

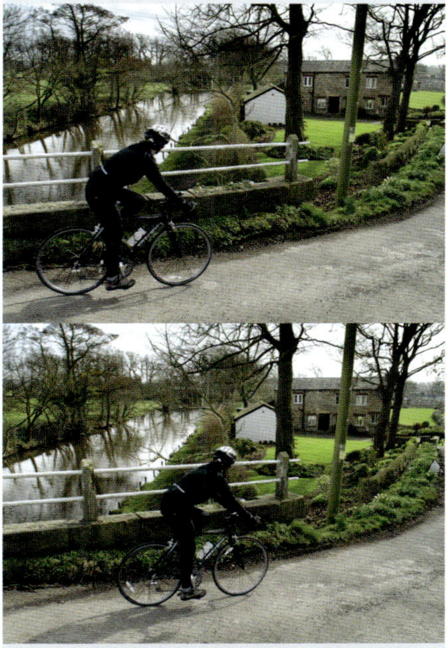

Cycling near Forton, Lancashire, UK
The only real difference between these shots is the position of the rider: do I really need to keep both?
Nikon D700, focal length 24mm, ISO 640, 1/320sec at f/11

Back up as soon as possible and as often as possible. Exactly how and where you do it is a matter of choice, and there's a lot more about it on p140 – but not backing up regularly, let alone not backing up at all, is asking for trouble.

EDITING IMAGES

We have to be careful with a word like 'edit', as it can be used in two senses, and often the distinction isn't immediately clear.

First, 'edit' can refer to the process of reviewing your images. As in the workflow examples, you can do a preliminary Field Review on the camera back. However, unless you're running short of card space, be conservative about this. It's safe enough to delete blatant duds and obvious duplicates, but many images that look uninspired on the camera screen may reveal more subtle qualities on the computer monitor. The bigger monitor also makes it much easier to do a side-by-side comparison of 'similars'. This helps both to flag up the best images and to identify redundant duplicates. This kind of editing can be a dull job, but a vital one. At the very least, it helps to postpone the day when your hard drive bursts at the seams.

Editing in its second sense – often called image-editing – addresses the fourth workflow grade: Enhance. Other words we might use are adjustment or fine-tuning. Although the best way to do this is to get things right at the shooting stage. Image-editing software, even the mighty Photoshop, is not a magic bullet. Also remember, that you will have more room for manoeuvre at this stage if you shoot RAW, less if you shoot JPEG. Which underlines the point: setting up the camera is the foundation of good workflow.

The workstation

The most important tool in digital photography is the camera, but for most of us the computer comes a close second. Getting the best out of our images, and getting them seen by others, nearly always means time at the screen.

THE SOLO DSLR

Can a DSLR live alone? That is the question. That is to say, is it viable to use a DSLR without hooking it up to a computer at least occasionally? Well, in theory, it is. If your end-point is the hard-copy print, you can take the memory card straight to a high street lab, or plug it into a desktop inkjet printer. With the latest in-camera processing, it's possible to crop, straighten and otherwise enhance your shots beforehand (on most new DSLRs). But then what? You've got a set of prints, and a set of images on your memory card. But memory cards are just about the worst place for long-term storage. They're a lot cheaper than they used to be, but still relatively expensive compared to other forms of storage, not to mention being easily lost – and if that happens, where's your backup?

Things will develop in the next few years. Camera phone users can already transmit images directly, albeit heavily compressed and poor quality. Press photographers can transmit their images back to the office, though usually via a laptop. How long before your DSLR can connect directly to the Internet, so you upload to online storage as you shoot? Even having done so, retrieving the shots still requires a computer.

Camera screens have got bigger and better in the last few years, but unless cameras get a lot bigger or some form of fold-out screen or holographic projection comes along, they've pretty much reached a limit. Both for viewing and for editing these screens can't really compete with a much larger computer monitor. For most of us, for the foreseeable future, the computer will remain an indispensable part of digital imaging.

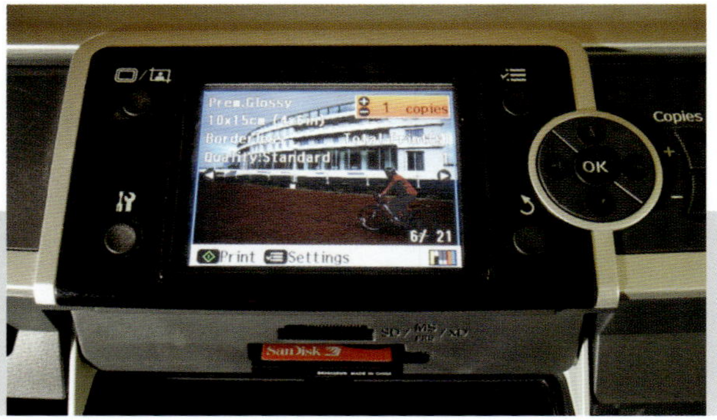

Printing
It's possible to print directly from the memory card on many desktop printers.

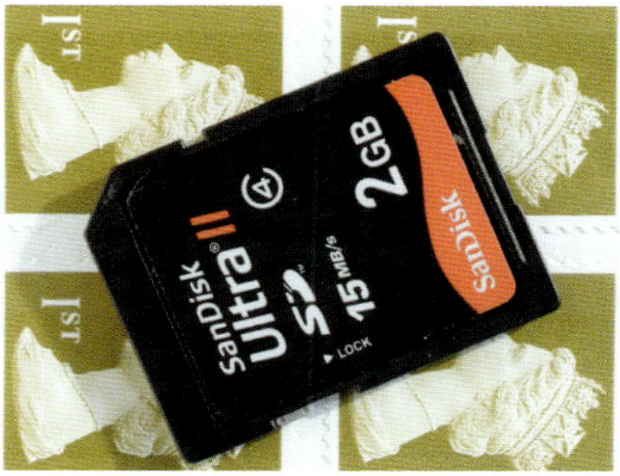

Storage
Memory cards are not ideal for long-term storage. They are relatively expensive and their tiny size makes them easy to lose.

WORKSTATION REQUIREMENTS

Workstation is a handy catch-all term, even if you view your images purely for pleasure. It's vital that your computer is up to the task, but your exact requirements will depend on your workflow: do you shoot large numbers of images? JPEG, RAW or a bit of both? Do you expect to do a lot of image-editing or leave the pictures generally as they are?

In the last few years laptop sales have outstripped desktop systems. This may be partly because more and more of us already have a decent desktop system; it's also undoubtedly because laptops have got a lot better. Today's laptops are certainly fast enough, and many have a respectable hard-drive capacity and a large screen. However, a laptop good enough for serious imaging work is still an expensive proposition, and unless you really need to be able to work on your photos on the move, a desktop system represents much better value.

THE SCREEN

It's no mistake that I've come to the screen (aka monitor) before the computer; it's that important. This is where you view your images, assess them and make decisions about them, so it makes no sense to skimp on it. A poor screen won't just make your images look less good than they are: it can also make it difficult to get satisfactory prints. Size matters, for two main reasons: it lets you browse large numbers of images simultaneously without the thumbnails becoming microscopic, and gives more space for editing, when you may have several palettes open. Anything smaller than the 17in screens of the (currently) largest laptops is going to feel cramped sooner or later. I've travelled widely with a 12in iBook – and written chunks of this book on it – but I'd never expect to do serious editing on it.

But if size matters, quality matters even more; if it's a choice between a good 17in screen and a less good 20in or larger, I'd go for the smaller screen. Quality factors include the maximum brightness, contrast level, colour saturation and resolution. More specifically, look at the 'native resolution' as this is where images and text will display most crisply. Higher resolutions will display images well but may make text, in documents and in menus, uncomfortably small. A key factor for imaging work is gamut, which describes the total range of colours that a screen can display. This is closely related to colour space: see p78. If you'll only ever use sRGB colour space then a wide gamut is less vital, but if you'll ever shoot RAW, prepare images for high-quality printing, or just want the best results from your DSLR, a wider gamut means you can see much more of the image information your DSLR can capture.

Calibration

A good-quality monitor is hobbled, if not completely wasted, without proper calibration. Calibration means measuring the actual colours that a specific screen can display to create a colour profile. The use of colour profiles, along with software that understands them, allows different devices (e.g. camera, computer and printer) to communicate with each other about how colours should be displayed. All serious imaging software understands colour profiling.

This may seem complex and time-consuming at first, but will save massive amounts of time and frustration in the long run. Detailed advice is beyond the scope of this book (there's a useful overview of colour management at cambridgeincolour.com). In Mac OS X there's a handy Display Calibrator Assistant which performs basic calibration; for Windows you may find that the maker of the monitor provides some equivalent software; many users also recommend the free Monitor Calibration Wizard from hex2bit.com.

Hardware calibration devices like the x-Rite Eye-One, Datacolor Spyder or Pantone Huey are far more powerful. For professionals, hardware-based calibration is essential but for the enthusiast it's also a worthwhile investment; it's a big help in avoiding the frustration and waste of prints that don't look right.

TIP

Don't rely on which screen looks brightest or most colourful in the showroom. It may be showing images specifically chosen to look punchy on a screen with a limited gamut. Look for objective comparisons in magazines or on the Web.

MEMORY (RAM)

RAM (Random Access Memory) is where the computer holds the data it's currently working on. Computer experts say that you can never have too much RAM, and for photography it's certainly true, especially with the large files that DSLRs can produce. One gigabyte of RAM is a bare minimum to run modern operating systems (Mac OS 10.5 or Windows Vista) and for comfortable imaging work 2GB is a modest amount. Fortunately extra RAM is relatively cheap these days and on many computers it's also fairly easy to install it yourself, though most vendors will do it for a small charge. If you are buying a new computer it's often possible to specify extra RAM at time of purchase and you may even see RAM upgrades offered free or very cheaply as a promotional sweetener.

HARD DRIVE SPACE

Anyone who's used a digital camera for any length of time knows how quickly you can amass thousands of images. With the large file sizes produced by today's DSLRs this soon adds up to a lot of gigabytes. And that's not all. Imaging applications like Photoshop also use spare hard disk space as a 'scratch disk' – another form of temporary memory to hold data that may be needed at short notice.

Allowing hard drives to fill close to capacity also slows the reading and writing of data. So, a 500GB hard disk can't really hold 500GB of data, or at least not without penalty. Any regular DSLR user can fill a 500GB hard drive in a year or two, even if you don't use the computer for anything else – unless you're ruthless in your editing.

PROCESSOR SPEED

Processor speed on computers is a bit like megapixel numbers on cameras – a glib numerical headline that is far less important than it purports to be. Like megapixels, other things being equal, more processor speed can't hurt, but it is unlikely, on any modern computer, to be a real limitation. Of course, if you do a lot of imaging work with large files, especially if you work in 16-bit (p44) or with lots of layers (p152), this will place high demands on the processor. Speed is never a bad thing, just relatively low down the priority list. Dual-core and quad-core processors also speed things up.

EXTERNAL STORAGE

We've said it before and we'll say it again: backup, backup, backup. And therefore one hard drive is not enough. You can back up to CD or DVD but using a second hard drive is far more convenient and no longer prohibitively expensive. Some computers have space to fit extra hard drives in internal expansion bays, which is a cheap solution but leaves you exposed if your computer is stolen or goes up in flames (rare, but it happens).

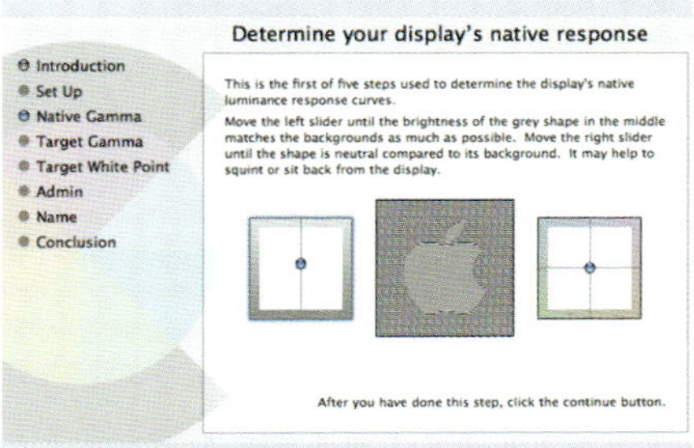

Software display calibration
This is built in to Mac OS X.

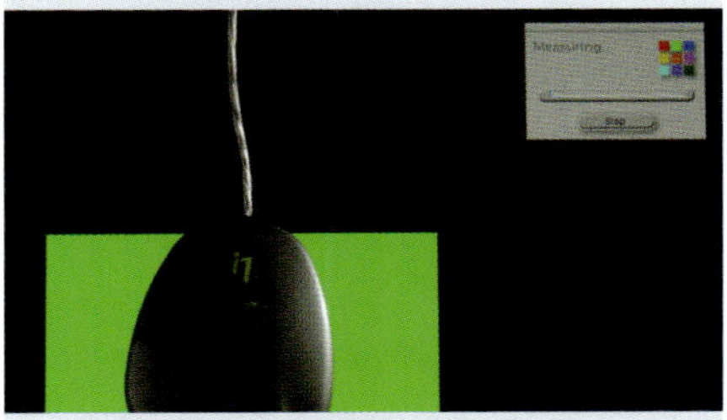

Hardware display calibration
Calibrators like this i1 measure the screen output for the greatest accuracy.

CRT OR LCD

Traditional CRT (Cathode Ray Tube) monitors have all but disappeared, though some high-end users still prefer them. For the average user a flat screen (LCD or TFT) is now really the only choice and on the average desk it makes a lot more sense.

Glossy screens

Glossy screens have become widespread; with many brands of laptop, and all-in-ones like Apple's iMacs, glossy is what you get. Not everyone welcomes this trend. There's some dispute about colour accuracy, but there's no doubt that they can be plagued with reflections. This may be a minor problem in a home or office setting where you can control the lighting, but if you're working on a laptop in changing settings it can be a real pain. Maybe it's significant that a matt screen is once again available as an option on Apple's latest MacBook Pro – probably the best laptop money can buy.

OPERATING SYSTEMS

The operating system is the bedrock software on any computer, providing the environment in which everything else operates. The choice boils down to Mac or Windows. The Mac operating system OS X, now at version 10.5 ('Leopard'), is only available on computers made by Apple, while Microsoft's Windows OS is found on PCs from a wide array of manufacturers.

The Mac is the traditional choice of photographers and other graphics professionals; for instance, the very first version of Photoshop appeared only on the Mac. The inbuilt colour management (called ColorSync) of Mac OS also gave it a crucial advantage. It's a myth that Macs never get viruses, though far more viruses and other malware are created for the Windows OS. Whichever system you choose, you should always install proper virus protection.

Today any advantage is less clear cut, though the Mac still commands tremendous loyalty among professional photographers. Virtually all significant imaging software is available on both platforms and works equally well. There is a perception that Macs are more expensive than PCs but this does not really stand up on a like-for-like comparison. Apple is absent at the low end of the market but its mid-range products (MacBook and iMac) are competitive in value terms and the top-end Macs (Mac Pro and MacBook Pro) are excellent value for the demanding user.

THE WORKING ENVIRONMENT

There are two key elements for the working environment: ergonomics and the right lighting. There's more to ergonomics than simply feeling comfortable, important though that is. Having chair, table and screen at the right relative heights to each other reduces strain on the back, shoulders, wrists and so on.

The ideal viewing distance will vary with individual eyesight, but is almost always greater than the diagonal measurement of the screen: i.e. on a 20in screen, sit at least 24in back.

RAID STORAGE

Something of a gold standard for safe data backup, RAID stands for Redundant Array of Inexpensive Disks. A RAID requires several hard drives plus some management software which works in the background to distribute the data across the disks. To the user it appears as a single disk and allows fast access to files. 'Inexpensive' is a relative term and a RAID is almost certainly beyond the needs of the average enthusiast photographer, but it is a good solution for the professional.

SYSTEM VERSIONS

Many professionals continued using Windows XP long after the underwhelming arrival of Windows Vista, though you can no longer buy a new PC with XP installed. Go for the Home Premium version of Vista rather than Home Basic. The Mac scene is far less confusing with only one, full-featured, version of the OS available at any time.

There's no point in having a big screen if you can't view it as a whole. If you want to inspect fine detail, zoom the image to 100 per cent; this is more accurate than leaning in closer, as well as reducing eyestrain.

Lighting is a crucial consideration for photographic work. Ambient light affects your perception of the screen image. There's little point in carefully calibrating a monitor if it sits next to a window bathed in sunlight one day and the cool tones of an overcast sky the next. Ideally, the screen should be the brightest thing around you, by a clear margin. My workstation is next to a window and when I'm writing or reading emails I'll often have the blind up so I can be distracted by boats passing on the canal outside – but when I need to work on photos, down comes that blackout blind.

POINT OF VIEW

The Mac still has the edge for me, and I've done enough work on Windows systems to speak from experience. Some of it is just the appeal of really good design, evident in both the hardware and the software. The Mac operating system is still more intuitive and more elegant, and it's extremely stable (it hardly ever crashes). New Macs also come with a decent suite of software, including iPhoto (see p155). They hold their resale value better too.

Uncluttered working environment
Note that the main screen is brighter than the surroundings and sits well back on the desk to allow comfortable viewing.

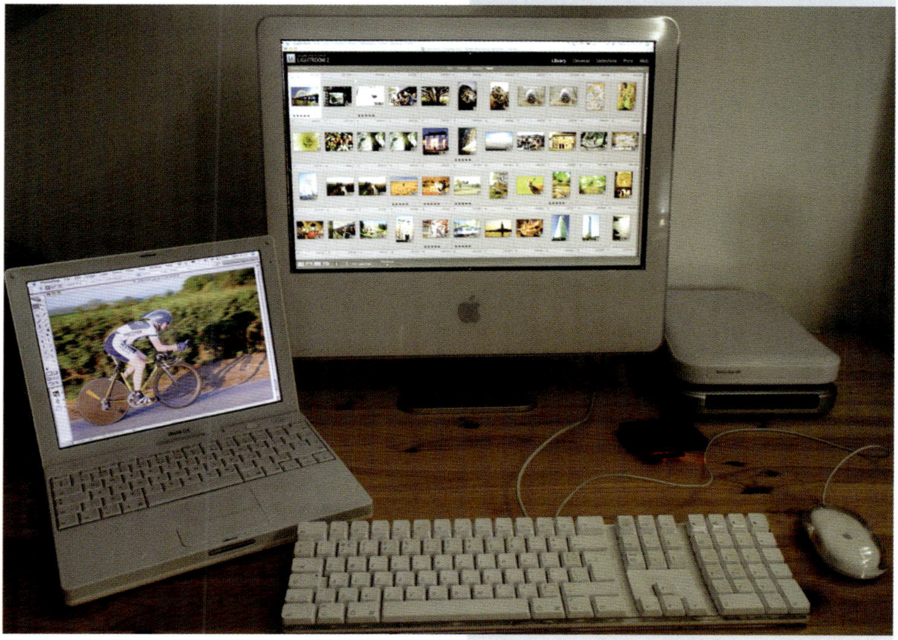

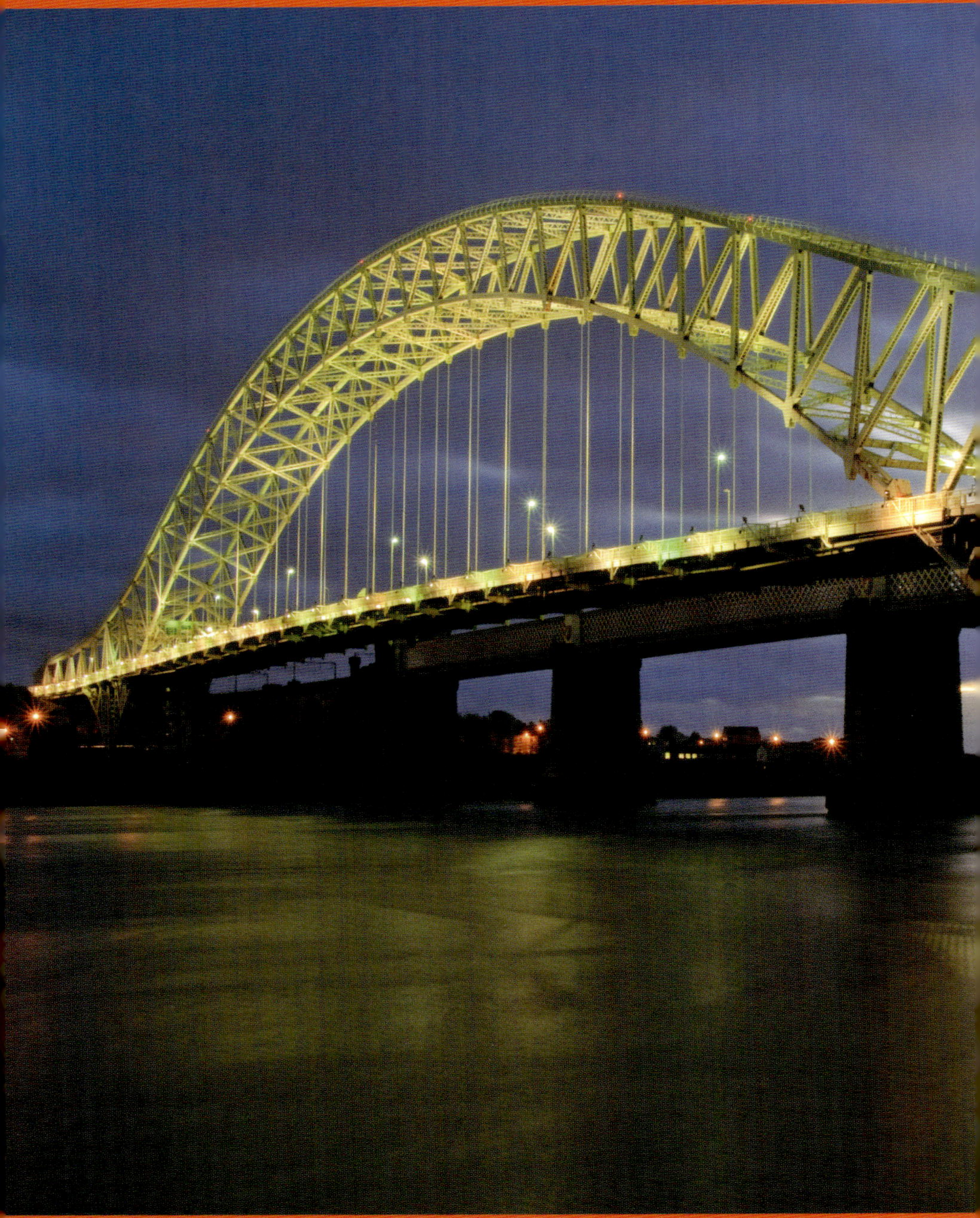

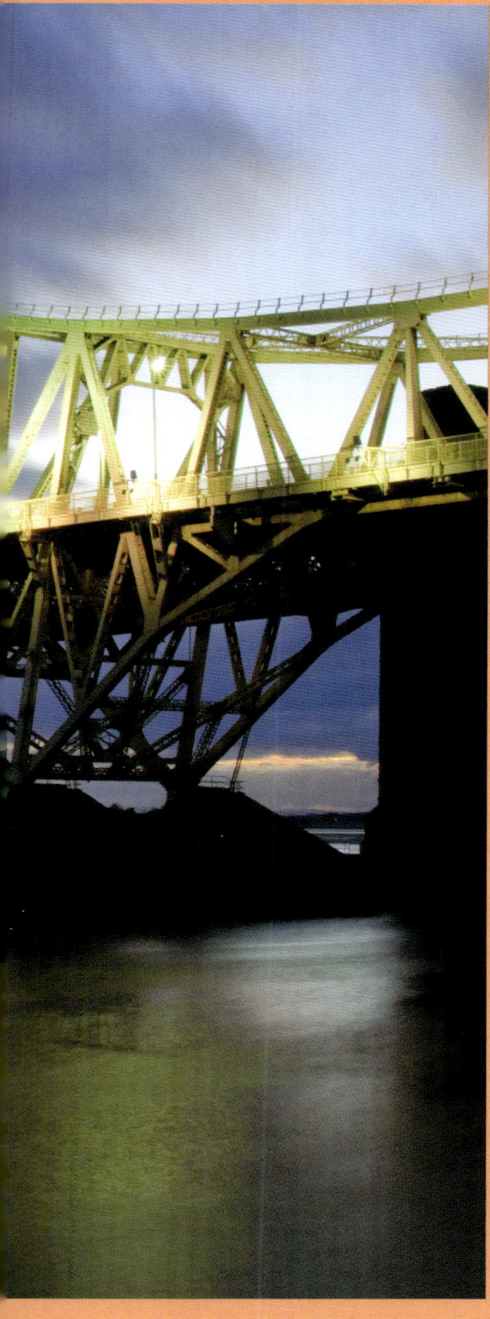

04:
SETTING UP YOUR DSLR

There's a saying, 'Chance favours the prepared mind,' and, we might add, the prepared camera. Digital SLRs can react with amazing speed to changing light and fast-moving subjects, but they still need to be set up in the right way to deliver the kind of results we are looking for.

The Bridge, Runcorn, UK
Nikon D2x, focal length 23mm, ISO 100, 15secs at f/16

Key parameters

There's an ever-growing number of photographers who never shot on film, or at most only took snapshots. I'm well aware that for anyone in this category constant comparisons between film and digital can be irritating, and certainly don't shed much light on the things you want to know. But in terms of setup it is worth making a brief comparison, if only to illuminate the fact that working with a digital camera, and especially a DSLR, really is a new ball game.

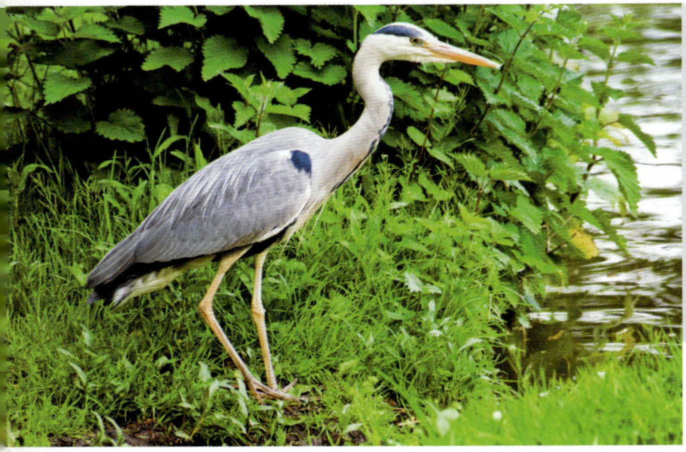

Heron, Bilsborrow, Lancashire, UK
It's rare to get this close to a heron, rarer still for it to stand and have its picture taken. Fortunately the camera was ready and I didn't need to waste any time fiddling with settings.
Nikon D700, focal length 16mm, ISO 6400, 1/160sec at f/5.6

If there was a chapter on setting up your SLR in a book on film photography, it would be a pretty short one. You chose the film you wanted to use, loaded it and made sure the film speed dial was set to the correct ISO. If you wanted finer control over the way the image was going to look, this might mean packing a few coloured filters; it might also mean planning to develop the film differently (especially if you were shooting in black and white). On some 35mm cameras you would have choices of focus mode, exposure mode, metering pattern and drive mode, but I shot happily for a decade on a Nikon FM2 which had none of these (except for the option of bolting on a motordrive).

It's different now. Just take a look at the list of key parameters opposite; in the top half of the list, i.e. down to and including custom settings, the only one with a direct equivalent on a film camera is the first one, ISO setting. It might look more complicated, but that's because we have more options, and that means we have more control.

PARAMETER	BASIC OPTIONS (*available on most cameras*)	EXTRA OPTIONS (*may not be available on all cameras, or may be tucked away in menu system*)
N THIS CHAPTER		
ISO RATING	Variable Range	Auto ISO
IMAGE QUALITY	RAW JPEG	12/14 bit Uncomp/Compressed TIFF Fine/Normal/Basic
IMAGE SIZE	Small/Medium/Large	DX Crop, Vary aspect ratio
WHITE BALANCE/COLOUR TEMPERATURE	Auto; Range of presets	Set manually; Fine tune; Copy from photo
COLOUR SPACE	sRGB, Adobe RGB	
IN-CAMERA PROCESSING	Varies; usually includes picture controls/film simulation; monochrome	There may be many further options, e.g. for retouching images after shooting
SHARPENING	Off; Low; High; etc.	
NOISE REDUCTION	ON (JPEG): Off (RAW)	Long Exp NR; High ISO NR
CUSTOM SETTINGS	Extremely varied	
'N NEXT CHAPTER		
EXPOSURE MODE	Program; Aperture priority; Shutter priority; Manual	Range of 'Scene Modes' etc. Program shift Exposure compensation
METERING PATTERN	Matrix; Centre Weighted; Spot	
FOCUS MODE	Manual; Auto	Auto-SS; Auto-Cont; Focus Point
DRIVE MODE	Single shot; Continuous	Variable Speed for Cont mode; Self timer; Mirror up; Live View

ISO rating

One of the truly liberating aspects of digital photography is that you can change the ISO rating from one shot to the next.

This was effectively impossible on 35mm film. Memories of struggling with slow film on dull days fill me with appreciation for this advance. Yet I'd bet that most DSLR users don't touch the ISO setting nearly as often as they could, and arguably should. It follows that good camera design makes the ISO setting easy to access and to change.

Unlike settings such as White Balance, ISO is not something you can forget about when you're shooting RAW. (Not that I recommend forgetting about White Balance, but you can get away with it). RAW is more forgiving in exposure terms than JPEG, but only to a degree. Whether you shoot RAW or JPEG, be aware of the ISO setting and make sure it's appropriate to the conditions and the type of shot you're taking.

It's also useful – vital even – to have a good idea of the highest ISO which still gives acceptable quality. This varies between cameras and to some extent also according to how critical you are and what use your images are destined for; some imperfections will show up more readily in big prints, and so on. It's worth taking some test shots across the ISO range and assessing them carefully.

A key issue at higher ISO ratings is image noise (see p85). On many compacts it rears its ugly head at anything above base ISO, and certainly becomes prominent at values above 400. With their larger sensors, DSLRs should perform better, though DSLR users are also likely to be more critical and to make larger prints. With my dear old Nikon D2x, I know that anything shot above 400 ISO is probably going to need some noise reduction applied, and that above 800 it gets tricky to produce images that bear close scrutiny. But with a D3 or D700, ISO 1600 is near perfect (though there's some reduction in dynamic range), 3200 is quite usable, and I can go well beyond if need be. Most current DSLRs will fall somewhere between the two.

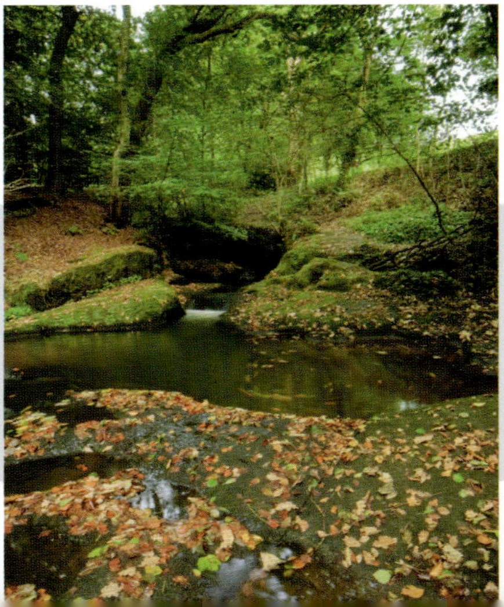

Low ISO shooting
A low ISO (200 in this case) is no handicap when shooting on a tripod anyway, and helps to ensure best colour fidelity and dynamic range.
Canon EOS 1Ds Mk II with 500mm lens, 1/400 sec at f/6.3

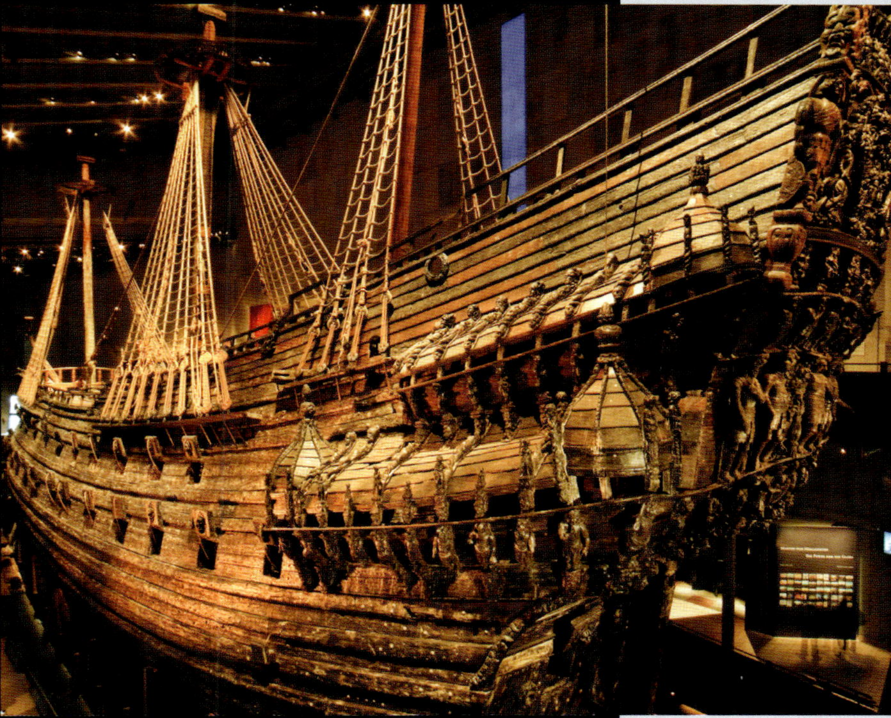

High ISO shooting, Vasamuseet, Stockholm, Sweden
This mighty warship was raised virtually intact after 333 years in the mud of Stockholm harbour. I couldn't use a tripod but knew the D2x was prone to noise above ISO 400, so used a bean-bag and carefully braced the camera on a railing. These decisions are too important to leave to chance.
Nikon D2x, focal length 12mm, ISO 400, 8secs at f/11

AUTO ISO

Most DSLRs have an Auto ISO option, which does what it says on the tin; the camera automatically varies the ISO rating to keep aperture and shutter speed within a deemed-to-be-acceptable range. If you're happy letting the camera make all the decisions about exposure, then it may make sense to let it decide the ISO as well. If you prefer to be in control – i.e. you shoot in Aperture Priority or Shutter Priority mode – it seems much less appropriate. And using Auto ISO when shooting in Manual mode seems completely self-contradictory.

Image quality and size

Image quality is not a magic button that you can press to guarantee great shots. This is quality in a purely technical sense. The basic choice is between RAW and JPEG. It should be possible to switch easily between the two; if it can't be done without delving into the menu system that's a black mark against the camera. The same could be said about image size, though most of us probably change this less often.

RAW OPTIONS

Many cameras have no further options for RAW shooting; any that do exist may be well buried in the menus. This is not usually a problem: most users will change these settings rarely, if ever. The usual choices relate to file compression and bit depth. It's usually safe to accept compressed RAW files, but check the maker's manual for assurances that the compression method is lossless. Uncompressed files take longer to write to the card and consume more space there.

Some cameras offer a choice between 12-bit and 14-bit RAW recording. Shoot 14-bit for the ultimate in quality, but note that there's usually a speed penalty. The file size also increases.

JPEG OPTIONS

Nearly all DSLRs offer a choice of JPEG file quality, usually denoted as Fine, Normal or Basic. These refer to different levels of file compression. Basic files are highly compressed and are all too likely to exhibit JPEG artefacts (see below) if blown up to large sizes. The only use for such files is for images that are to go straight to email or the Web, and when you're quite sure there will never be any need to use them at larger sizes.

In any case, the only reason to shoot Normal or Basic is because they take up less space on the memory card. Given the low cost and high capacity of memory cards now, this is far less of an issue than it was when 512-megabyte cards cost as much as a good restaurant meal. Now you can get 4-gigabyte cards for the price of fish and chips, there's no real reason not to shoot JPEG Fine all the time (unless you shoot RAW, of course).

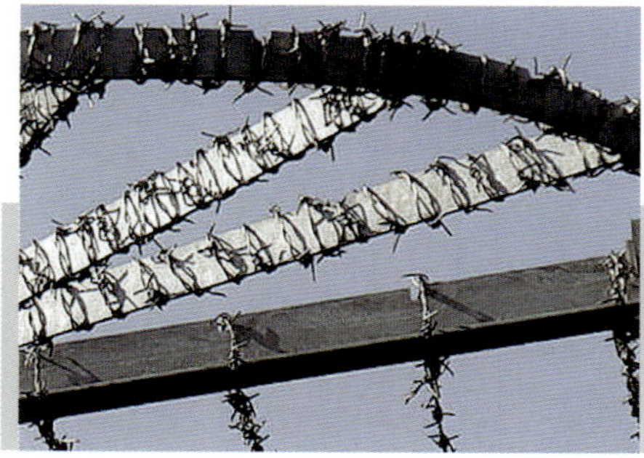

Compression artefacts
Heavy or repeated JPEG compression creates 'artefacts' like the blocky effect along edges seen here.
Nikon D700, focal length 170mm, ISO 320, 1/800 sec at f/10

IMAGE SIZE

The choice of image size generally applies only to JPEG images. RAW images are normally recorded full size, i.e. at the camera's full pixel count. The same is true of JPEG Large; they could be called JPEG full size. The other options scale down the image to a smaller pixel count. The figures below are for a Nikon D700.

Don't confuse this with in-camera cropping, which some cameras offer (for example, Sony's misleadingly-named Smart Teleconverter function). Large, Medium or Small images still use the full area of the camera's sensor, while cropped images use only a part of it.

LARGE	MEDIUM	SMALL
4256x2832	3184x2120	2128x1416

To illustrate additional options that may arise, let's stick with that Nikon D700. This is a full-frame camera (Nikon calls it FX) with sensor dimensions of approx. 36x24mm. It has an option for DX crop, (see p35) which uses the central 24x16mm area, allowing the use of DX lenses. Its big sister the D3 also offers a 5:4 crop using an area approx. 30x24mm, corresponding more closely to many common print sizes.

City Hall, Stockholm, Sweden
The full frame is the image as shot, with the 3:2 ratio that digital cameras have inherited from 35mm. The brighter area indicates a 5:4 crop; this aspect ratio corresponds to many traditional paper sizes – a lot of people consider this to be more appealing than 3:2.
Nikon D2x, focal length 50mm, ISO 250, 1/320sec at f/9.0

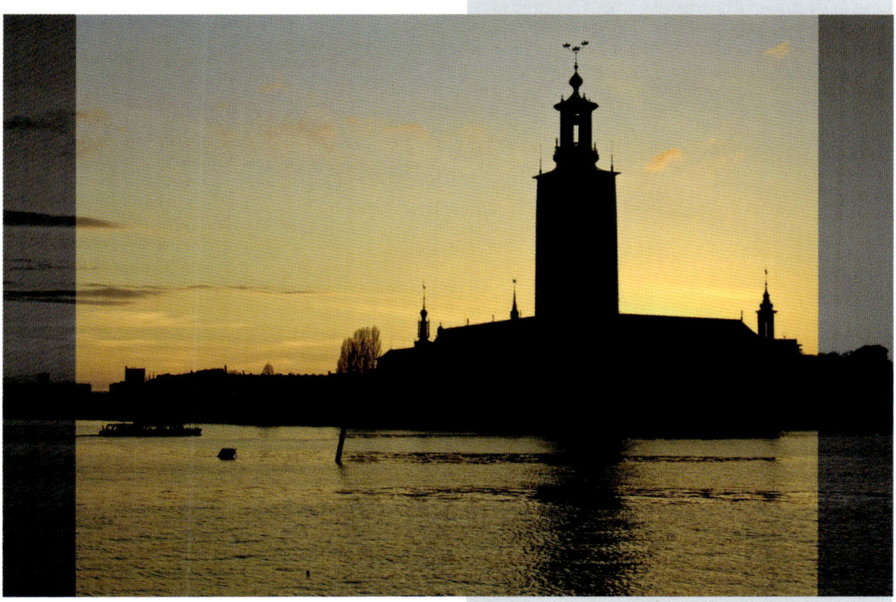

White balance and colour temperature

White balance and colour temperature are really two ways of talking about the same thing: how we ensure that the camera records colours the way we see them, or the way we want them to appear (these are not necessarily the same thing!).

This is important because we see things by the light they reflect, but the light that falls on them can vary enormously in colour. If there was no allowance for this, then the same object could appear in widely differing colours when photographed in different weather conditions, times of day or using different light sources such as flash. Our eyes (or really, our brains) are very good at making such allowances, so that we go on seeing grass as green, snow as white, and so on. Cameras are not so clever and need a little help. This is done through the White Balance settings.

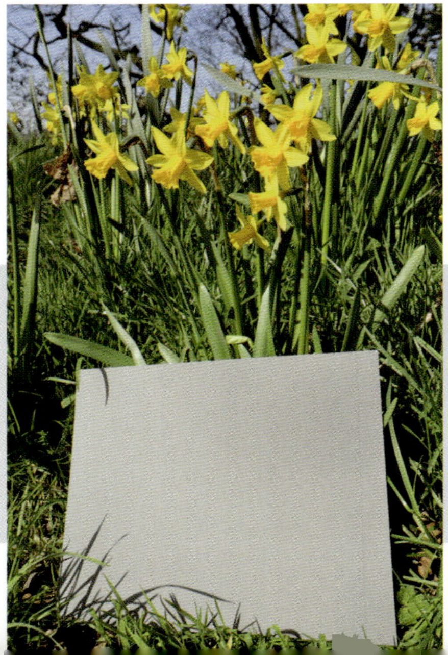

In most cases the basic settings are fairly self-explanatory, though different makers use slightly different terminology. For instance, Canon refers to 'Daylight' while Nikon uses the more precise term 'Direct Sunlight' for the same setting. On overcast days the 'Cloudy' setting is appropriate.

When it is necessary to get the balance exactly right, then most DSLRs, certainly the more sophisticated models, allow you to set White Balance with reference to a target known to be neutral, such as a genuinely white wall or, better still, a photographic grey card. In Canon-speak this is called Custom White Balance; Nikon calls it Preset Manual. In this case I think the Canon terminology is more lucid.

The table gives examples of settings and associated colour temperatures, with both Nikon's (N) and Canon's (C) terminology and figures. Other camera makers may be slightly different again, but the general outlines will be similar.

Taking White Balance
Colour accuracy was highly desirable, and taking White Balance from a photographic grey card left nothing to chance. This image was shot as a JPEG using Preset Manual White Balance. It would have been equally easy to shoot RAW and use the grey card to set White Balance at the conversion stage.
Nikon D700, focal length 32mm, ISO 500, 1/250 sec at f/13

COLOUR TEMPERATURE

Colour temperature, measured in degrees Kelvin, does give a much more precise way of describing white balance than vague terms like 'Daylight' or 'Shade', especially as different manufacturers don't always agree on what these mean (Nikon's 'Shade' is 8000ºK, Canon's is 7000ºK). However, this precision may be more than most users need, or want, most of the time. If you want to know about the physics behind colour temperature, a quick web search is all it takes.

MENU OPTION	COLOUR TEMPERATURE (ºK)	DESCRIPTION
AUTO 3000 – 7000 (C)	3500 – 8000 (N)	Camera sets WB automatically, based on information from imaging and metering sensors.
Incandescent (N) Tungsten (C)	3000 3200	Use in incandescent (tungsten) lighting, e.g. traditional household bulbs.
Fluorescent (N) White fluorescent (C)	Variable 4000	Fluorescent light varies widely. Nikon's sub-menu offers seven options.
Direct sunlight (N) Daylight (C)	5200	Use for subjects in direct sunlight
Flash	5400 (N) 6000 (C)	Use with built-in flash or separate flashgun. Values should reflect different output of Nikon and Canon flash units and may be incorrect with other maker's flashguns or studio flash.
Cloudy	6000	Use in daylight, under cloudy/overcast skies.
Shade	7000 (C) 8000 (N)	Use on sunny days for subjects in shade, i.e. mostly lit by the blue sky.
Choose color temp.	2500 – 10000	Specify exact colour temperature.
Preset Manual (N)	n/a	Derive white balance direct from subject or neutral target, or from an existing photo.

'Correct' colour is not always desirable. We may not always want grey rocks to appear as a neutral grey; for instance, when they're bathed in the reddened light of the setting sun, correcting this to a neutral hue may be the last thing we want. This is one of the main reasons why Auto White Balance won't always give the desired result, and if you are shooting JPEGs there's limited scope to fix the colours afterwards. Auto White Balance is typically less reliable under artificial light than natural light.

It's worth trying to evaluate how accurately the camera's LCD screen portrays colours: in other words, how reliable it is as a guide to the colours of the final image, as they'll be seen on your main computer screen (which is, of course, properly calibrated – see p62). Most current DSLR screens are at least somewhere in the ballpark. However, your perception of the screen image can be affected by your surroundings and it may be advisable to use a shade or hood to ensure an unbiased view of the screen.

TIP

Those shooting RAW have full scope to adjust the White Balance at the processing stage, and it might therefore seem unnecessary to fiddle with WB settings on the camera. However, it is worth getting these at least approximately correct, as they do influence both the preview image on the camera's screen, and the histogram display associated with it.

WARNING

It's very easy to get confused by colour temperature; the red end of the spectrum, which we call 'warm' light, has the lowest colour temperature, while the blue end, which we'd casually refer to as 'cool', has the highest colour temperature. That's human perception versus scientific exactitude.

Albert Dock, Liverpool, UK
Auto White Balance is generally less reliable when dealing with artificial light, and strong subject colours won't help.
Nikon D2x, focal length 12mm, ISO 250, 1/60sec at f/11

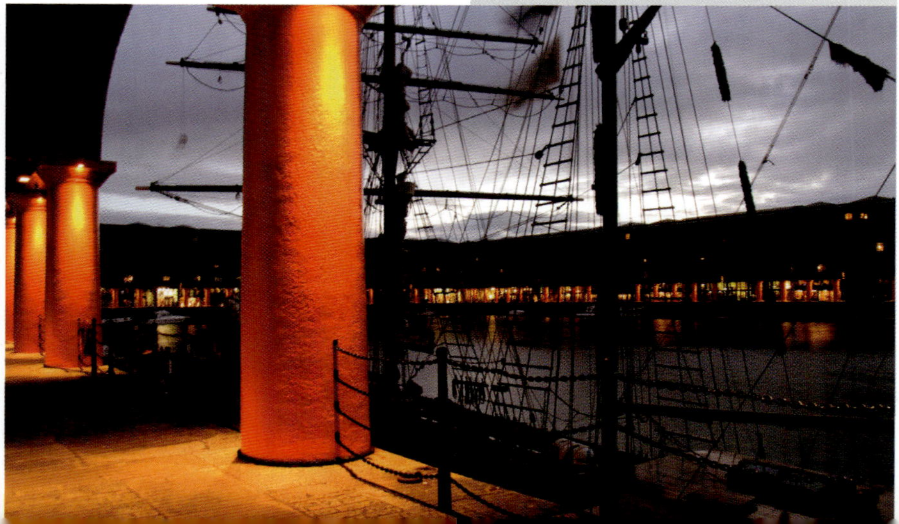

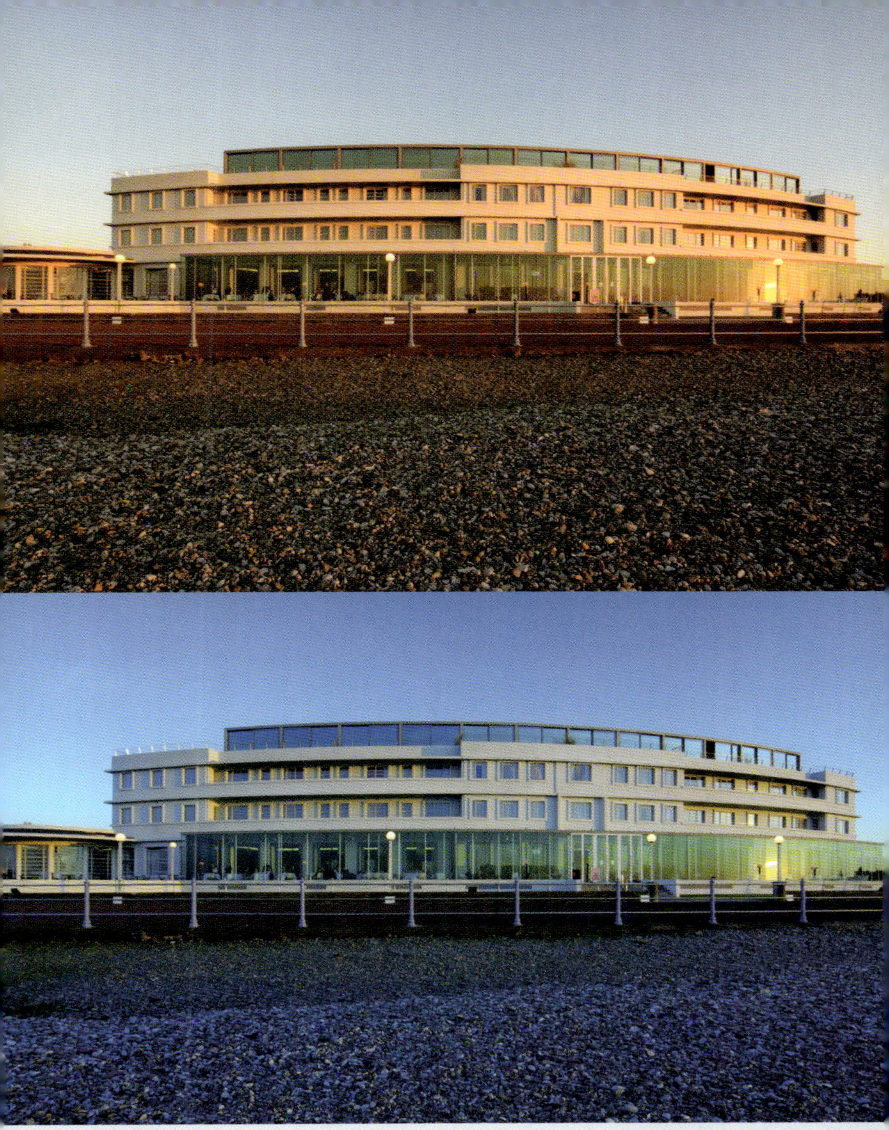

The Midland Hotel, Morecambe, UK

This Art Deco landmark is basically white, and in the bottom photo it is perfectly neutral (R,G, B values are equal, measured at the midpoint of the hotel frontage). 'Correct' perhaps, but which shot is more pleasing?

Nikon D2x, focal length 18mm, ISO 125, 2.5secs at f/11

Colour space

Colour spaces are simple, at least in the sense that you have – at most – two choices when setting the camera (on many compact cameras there is no choice). Understanding what they mean, however, is not quite so simple.

sRGB AND ADOBE RGB

Colour spaces are standardized definitions of a range – or gamut – of colours. The most common colour space in general use is known as sRGB which was designed to approximate the colours that could be displayed on a typical computer screen. As no two screens are exactly alike, it can only ever be an approximation, and some of today's screens are capable of displaying a significantly wider gamut. However, sRGB remains the standard for images on the Internet. Most high street photo-printers and many online services will also assume that images are sRGB. It's also safe to assume that any new camera will be set to sRGB by default.

The alternative colour space is Adobe RGB. This was designed as an approximate equivalent to the colours that can be reproduced by an 'average' printing process. Again, printers vary considerably and the issue is further complicated because printers don't use the RGB colour model; the standard ink colours

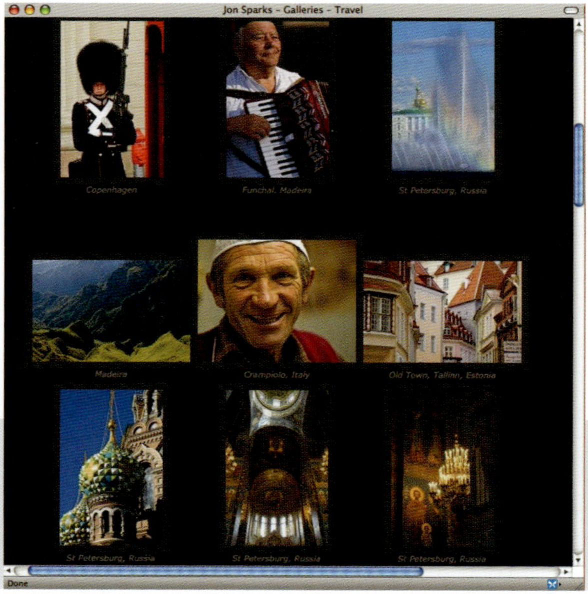

Screenshot from the author's website
Images are all uploaded as sRGB, as this works in all web browsers.

are cyan, magenta, yellow and black. (Black is called 'key', hence the acronym CMYK). Though it may not be perfect, Adobe RGB covers a substantially wider gamut than sRGB, and is a standard colour space for many professional uses, especially for photos destined for books and magazines. You might also use it if you're aiming to make high-quality prints through a professional lab or on a high-end photo inkjet printer. Generally, if you need Adobe RGB for a specific reason you'll probably already know about it. If you don't have such a reason, you're probably safe shooting in sRGB, and it saves having to convert images to sRGB before uploading to a website or printing through a high street outlet.

It's sometimes asserted that Adobe RGB is 'better' than sRGB, but this is misguided. In many instances it has nothing to recommend it but snob value. Yes, it can accommodate a wider range of colours, but there's no advantage in setting your camera to capture those colours if they can't be seen at the output stage. If you're printing to an sRGB device, or publishing on the Internet, you lose nothing by sticking to sRGB, and there can be advantages in doing so.

Assuming that your camera is recording 8-bit JPEG files, then it records the same finite amount of data whether using Adobe RGB or sRGB. As Adobe RGB captures a wider colour space, that data has to be spread more thinly to cover it all. Adobe RGB will capture colours that sRGB can't, but sRGB may pick up finer distinctions and show better contrast within its narrower gamut. If an Adobe RGB file is displayed or printed on a device that assumes everything is sRGB, then the 'extra' data is simply ignored. When this happens, Adobe RGB images tend to look flat and dull.

COLOUR PROFILES

Colour profiles are not an issue you'll face directly when setting up the camera, but it's worth introducing the concept at this stage as they are related to colour spaces. We've already observed that colour spaces are standardized definitions of a range – or gamut – of colours. Colour profiles are specific definitions of the range of colours that can be captured or displayed by a particular device, whether it's a camera, monitor or printer, and they're key to insuring consistent and predictable results as you progress along the imaging chain – for more on this see p62.

ADOBE RGB ON THE NET

Saying that sRGB is standard on the Internet does not mean that other colour spaces such as Adobe RGB are banned or can't be used. Some web browsers, such as Safari and Firefox (from version 3.0) are colour-managed and should display Adobe RGB files correctly, and you can of course send Adobe RGB files by email and other forms of internet transmission – but it's wise to check that the recipient is using the right software and settings to view them.

In the RAW

If you shoot RAW, the choice of colour space at the shooting stage is irrelevant. RAW files capture all the colours that the sensor is capable of recording and RAW conversion software normally works in a wide colour space; the choice must be made when exporting files for final use. However, it's still worth setting the colour space appropriately, to be prepared for those occasions when you do switch to JPEG or shoot simultaneous RAW + JPEG.

In-camera processing

In-camera processing is nothing new. Any camera that produces JPEG files performs extensive processing on the raw data from the image sensor. What has changed with the latest generations of DSLRs is that the user now has much more control over the way this processing is done.

For instance, possible options may include making images more vivid or more subtle, as well as more 'traditional' parameters like White Balance, sharpening and noise reduction. In essence, what these do is offer the JPEG shooter at least some of the fine control over the character of the image that the RAW shooter already has.

Some of these options are selected before you take a shot, which means that they belong fully in this chapter, while there may also be a chance to modify the image (or create an adjusted copy) after the shoot.

This is not an area where the camera makers agree on what controls to offer or what to call them, so to be sure what's available for your DSLR you will need to consult the maker's manual or look for one of our Expanded Guides (at least for Canon and Nikon DSLRs). However we can at least give a general idea of the sort of thing to look for.

TONAL CONTROLS

Tonal controls offer a way of dealing with areas where detail may easily be lost, i.e. shadows and highlights. Highlight detail in particular is often a weak point in digital capture; with film, there was a gradual transition into 'blown' or 'clipped' highlights, whereas with digital we can often see quite an abrupt cut-off, making the loss of detail in these areas all too conspicuous. This has long been a preoccupation for wedding photographers faced with white dresses, but it can make or break many other shots, such as landscapes shot in high-contrast lighting.

Hence we see functions such as Canon's Highlight Tone Priority and Nikon's Active D-Lighting – different names for what appear to be very similar processes, though Canon's only has On and Off settings, while Nikon has (in the latest models) Off, Low, Normal, High, Extra High or Auto. The makers are a bit coy about exactly how the processes work, but it's basically down to image-processing algorithms that fully exploit any extra detail captured in the raw image data. Nikon also state that there is a slight reduction in overall exposure when Active D-Lighting is enabled. It looks as if the same is probably true for Canon.

However it's done, the end result can be quite significant. With 'easy' shots, where the JPEG could comfortably capture a full range of tones anyway, there should be no visible difference, but in more challenging situations the extra highlight detail can be very obvious.

Because of the overall exposure reduction, this feature does make a difference to RAW files too, and may result in a small increase in noise

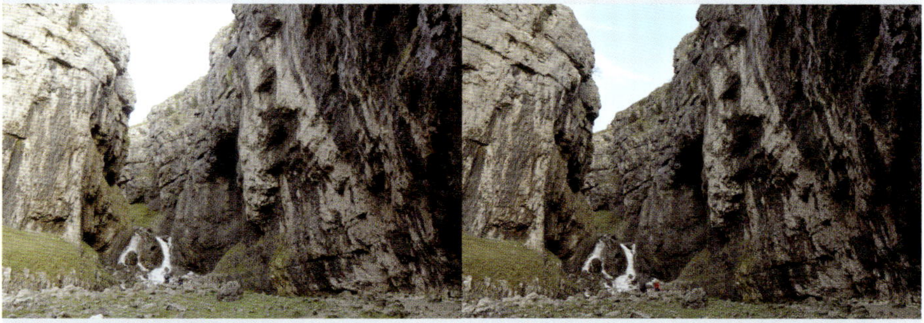

Goredale Scar, Yorkshire Dales, UK

Both images were shot in Aperture Priority mode, allowing the camera's metering to determine exposure. In the photo on the left, Active D-Lighting was Off, in the one on the right, it was set to High. There's a very clear difference in the amount of highlight detail captured, both in the sky and the left-hand rockface.

Nikon D90, focal length 18mm, ISO 400, 1/30sec (left) and 1/100th sec (right) at f/9.0

in shadow areas. It's probably safe enough to leave it enabled for most normal shooting (in which case Nikon users should stick to Auto or Normal), but turn it off whenever good shadow detail is a higher priority than highlight detail.

PICTURE CONTROLS AND STYLES

Nikon's Picture Controls and Canon's Picture Styles functions bring together predefined settings for contrast, colour (hue and saturation), sharpness and so on. For instance when shooting portraits you might prefer a relatively subtle level of contrast and colour for a natural look, while for landscapes you might want something more punchy. So, on the latest cameras, Nikon has presets called Standard, Neutral, Vivid, Monochrome, Portrait and Landscape, while Canon offers Standard, Portrait, Landscape, Neutral, Faithful, and Monochrome: the similarity is obvious. On some cameras, in certain exposure modes, a suitable Picture Control/Picture Style is applied automatically. On Nikons this applies to the Scene Modes such as Landscape and Portrait; on Canons the equivalent modes are found in the Basic Zone. Shoot in Landscape mode and the image automatically gets the Landscape treatment, and so on. This is fine if you want your landscapes to have the punchy sort of look that is deemed appropriate: saturated colours and fairly strong contrast. If you'd prefer a more subtle effect, or just want to have the choice, it's only a matter of switching to one of the more flexible modes (such as Aperture Priority) and making your own decisions about Picture Controls – or even shooting RAW.

You don't have to stick to predefined Picture Controls; you can modify the settings through the Shooting Menu (Shooting Menu 2 on Canon). You can also download additional picture controls through the camera-maker's website. Canon also has a piece of software called Picture Style Editor, which is supplied with current DSLRs.

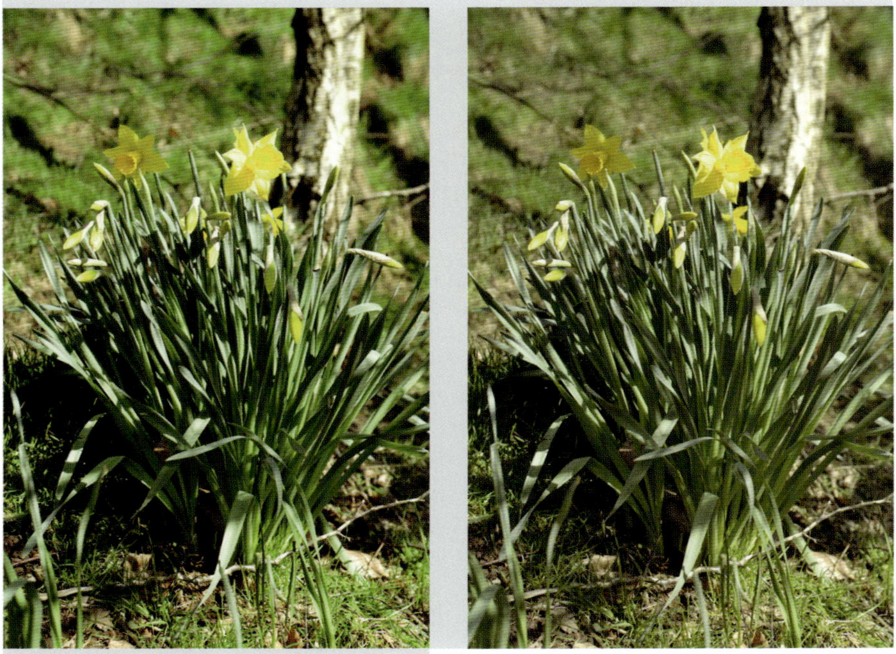

Daffodils in sunshine
The same setup, seconds apart; the difference is that the left photo was shot with a Vivid Picture Control and the right with Neutral.
Nikon D700, focal length 70mm, ISO 320, 1/500sec at f/5.0

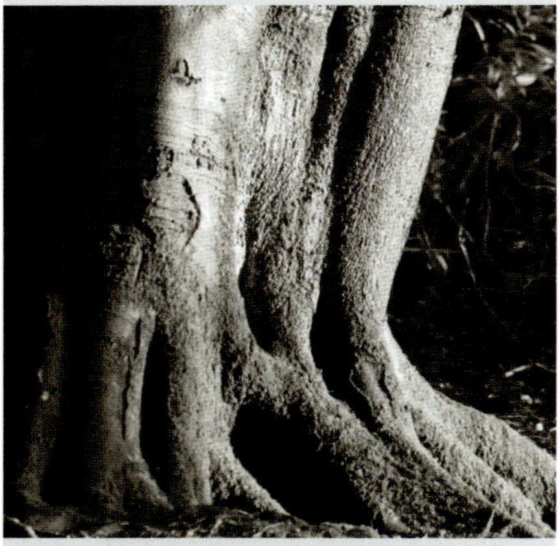

Tree base
A monochrome image; just try putting the colour back!
Nikon D300, focal length 200mm, ISO 400, 1/125sec at f/5.6

WARNING

Picture Control/Picture Style settings are like any other processing setting; the results are locked into the JPEG file and there's limited scope to change things afterwards. This is most obvious if you use a Monochrome setting; you can't put the colour back into the shot later. Likewise, if strong sharpening is applied it's virtually impossible to undo.

RETOUCHING

Most DSLRs now have onboard retouching facilities, allowing various changes to be made to images after they have been captured.

Nikon has a Retouch Menu, Pentax has Digital Filters, and so on. The Nikon approach is that when you use the Retouch Menu, the original image is untouched and a modified copy is created. You can apply this to RAW originals but the copy is always a JPEG.

Most of Nikon's retouching options are fairly self-explanatory: Red-eye correction, Trim, Monochrome, Straighten and so on. One of the more intriguing is D-Lighting, not to be confused with Active D-Lighting, already discussed (p80). D-Lighting attempts to do the same job but because it can't affect the base exposure its ability to recover highlights, in particular, is presumably more limited, especially when applied to an original shot as JPEG. On the other hand, it leaves the original (RAW or JPEG) untouched, so you may say there's nothing to lose.

In general, such editing is best done on the computer, but there may be occasions when you don't have access to a computer; you might want to take a memory card straight to a lab for printing, for example. In this case, the ability to do some 'quick and dirty' retouching on the camera itself does have real value.

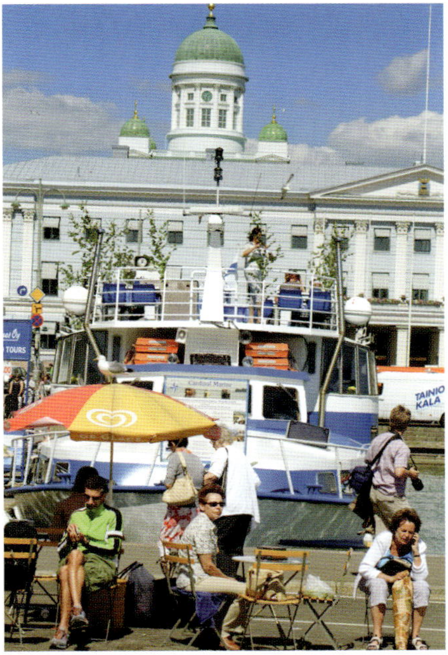

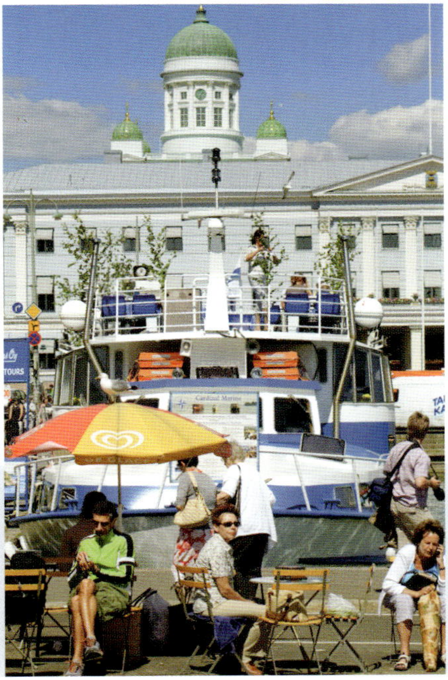

South Harbour, Helsinki, Finland
An image corrected using the Straighten option in the Retouch Menu. This crops the image, losing the top of the cathedral and the figure at bottom right; it's always better to get it straight at the shooting stage.
Nikon D2x, focal length 72mm, ISO 250, 1/1000sec at f/8

Sharpening and noise reduction

Sharpness helps us see fine detail; noise tends to obscure it. Clearly, they're important aspects of image quality, but it is possible to become obsessive about them, scrutinizing every image at 100% magnification for tiny imperfections that will never be visible in normal viewing.

SHARPENING

It's become a Hollywood cliché: some computer whizz turns a blurred mishmash of an image into a crisp detailed shot where the villain can easily be recognized. This is fantasy, and has promoted completely unrealistic expectations of what sharpening can do. In fact it can be argued that you can't make an image sharper: you can only make it *look* sharper.

Since the essential issue is how our images look, it might seem that this bold assertion is really a paradox. But it's true in essence. You can't restore detail if an image failed to capture it in the first place. The best that any sharpening action can do is take fuzzy detail and turn it into detail that's easier to see.

All digital camera images need some sharpening; this is because the anti-aliasing (or 'low-pass') filter in front of the sensor has a slight softening effect. Modern sharpening software uses complex algorithms which analyze the image in diverse ways, but the process can be summarized by saying that the software looks for edges and increases contrast along them. This underlines the point that there has to be some discernible edge to find in the first place.

Being slightly more pedantic, sharpness is a perceived quality and so isn't readily measurable, but it derives from two measurable qualities: resolution and acutance. Resolution is the level of fine detail that can be distinguished (like the number of lines on a test chart); acutance is the contrast at the edges which makes the resolution more or less visible. Sharpening can't add resolution, only acutance.

The risks with sharpening are twofold. Over-sharpening – too much acutance – can over-emphasize edges, so that lines and objects appear to possess halos. And in-camera sharpening is not readily reversible; you can't just subtract acutance and get back to where you wanted to be.

The second issue is that sharpening is sensitive to the size of the image. A level of sharpening that looks fine on a small image (or an image viewed on a small screen) can look awful when the image is enlarged.

For both these reasons, the general principle to follow is 'less is more'. It's relatively easy to add more sharpness later on, but virtually impossible to remove it. Keep in-camera sharpening to a minimum, especially if some or all of your images may subsequently be reproduced at large sizes. If the same image needs extra sharpening to look good on the Internet, add sharpening when you prepare it for upload.

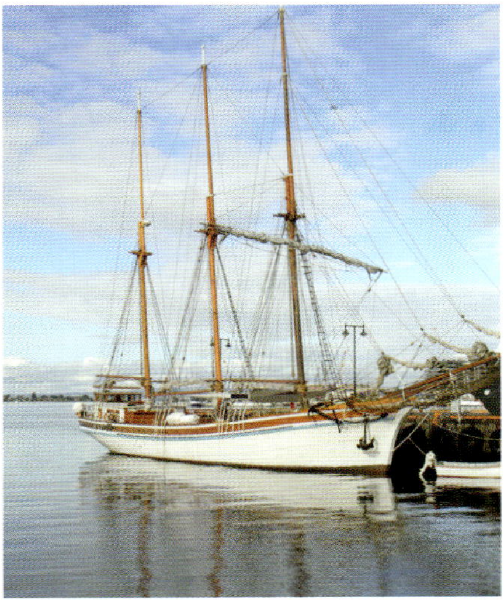

Oslo, Norway
Over-sharpening creates a halo effect along the edges.
Nikon D2x, focal length 72mm, ISO 320, 1/200sec at f/13

NOISE REDUCTION

We've already said quite a bit about noise, particularly in relation to sensor size and pixel pitch. Bigger pixels reduce one component of image noise – the random fluctuations in numbers of photons hitting each photosite. This is most evident when light levels are low and ISO settings are cranked up to the max. More efficient sensor design impacts on the second component of noise, the base-level electrical activity within the sensor itself. Because noise has these two main sources, many DSLRs offer not one but two sets of options for noise reduction (often abbreviated to NR). These are called, respectively, High ISO NR and Long Exposure NR. In this case both Canon and Nikon use virtually the same terminology and other manufacturers' jargon is generally similar too.

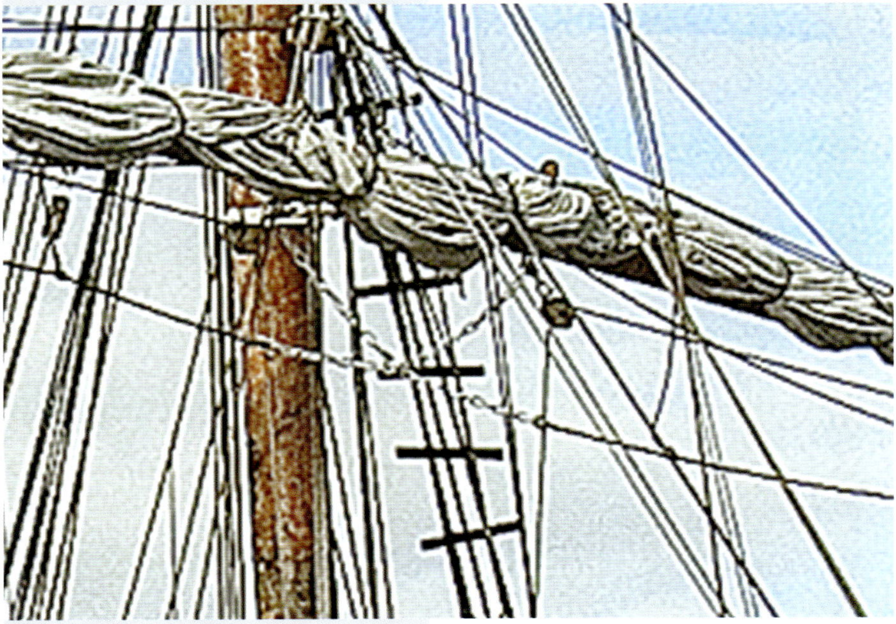

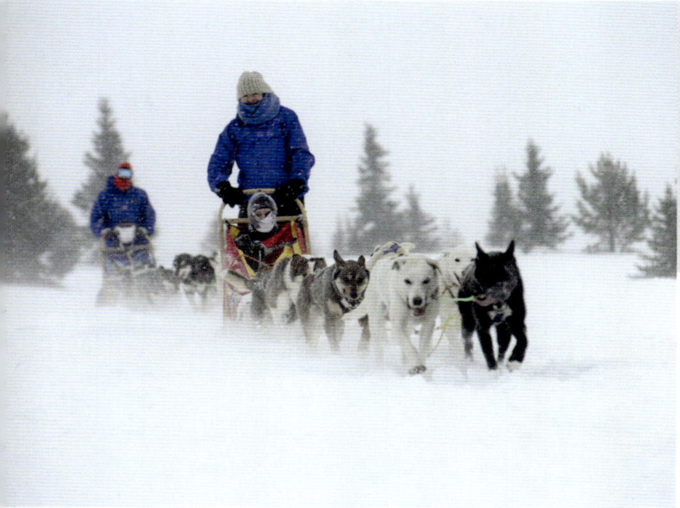

Huskies at Gålå, Norway
This shot was taken at ISO 1000 In difficult weather conditions. The darkest areas may benefit from a little High ISO NR.
Nikon D700, focal length 200mm, ISO 1000, 1/500sec at f/6.3

HIGH ISO NR

Most cameras offer the option to turn this high ISO NR on or off; some have further options such as High or Low. In most cases, even if you set this to Off or Disable, JPEG images shot at the highest ISOs will still receive a modest amount of noise reduction. If you want to see why, shoot a RAW image at the same exposure settings and make sure all NR is turned off in the RAW conversion software.

The NR software analyzes the image for random variations which it deems to be noise and averages them out. High levels of NR can obscure detail and soften the image, in some cases producing a rather plastic effect. As with sharpening, it's much easier to add more NR later than to undo what has already been applied, so a conservative approach to the camera settings is advised.

NOTE

High operating temperatures can increase base-level noise (Long Exposure noise). This is an obvious issue when shooting in tropical climes or other hot places, but the camera's internal temperature can also increase during long periods of intensive use. For this reason some cameras will automatically 'take a breather' after shooting long continuous sequences, perhaps 100 images at high speed.

WARNING

Remember that Picture Controls/Picture Styles include a Sharpening element that will override any general settings you make, so if you use any of these presets, ensure that Sharpening is set appropriately here too.

LONG EXPOSURE NR

Because Long Exposure NR is tackling electrical noise generated within the sensor itself, it works rather differently. At long exposures (typically defined as one second or more) the camera will take the normal exposure and then effectively take a second exposure with the shutter closed. With no light entering, it records only the sensor-generated noise, which is then 'subtracted' from the first exposure. There's an obvious drawback with this; if you're making a 10-second exposure, the camera is locked for a further ten seconds for the second exposure. This may not matter if you are shooting static subjects, but it does if shooting something like a fireworks display.

World Fireworks Championship, Blackpool, Lancashire, UK
Even major fireworks displays usually last no more than 15 or 20 minutes; you certainly don't want the camera locking you out for half this time while it chunters through Long Exposure NR. Turn it off!
Nikon D700, Focal length 24mm, ISO 200, 65secs at f/22

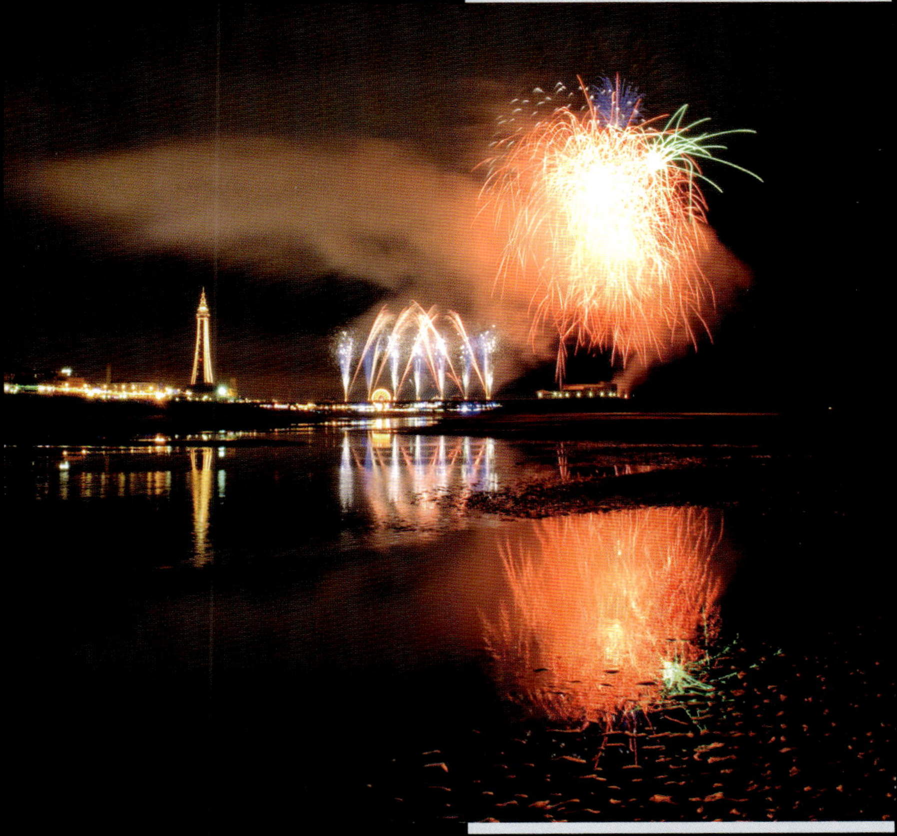

Into the Menus

The settings we've covered so far are essential: you can scarcely avoid making decisions about them. Don't leave them on default just by default! In a well-designed camera most if not all of them should be quickly accessible through buttons and/or dials. But they're just the tip of the iceberg; there are many more ways in which you can determine how your DSLR operates, making it exactly the camera you want it to be.

The majority of these settings are only revealed by delving into the menu system. Makes and models differ, but the main menu groups are usually called something like Playback, Setup, Shooting (or Record) and Custom; Nikon, for one, also has a separate Retouch Menu for in-camera processing. There may also be a Recent Settings Menu or My Menu, which collects favourite or recently used items from other menus in a handy one-stop shop.

Camera makers approach the organization of their menus slightly differently, and there are also variations between different models from the same maker. A book of this size can't possibly cover them all. The camera's manual will list them and, if you're lucky, give clear explanations of what they actually do. Nikon or Canon users can also look for the appropriate volume in our Expanded Guide series, which gives detailed explanations of the menus (and many other things) for each camera model; other makes may join the series in the future.

Many menu items are pretty self-explanatory, like Time or Language in the Setup Menu. (Language is almost certainly set to English by default). Other items may be an alternative route to settings that you can also reach through buttons and dials, like ISO or White Balance.

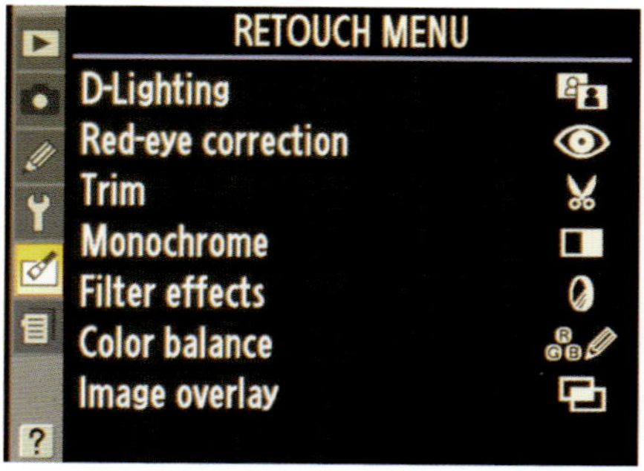

Retouch Menu from a Nikon D700

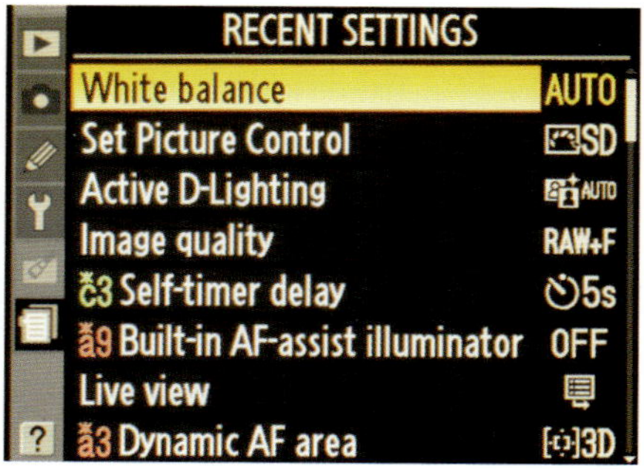

Recent Settings Menu

Beyond that, though, there are dozens more. All we can do is outline the main groups and suggest a few of the settings that you're most likely to be concerned with. However, items that are in the Setup Menu on a Canon may lurk in the Shooting Menu or Custom Menu on a Nikon, and so on. I've followed Nikon's scheme in what follows, because that's what I'm most familiar with, but whatever camera you use you'll have to do some exploring for yourself.

PLAYBACK MENU

The Playback Menu, naturally, contains options for image review and playback. These will include options for the way images are displayed on playback, probably allowing extra screens of information to be made available, such as a detailed histogram or highlight-clipping warning (see pp94–98). You may be able to hide certain images, protect images against accidental deletion, and select images for printing; this may be headed 'print order' or 'DPOF', which stands for Digital Print Order Format.

SHOOTING MENU

This menu is where you find key parameters such as ISO Settings, Image Quality, Image Size, White Balance, Colour Space, Tonal Controls, Picture Controls/Styles and Noise Reduction, most of which have already been covered. A lot of them can be approached using buttons and/or dials, which is often easier than using the menu.

The Shooting Menu may also have options for features such as multiple exposure or interval-timer shooting. On DSLRs that can shoot video, this is probably where you'll find options to set the size of the video image and perhaps whether sound recording is on or off.

Some cameras may enable you to amend the way files are named and/or numbered. By default, an image might have a name such as _DSC.3456.JPG. The JPG suffix indicates it's a JPEG file and 3456 is a unique sequential number. The initial three-letter string is the bit you can edit. As I shoot with lots of different cameras I use it to identify each one. Some pros may change this for each assignment (presumably why it's in the Shooting Menu). You can also change the way the camera assigns those sequential numbers – on a Nikon that's found in the Custom Settings Menu.

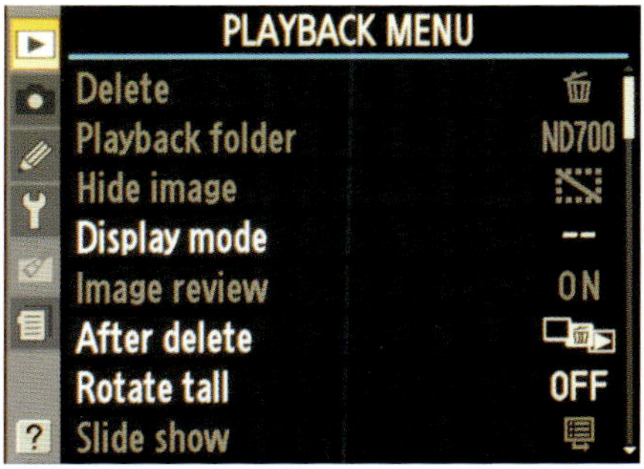

Playback Menu

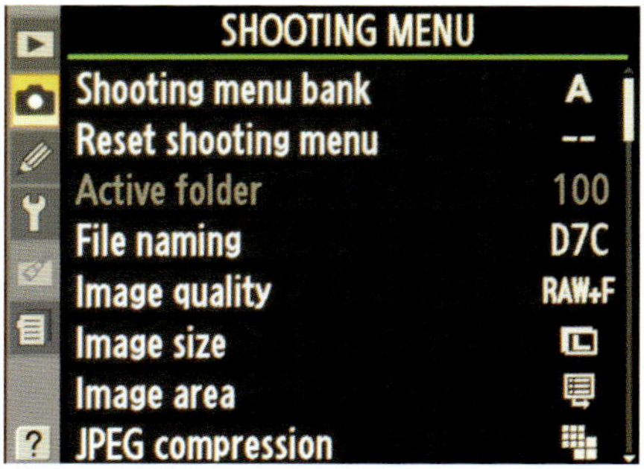

Shooting Menu

CUSTOM MENU

In the Introduction I noted that a Nikon D90's Custom Settings Menu has 41 items, offering anything from 2 to 10 options. This is quite normal; the Canon EOS 40D has 25 items in its Custom Function Menu, while the EOS 1Ds MkIII has 57. On some cameras many are hidden (on some Nikons you need to use the CSM item in the Setup Menu, changing Simple to Detailed). This menu is often subdivided into groups. Nikon's main headings are Autofocus; Metering/Exposure; Timers/AE Lock; Shooting/display; Bracketing/flash and Controls. Canon's are – usually – Exposure; Image/Flash exp/Display; Autofocus/Drive and Operation/Others. Neither of these lists is totally self-explanatory, but it's a start. Let's look at a few of the most important options.

Autofocus

This controls the way autofocus operates, fine-tuning it to the different needs of landscape, wildlife, sports and other shooting situations. A landscape photographer probably wants to be able to manually select a single focus point, while a sports shooter will often benefit from focus points that dynamically track moving subjects. If you shoot the same kinds of subjects all the time you may be able to make a one-time selection here and then forget it, but if you shoot portraits one day and wildlife the next, you may need to visit this menu more often. This is exactly why it's so handy to have a Recent Settings Menu or other short-cut to the menu items you visit regularly.

On cameras with Live View, i.e. most current DSLRs, autofocus usually operates differently in Live View and there are separate sets of menu options to cover it.

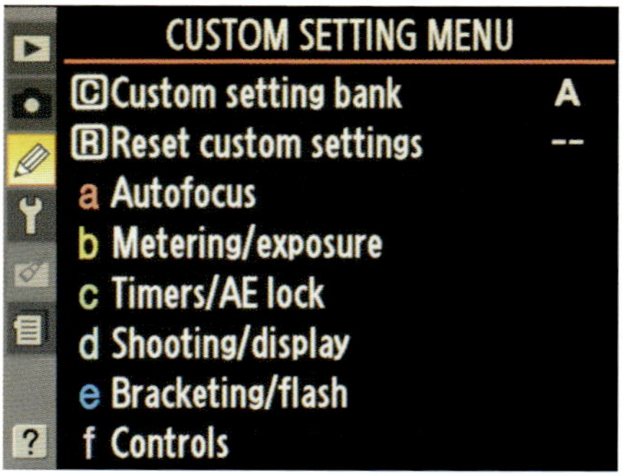

Custom Settings Menu from a Nikon D700

Metering/Exposure

This menu governs how metering and exposure operate. On a Nikon, for example, you can change the steps between aperture and shutter-speed values (normally ⅓ EV but you can select ½ or 1EV), the size of the dominant area in centre-weighted metering, and so on.

Timers/AE Lock

This covers a more diverse set of options. Does holding the shutter-release lock focus and exposure, or just focus? How long before the meter and displays turn off when the camera's idle? How long is the self-timer delay? And so on.

Shooting/display

This menu enables you to determine whether the camera beeps at you and what for to decide if you want to see grid lines in the viewfinder (useful for squaring up architectural subjects); whether you want the camera to warn you when it thinks flash is needed; and much more.

Bracketing/flash

Bracketing is a really helpful facility; sometimes it feels like a life-saver. It's the ability to quickly and automatically vary selected parameters and is often applied to exposure, but may alternatively apply to flash power, White Balance and other values. The menu may also govern the order in which bracketed shots are taken. Canon has an item which lets you decide whether or not bracketing remains set if you turn the camera off and on again; I wish Nikon would copy this.

Flash options cover areas include the range of shutter speeds that can be used with flash, whether you can see a preview (modelling) flash before the actual exposure, and so on.

Controls

This menu lets you change or reassign the functions of many of the camera's buttons and dials. Probably one of the most under-used and underrated menus on most DSLRs, it gives you wide scope to set up the camera so that its operation feels intuitive, and the functions you need most often are accessible through a single button-press. In other words, use this menu once to avoid having to use one of the other menus repeatedly.

Most Nikons have both a depth-of-field preview button and a function (Fn) button. For landscape shooters, DOF preview is sacrosanct. However, a sports photographer may work mostly with the lens wide open, and so have little need of this preview. In this case it could be handy to reprogram this button to lock exposure or to initiate a bracketing burst.

SETUP MENU

Setting up the DSLR does not begin or end with the Setup Menu; indeed, some items are ones you'll rarely use. Others may crop up more frequently; for instance, both Canon and Nikon have options here – on recent models – relating to sensor cleaning, allowing you to set the camera to clean the sensor automatically on startup and/or shutdown. (The camera does this by vibrating the low-pass filter over the sensor to shake off the dust.) You might set this once and forget it, but there are also options enabling you to manually clean the sensor if the automatic dust removal hasn't worked (see p21); if you're unlucky or work in dusty environments these might be needed more often.

Another item located in this menu that can be useful is Firmware Version. Firmware is the onboard software that runs the camera; the manufacturers release updates from time to time to tackle 'bugs' or to add new features. These can be downloaded from the maker's website then copied to a memory card for installation into the camera.

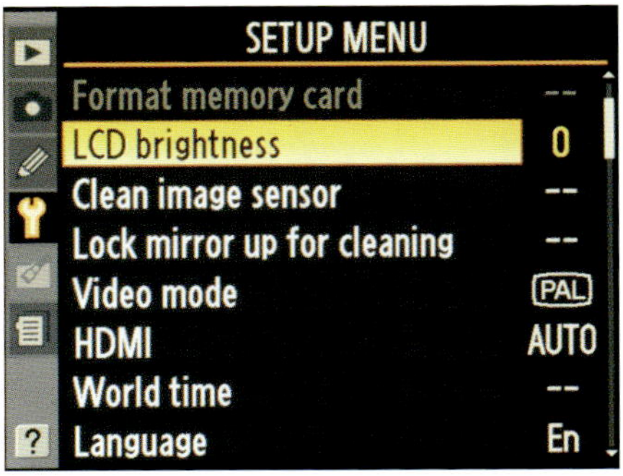

Setup Menu from a Nikon D700

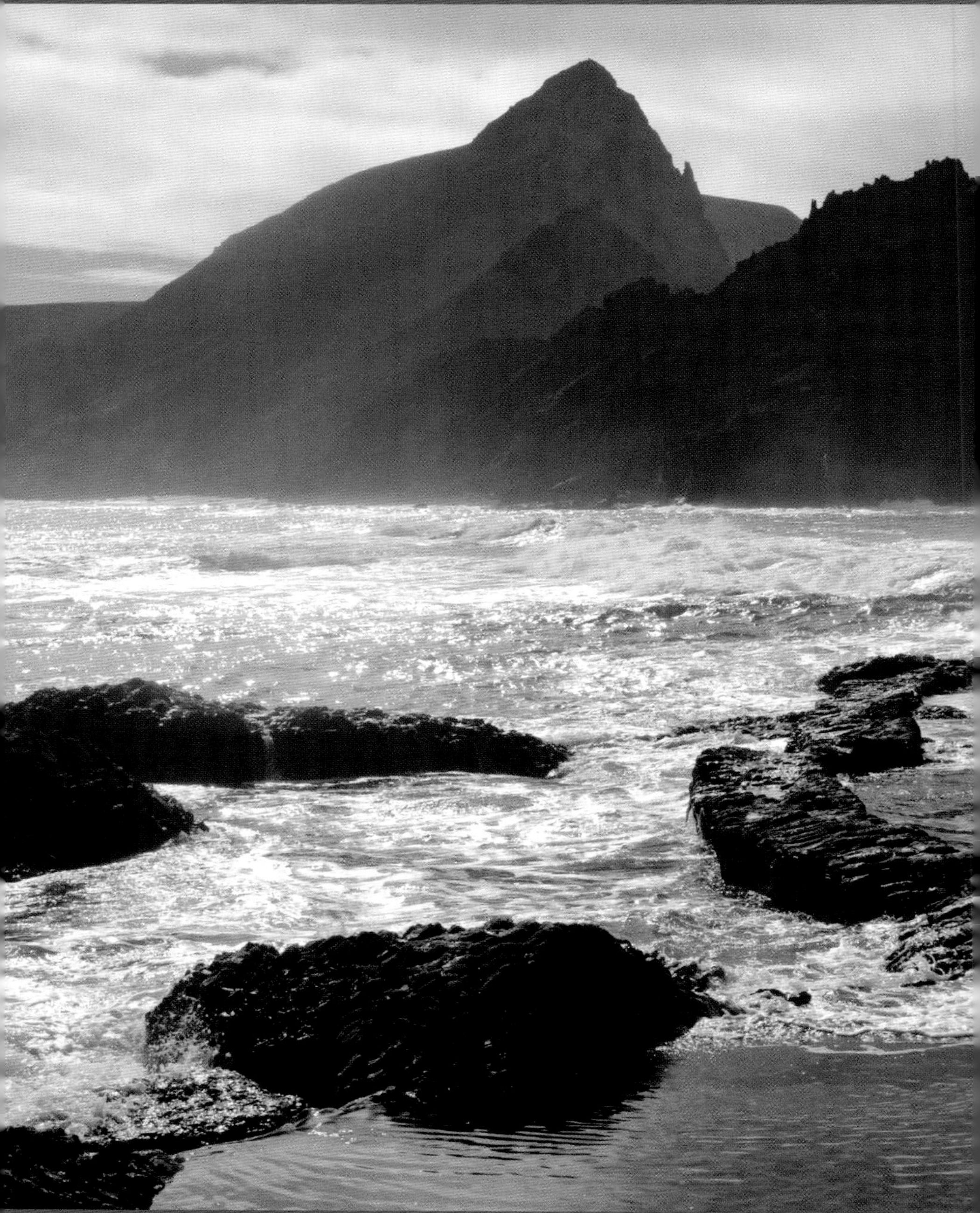

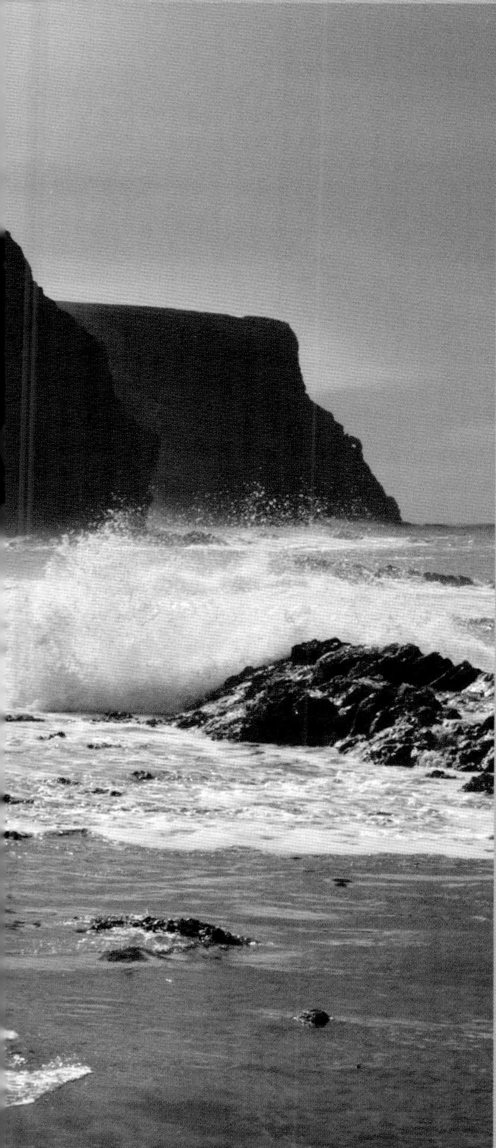

05: SHOOTING WITH YOUR DSLR

The last chapter looked at settings that affect the way in which the camera processes the image. We will call these 'processing settings'. In this chapter we turn to settings that affect the raw data that the camera captures. We'll call these 'shooting settings'. An active photographer may change processing settings from day to day or even hour to hour, but shooting settings often change from shot to shot.

Cabo Calheta, Porto Santo, Madeira Islands
Nikon D300, focal length 35mm, ISO 200, 1/250sec at f/16

Exposure

The term 'exposure' goes dates back to the origins of photography, reminding us that all photography is about exposing light-sensitive material, be it a digital sensor or a chemical emulsion on glass, film or paper, to the required amount of light. What we usually mean when we talk about exposure is the process of determining exactly how much light is needed to produce the desired image of a subject under the conditions that apply at that place and time.

In many respects, the fundamentals of exposure are the same as they have always been. Levels of illumination vary hugely (bright sunlight to night, for example) as do scenes and subjects; some reflect much more light than others. And the ways we deal with this still boil down to three main elements: shutter speed, aperture and the sensitivity of the sensor (or emulsion) to light.

However, digital sensors do respond to light in a somewhat different way from chemical emulsions, and the options that are available to us for dealing with exposure are also different. Digital photographers can, in general, dispense with hand-held meters and other gubbins that was often required to obtain perfect exposures on film, but that does not mean that there is no skill required to get the exposure right. The skills are different, that's all.

In particular, digital photography offers us a really powerful tool for assessing the exposure of any image. It's called the histogram, and being able to understand and interpret it is one of the most important skills in digital photography.

THE HISTOGRAM

If you hated maths at school, then words like 'histogram' may be a turn-off, but it really isn't hard, and you don't even need to tangle with numbers. A histogram is just a graph, and a very simple one at that. It shows how much of an image is made up of dark, medium or light tones. You might say that looking at the image itself on screen can tell you that, but the image on the camera back can be hard to see clearly, especially in bright conditions. The histogram is much more objective and much more precise.

The RGB histogram

A single summary histogram can tell us a great deal. Looking at individual histograms for the three colour channels (red, green and blue) can tell us even more. If an average subject is exposed with the correct White Balance, all three channels should look similar, but strongly coloured subjects will naturally produce histograms with a bias to one or two channels – a shot of a cricket pitch will be strong in the green, for example. Be extra vigilant for clipping in the dominant channels.

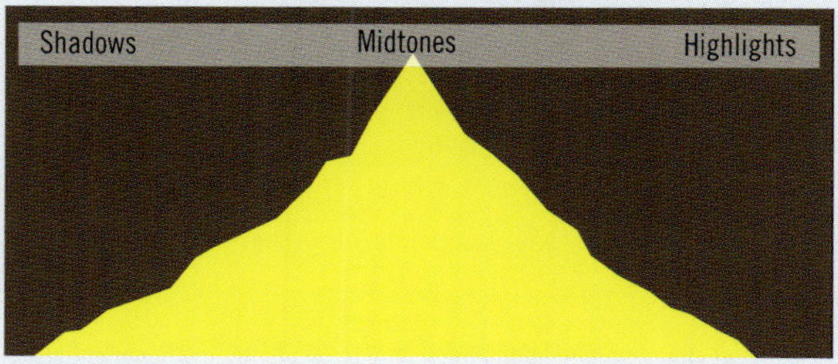

Good histogram

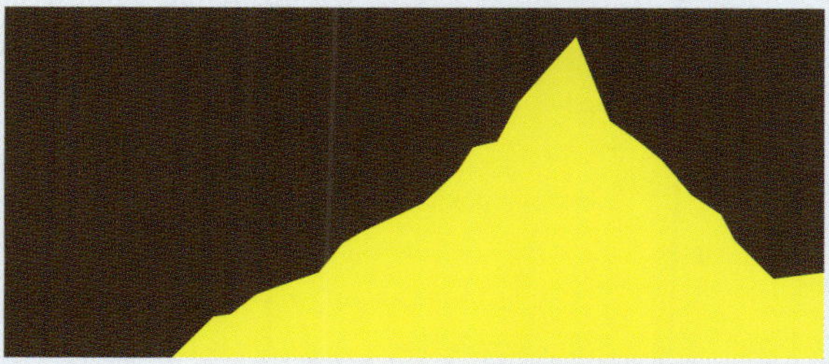

Overexposed

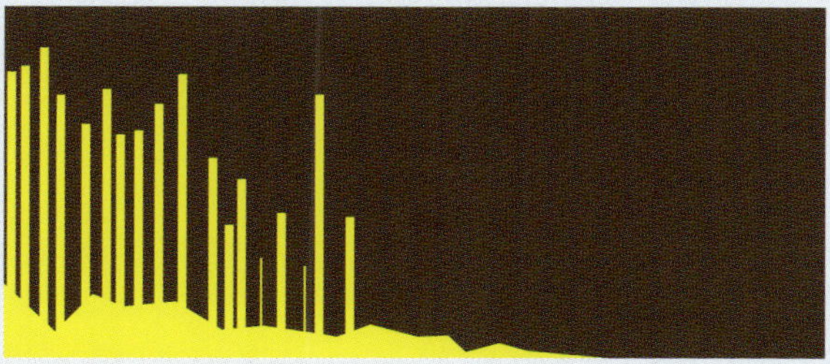

Underexposed

Histograms
The top histogram shows the distribution of tones centred around the middle values. The middle example shows tones skewed to the right, implying a much lighter overall image; worse, the tones are spilling off the end of the diagram, suggesting that some areas have no detail (highlight clipping). In the bottom histogram, tones are skewed to the dark side, there's shadow clipping, and worse still, the histogram appears spiky and comb-like, implying sharp tone-breaks – which are often seen in an over-processed image.

A good histogram

A good histogram does not always have a single peak, nor do the peaks in the three colour channels always have to be aligned. Many landscape images, for example, may show a 'twin-peaks' histogram, with a right-side peak representing bright tones in the sky and a left-side peak for the darker tones of the land.

ISO

I'm well aware that ISO is a shooting setting, not a processing setting; my reason for including it in the previous chapter is that it relates closely to some of the processing settings, notably High ISO NR. But ISO should be always on the mind of the active photographer; don't 'set it and forget it'.

REAL-WORLD HISTOGRAMS

The best way to get to grips with the histogram is to look at some real-life examples.

Metered exposure (top): Tones in the red and green channels are well distributed across the histogram, but the blue channel is skewed to the left. Looking at the preponderance of green, yellow and brown tones in the picture, this is hardly surprising. The red and green channel histograms extend all the way to the right margin, which implies some highlight clipping (a look at the highlight warning would show that it's in the flower petals). Shooting in RAW, this could almost certainly be recovered.

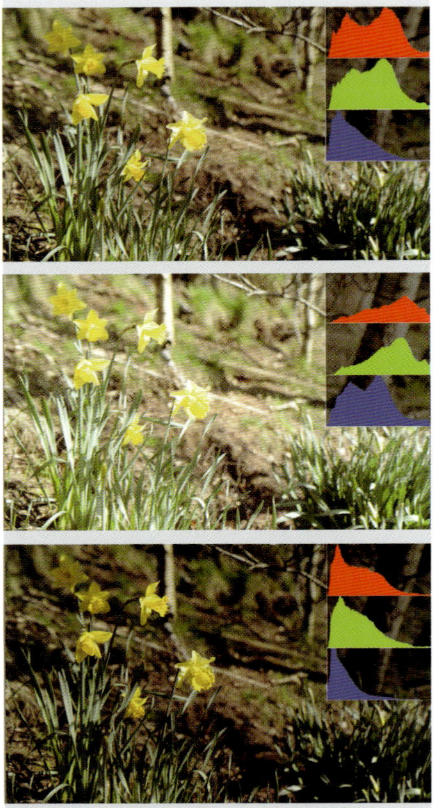

Near Garstang, Lancashire, UK
Nikon D700, focal length 70mm, ISO 320, 1/250sec, 1/500sec and 1/1000sec at f/5.6

Overexposed +1EV (middle): The slope of the left side is much more gentle, suggesting that shadow detail is much more open, but all three channels are now clipped at the right, with tall spikes appearing in the red and green; this suggests there is much less chance of recovering any highlight detail from a RAW image.

Underexposed -1EV (bottom): All three channels are now heavily skewed to the left and the blue channel is starting to show definite shadow clipping. Yet there is still some highlight clipping in the red channel. This apparently simple little scene is showing that it's actually quite challenging, with a wide dynamic range.

The 'normal' histogram (opp, top): Resembling the famous statistical 'bell curve', it is actually quite rare in most photography. To prove the point, it took me some time to find a suitable image to use as an example. This tree detail was originally shot to illustrate the use of fill-in flash and shows a nice peak in the mid tones, little divergence between the three colour channels, and no sign of any clipping.

Twin peaks (opp, bottom): This double-peaked histogram is quite typical of landscapes and many other images. Sharp peaks at the left represent the strong (but unclipped) shadows; the mid tones are dominantly red and green, while the sky is represented by another sharp peak in the blue channel.

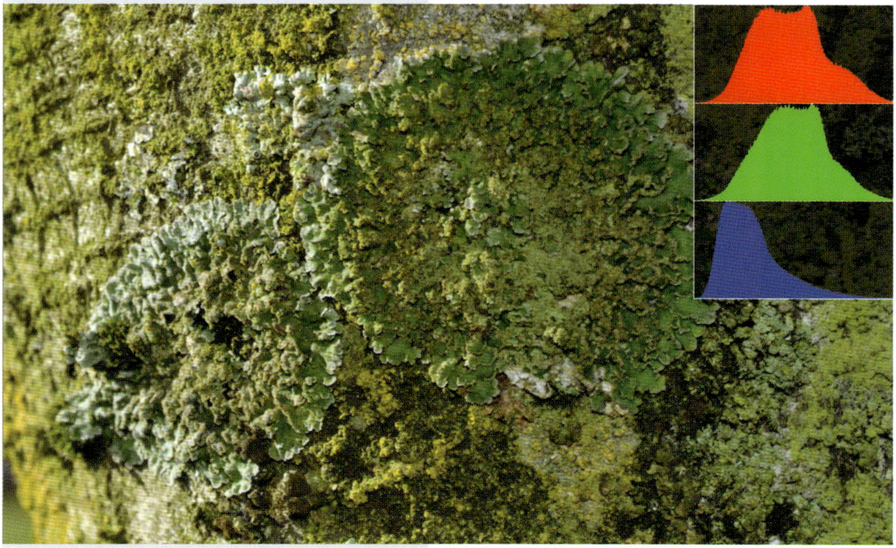

Garstang, Lancashire, UK
Nikon D700, focal length 70mm, ISO 200, 1/100sec at f/11

Blawith Fells, Lake District, UK
Nikon D2x, focal length 18mm, ISO 200, 1/100sec at f/16

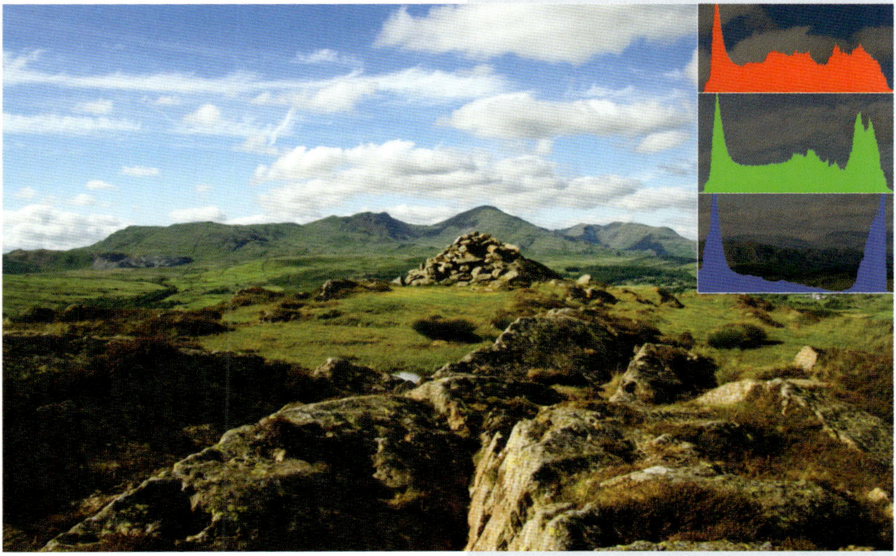

HIGHLIGHT WARNING

Most DSLRs can display a warning when highlights are clipped. This warning usually takes the form of flashing areas in the full-screen playback. For intelligent exposure assessment, this is not an alternative to the histogram, but can be a very useful adjunct as it tells you exactly where, and how extensive, the clipped areas are. If they're small and don't affect key subjects, you might decide to ignore the clipping and stick with an exposure that preserves shadow detail. If they're right at the edge of the frame you might simply decide to crop them out.

You might ask, if there's a highlight warning, why is there no shadow warning? Actually, in most RAW conversion and image-editing software, there is, but it's true that it's not included in camera displays. There's no technical reason why it could not be there, and some of us would like it to be available, but presumably the argument is that blown-out highlights are visually more objectionable than blocked-up shadows.

RAW RECOVERY

If you're shooting JPEG, then clipped shadows or highlights are gone forever. The JPEG file will have no detail in those areas so there is nothing for an image-editing program to work with. If you're shooting RAW, however, the situation is not quite so clear cut. There's often information there that can be recovered, especially if the histogram shows that not all the colour channels are clipped.

It's a myth that there's no skill in digital because you can always 'make it right afterwards'. Sometimes you can salvage a less than perfect image, sometimes it's beyond rescue. If the histogram is complete then it can at least be improved (although it's unlikely to be quite as good as one that was correctly exposed in the first place). If the histogram is severely clipped, no amount of Photoshop wizardry can make it right.

POINT OF VIEW

Switching from film to digital wasn't always easy. One of the key aspects of the process was learning to look at the histogram, and to interpret it. Now when I shoot, the RGB histogram is the first page that comes up in image playback. I may look at the highlight warning too, but I barely glance at the full-screen playback.

Detectorist, Blackpool, UK
Shown in red here (in Adobe Lightroom), clipped highlights are usually shown by blinking black areas on the camera display.
Nikon D2x, focal length 200mm, ISO 250, 1/800sec at f/10

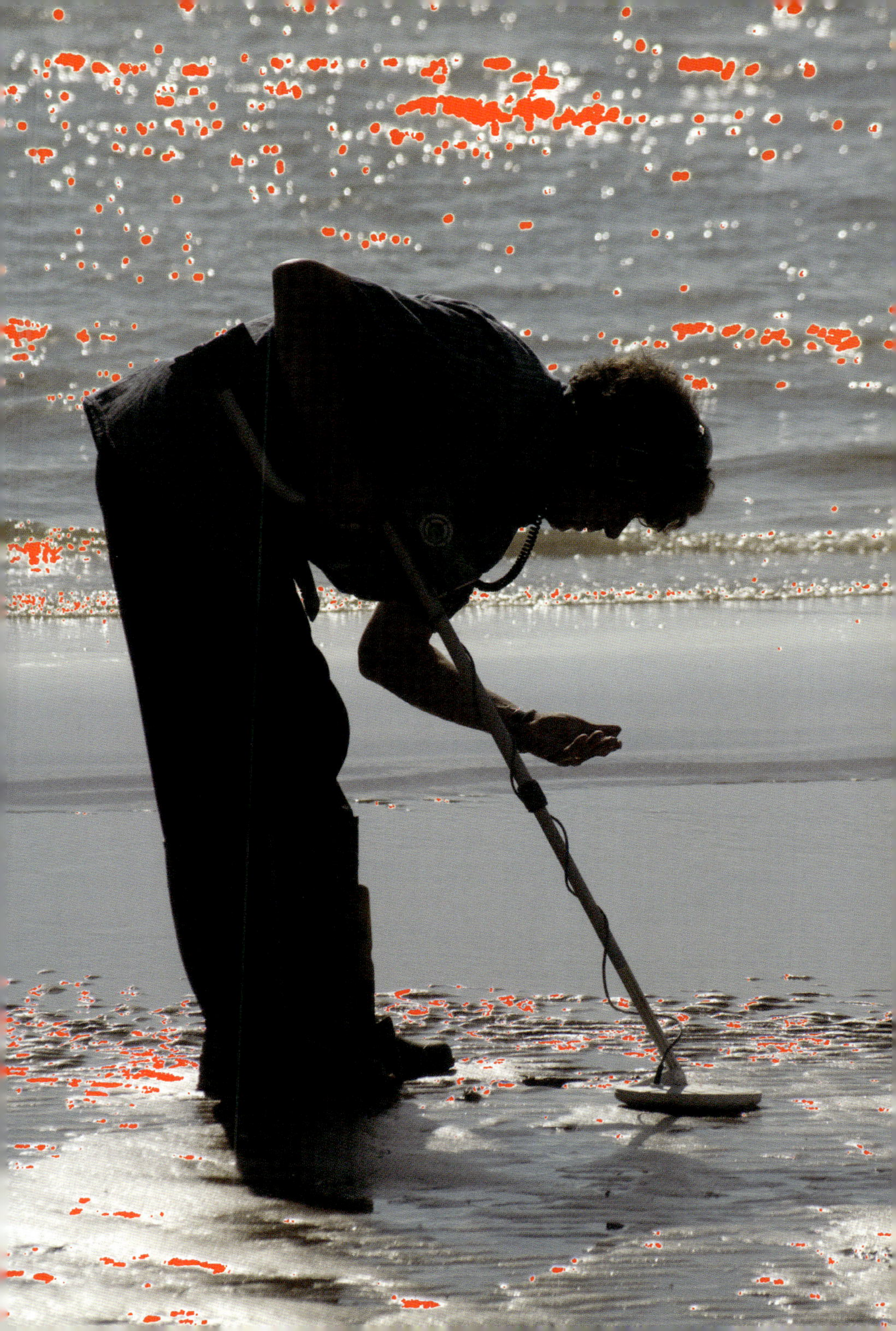

Metering pattern

You might think I've put the cart before the horse by discussing the histogram before looking at metering methods, but this is no accident. The histogram is that important. If I had to, I could shoot without ever taking a meter reading at all, as long as I had the histogram.

Nevertheless, the meters in modern DSLRs are wonderfully sophisticated and can be relied on to give very good results most of the time. Of course 'very good' may not be exactly the same as 'the way I want it', but at the very least the metered result should be well inside the ballpark. The review image and, above all, the histogram are there for fine tuning.

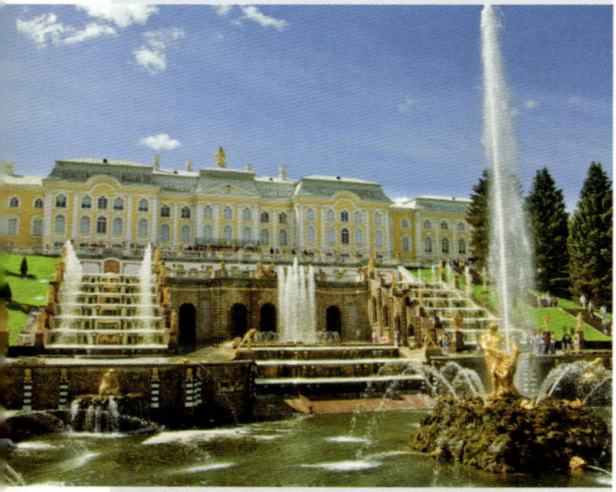

Peterhof Palace, St Petersburg, Russia
This is a good test for matrix metering, with a wide dynamic range. I checked the histogram carefully after the first shot and made a slight reduction in exposure to hold more detail in the fountain.
Nikon D2x, focal length 18mm, ISO 200, 1/200sec at f/11

MATRIX METERING

Matrix metering is Nikon's term; Canon calls it *evaluative*, Sony has *multi-segment*, and other makers have their own jargon. Names aside, these systems all work in the same general way: they calculate the overall exposure by comparing light levels at different parts of the frame. The latest Canons have 35 metering zones, Sony has 40 and Nikon claims 1005, which may look a bit like overkill. Sophisticated metering algorithms also take account of distance information (i.e. the active focus points) and, at least in Nikon's case, colour information too.

In effect, matrix metering takes all this information and compares it with a large database of real-world images. This is highly effective most of the time, but it's open to the charge that matrix metering is metering by committee. There is always room for interpretation in how an image should look, and relying uncritically on matrix metering means you're using someone else's interpretation.

CENTRE-WEIGHTED METERING

This is a very traditional form of metering; for much of the history of the 35mm SLR this was as clever as it got. Here the camera meters from the whole frame, but gives greatest weight to a central circle. The exact size of this area varies across different cameras, and in some cases can be changed to suit you (using the Custom Settings Menu). A good example of where you might use centre-weighted metering is in portrait photography, where the key subject occupies the central portion of the frame.

METERING IN RAW AND JPEG

When shooting JPEG images, to be used as they stand, we might focus on the general look of (getting the midtones right); when shooting RAW for further processing, we might give greater priority to ensuring that the histogram is complete (avoidance of shadow and highlight clipping). This implies that a truly sophisticated auto-exposure system might operate differently when shooting different file formats, but I'm not aware that any current system does this.

Red deer, Bowland Wild Boar Park, Lancashire, UK
A good candidate for centre-weighted metering, though matrix metering would also handle this shot comfortably.
Nikon D2x, focal length 300mm, ISO 400, 1/400sec at f/10

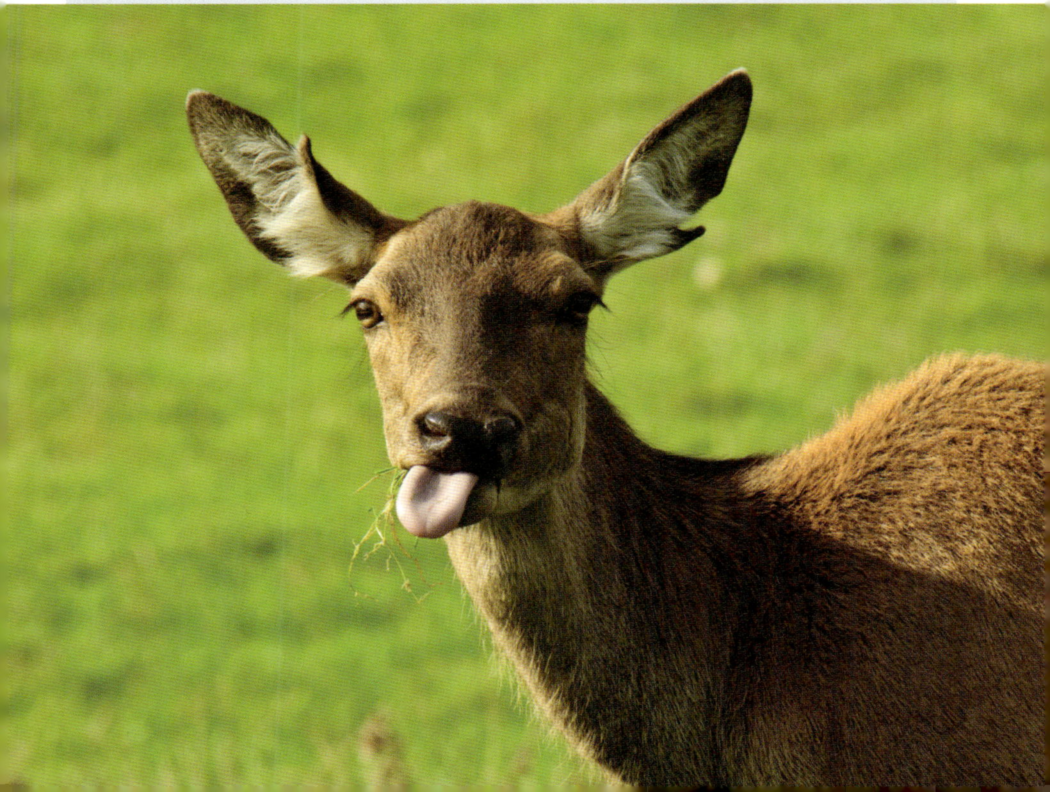

SPOT-METERING

As the name suggests, spot-metering takes the light reading from a very localized area, usually a spot just 2 or 3mm in diameter. On many cameras this can be linked to the active focus point, allowing the reading to be taken from a key area or subject.

Some discussions of spot-metering make it seem like one of the dark arts. It doesn't need to be that bad, but making good use of it undoubtedly takes a bit of experience.

An extension of basic spot-metering is to take two or more readings, e.g. one for the highlights and one for the shadows, with the aim of capturing a full tonal range. Or it may be that you decide that one or the other – highlight or shadow – is crucial. For instance, in a snow scene the priority may be to ensure that the snow looks clean and white but without highlight clipping, i.e. retaining readable detail. This requires giving considerably more exposure than the meter reading might suggest, typically 2–4EV; exactly how much will depend on the exact result required and on the dynamic range capability of the camera.

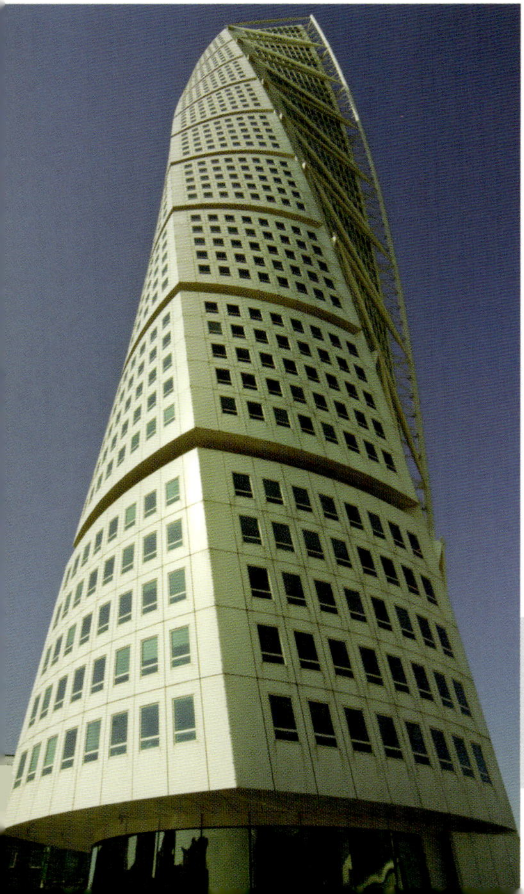

PARTIAL METERING

This is a variation found on some Canon DSLRs; the camera meters only from the central area, ignoring the rest of the frame. On high-end Nikons you can adjust the size of the spot-metering area (see below) in the Custom Settings Menu for a similar result.

Law of averages

Both centre-weighted and spot-metering assume that the metered area is a mid tone. Take a reading off an average subject and it will (should!) be accurate, but take a reading from a white flower or a black cat and both are likely to come out grey. To restore them to their correct values requires some adjustment of exposure – give more to make the white flower white, give less to make the black cat black.

The Turning Torso, Malmö, Sweden
I used spot-metering here to be sure of holding detail in the sunlit face of this amazing white skyscraper.
Nikon D2x, focal length 14mm, ISO 100, 1/125sec at f/16

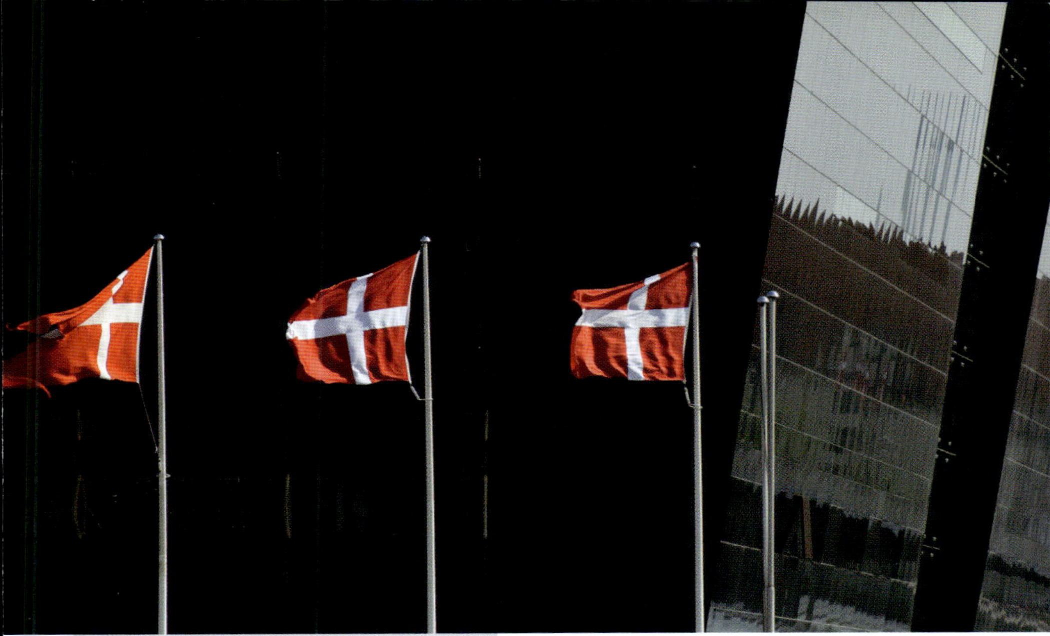

The 'Black Diamond', Copenhagen, Denmark
The mass of very dark tones fooled the meter into overexposure; around two stops of negative compensation was needed.
Nikon D2x, focal length 200mm, ISO 250, 1/640sec at f/8

EXPOSURE COMPENSATION AND EXPOSURE BRACKETING

Exposure compensation is a quick way to fine-tune the camera's exposure setting. You might use it because the playback image or the histogram aren't quite right, or because experience or intuition tell you it's required. The exact procedure for applying compensation varies from camera to camera but in most cases it just involves pressing a compensation button and rotating a control dial. Plus compensation makes the image lighter, minus makes it darker.

Exposure bracketing is a way of hedging your bets by getting the camera to shoot two or more frames with different exposure values. Depending on the particular camera you may have options for the number of frames in a bracketing 'burst', the difference in exposure between them and the order in which they are taken (e.g. Under > Normal > Over). It's very handy in tricky lighting situations, especially if you're pressed for time, but takes up card space and leaves you with extra frames to delete later. The three pictures on p96 are an example of bracketed exposures.

COMPENSATION TIPS

Exposure compensation should work with all metering patterns and in all exposure modes, with one exception: in manual mode, applying exposure compensation does not change the actual exposure settings but may affect the meter reading. Exposure compensation is not self-cancelling. The camera will go on applying it to subsequent shots. This may not be what you want, so remember to reset it to zero.

Exposure modes

Most DSLRs have a wide range of exposure modes, but they all boil down to two main settings: shutter speed and aperture. Aperture governs the size of the lens opening that admits light and shutter speed sets how long it's open for. Between them they determine how much light is admitted for each exposure. The other main setting to interlock with these is the ISO – the often-neglected third factor. Most DSLRs have a separate Mode dial, but some use a Mode button in combination with a control dial.

PROGRAM MODE

In Program mode, usually indicated by a P symbol, the camera sets both shutter speed and aperture according to predetermined rules. While this is ideal for casual shooting, it limits creative control. The combination of shutter speed and aperture is a compromise which may not be ideal for the sort of subject you are shooting. It's ideal when you're starting out but to learn more about the camera and how the basic values of shutter speed and aperture affect your results, Aperture priority and Shutter priority modes give much more power.

APERTURE PRIORITY

Aperture priority mode is usually indicated by an A symbol (Canon uses Av). Here you control the aperture, usually by rotating a control dial, and the camera sets the shutter speed accordingly.

The most obvious reason to use aperture priority mode is when depth of field is your primary concern (see p111). Aperture is one (but only one) of the key variables that determines depth of field.

Although aperture may be your priority, as the name suggests, try and keep an eye on the shutter speed that the camera is setting. If it's getting uncomfortably low, for example, raising the ISO level allows you to keep the aperture the same while gaining a faster shutter speed.

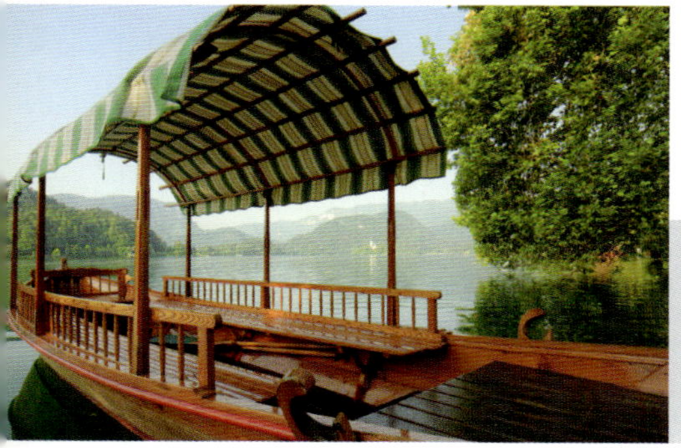

Pletna, Lake Bled, Slovenia
Aperture was key to controlling depth of field and ensuring that the pletna was sharp throughout.
Nikon D2x, focal length 12mm, ISO 160, 1/60sec at f/10

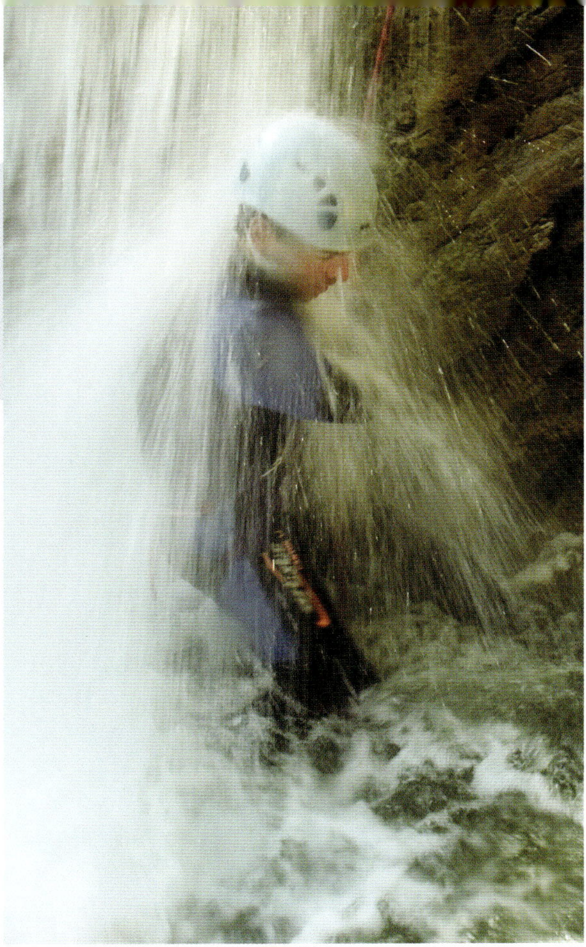

Canyoning in the Lechtal, Austria
The speed setting is critical to the way the falling water is recorded here.
Nikon D70, focal length 18mm, ISO 200, 1/50sec at f/10

PROGRAM SHIFT

Most DSLRs offer program shift (or flexible program), where rotating a control dial changes the combination of shutter speed and aperture. This is a handy feature when you're working fast, but if you find yourself using it all the time, which means you're paying attention to shutter speed and aperture, consider shooting in Shutter priority or Aperture priority instead.

POINT OF VIEW

My three favourite things about digital photography – the three biggest advances over shooting on film – are:

- The histogram
- White Balance control
- ISO control (i.e. not being stuck on the same ISO value for a whole roll of film). Being able to change the ISO at will is brilliant.

SHUTTER PRIORITY

Shutter priority mode is usually indicated by a B symbol, though Canon uses Tv (for Time Value). It's the converse of Aperture priority: here you control the shutter speed, and the camera sets the aperture accordingly.

Reasons to use Shutter priority include ensuring that the shutter speed is high enough to overcome camera shake, and tackling moving subjects. For example you may use a high shutter speed to freeze a fast-moving subject, or set a much slower speed for intentional, controlled blur.

MANUAL

Manual mode is universally indicated by an M symbol. In this mode, you set both aperture and shutter speed, with reference to the camera's meter reading. It's not complicated; there are only two variables to deal with. However, for anyone who's new to it all, Aperture priority and Shutter priority represent the best way to gain familiarity with these key controls.

SCENE MODES

While Program, Aperture priority, Shutter priority and Manual have the same names and work in much the same way on all DSLRs, it's not so easy to generalize about Scene modes. For a start, they may have different names: for instance, Canon refers to the Basic Zone. The choice of modes may vary, and so does the way they operate. For the full lowdown, you'll need to refer to the maker's manual, or perhaps one of the Photographers' Institute Press *Expanded Guides*. Yet, there is some common ground. First, all Scene modes are program modes, in the sense that the camera sets both shutter speed and aperture according to built-in rules. However, it will apply different rules for different scene modes; for a Landscape mode it will prioritize a small aperture to give good depth of field, while for a Sports mode it will prioritize a high shutter speed.

Second, Scene modes don't just affect the shooting settings (shutter speed and aperture); they also bring processing settings into play, especially Picture Controls/Picture Styles – for more information see p81.

Third, Scene Modes may dictate when flash is or is not used. Some modes may block the use of flash entirely, others may operate it automatically when light levels are deemed to be too low. It may be impossible to override this, or – at best – may require digging into the menus every time. To me this is one of the most infuriating aspects of Scene Modes; being able to decide for myself whether or not to use flash seems a basic human right. Which is one reason why I never use the Scene Modes for my own photography, just Program, Aperture-priority, Shutter-priority and good old Manual.

NOTE

Scene modes are usually absent on high-end cameras, on the assumption that professionals and experienced amateurs prefer the greater control of working in Program, Aperture priority, Shutter priority and Manual.

SPEED PRIORITY MODE

As far as I know, no DSLR actually offers a mode called Speed priority, but there's an easy trick if you want to be sure that the camera is always setting the fastest possible shutter speed. Instead of using Shutter priority mode, use Aperture priority and set the widest available aperture. If the shutter speed still doesn't look fast enough, increase the ISO.

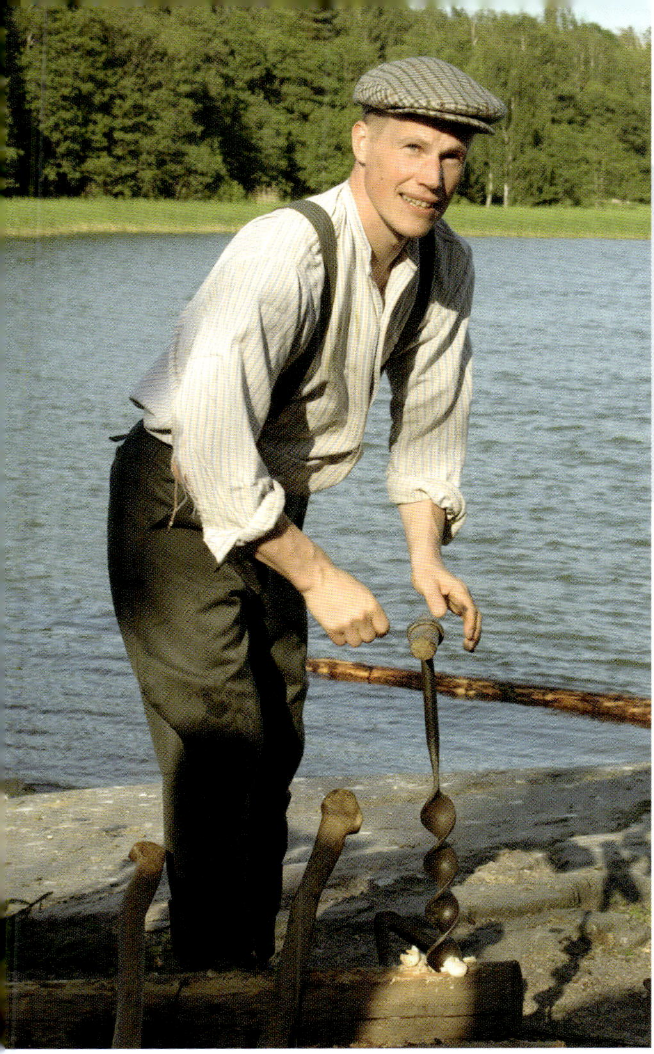

Woodcraft demonstration, Seurasaari, Helsinki, Finland
Portrait mode might seem an appropriate choice for a shot like this, but be aware that it produces slightly more muted colours and lower contrast.
Nikon D2x, focal length 56mm, ISO 250, 1/160sec at f/11

FULL AUTO MODE

Full auto is usually indicated by a green symbol and is the ultimate 'auto-everything' mode. It's not even a scene mode as it doesn't prioritize any particular kind of Scene or subject. It's compromise all the way. The camera is likely to be set to this mode when you unpack it, and one of your first actions should be to take it off this setting, never to return.

POINT OF VIEW

I still use Manual mode most of the time. This is partly force of habit, having spent my formative years shooting with cameras that gave me no other choices. As I shoot a lot of landscapes, where depth of field is a major factor, it might seem logical to use Aperture priority mode. However, I find that doing this in interesting light involves regular use of exposure compensation. To me, it generally seems easier and more intuitive to stay in Manual and tweak shutter speed myself. But that's a personal choice.

Focusing

Focusing is pretty simple, you might think – with modern autofocus, the camera makes sure that the subject is in focus and that's all there is to it. In fact, that's barely the beginning. DSLRs offer a range of focus options designed to maximize the chances that the right part or parts of the subject or scene are recorded in sharp focus.

MANUAL

Manual focusing has been around as long as photography itself, and the first SLR cameras allowed a more intuitive and natural method of focusing than anything that had gone before. Today's DSLRs still lend themselves comfortably to manual focusing, and some photographers still prefer to do it this way. However, it must be said, some viewfinders are better – bigger, brighter and clearer – than others, and on many contemporary lenses the manual focus ring may be narrow and awkwardly placed. Some DSLRs – Nikon in particular are noted for backward compatibility – still accept classic manual focus lenses.

AUTOFOCUS (AF)

The basic principle of operation is the same in virtually all DSLRs: halfway pressure on the shutter-release button activates autofocus. In some cases there may also be a separate focus-activation button as an alternative. However, that's just the beginning – most DSLRs have multiple options both for AF mode and for selecting the focus point.

POINT OF VIEW

While I still use manual exposure mode most of the time, I rarely use manual focus these days. With today's DSLRs I can autofocus on exactly the point I choose, more quickly and more accurately than doing it manually.

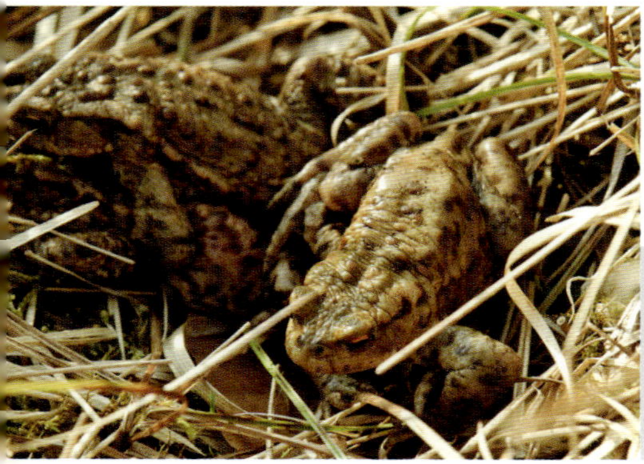

Common toads (bufo bufo)
At such close range, depth of field is slender. I focused on the eye of the nearest toad.
Nikon D700, focal length 70mm, ISO 400, 1/160sec at f/10

SINGLE-SHOT AF

This method is best suited to static subjects. Nikon calls it *Single-servo AF*, Canon calls it *One Shot mode*, Sony calls it *Single-shot*. They all do much the same job – on pressing the shutter-release button half way, the camera attempts to focus on the selected focus area. If it focuses successfully, you'll usually hear a confirmation beep or get a green light. If you keep half pressure on the shutter-release button, the camera stays focused at that distance; in other words, focus is locked. If you want to refocus, take the pressure off the button first.

CONTINUOUS AF

This method is intended for continuously moving subjects. Nikon calls it *Continuous-servo AF*, Canon calls it *AI Servo* mode, Sony calls it *Continuous AF*. Initial focus is acquired in much the same way as in Single-shot mode, but thereafter if the subject moves the camera attempts to keep it in focus, using information such as its colour and tone to track it. In some cases face-detection technology may also be employed.

When this works, it works brilliantly, but there are some limitations. In particular, the camera can only keep track of a moving subject as long as it remains within the area covered by the focus points.

AUTO AF

The operation of automatic AF varies more widely among different manufacturers, but in general it switches automatically between single-shot and continuous AF. Sony calls it *Automatic AF,* Canon calls it *AI Focus*, and Nikon calls it *AF-A*.

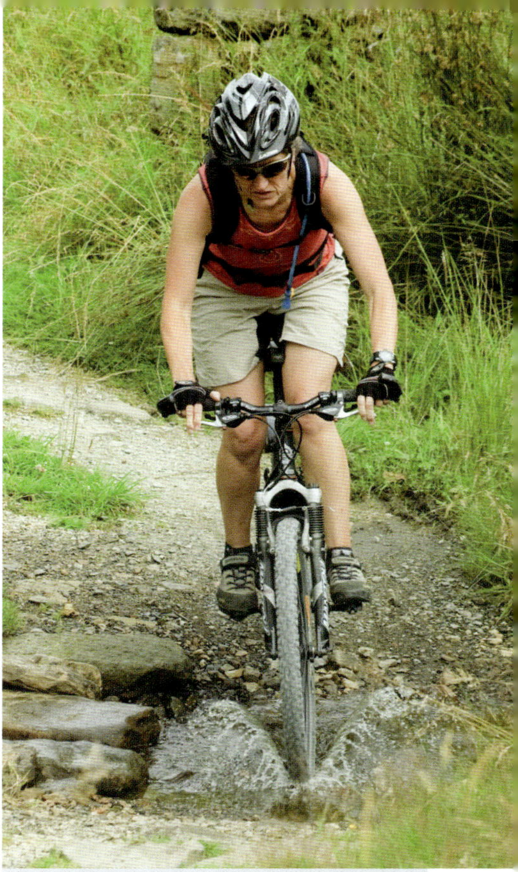

Mountain biker, Gisburn Forest, Lancashire, UK
The AF system in any modern DSLR should have no difficulty with a subject moving directly towards the camera.
Nikon D70, focal length 102mm, ISO 250, 1/400sec at f/7.1

WARNING

Many lenses have a switch (marked A-M or similar) which changes the lens drive mode. If the lens is set to A, manual focus may not work, and vice versa. There's also the possibility that attempting to focus manually while the AF drive is engaged may lead to damage, or at least excessive wear and tear. Use with care!

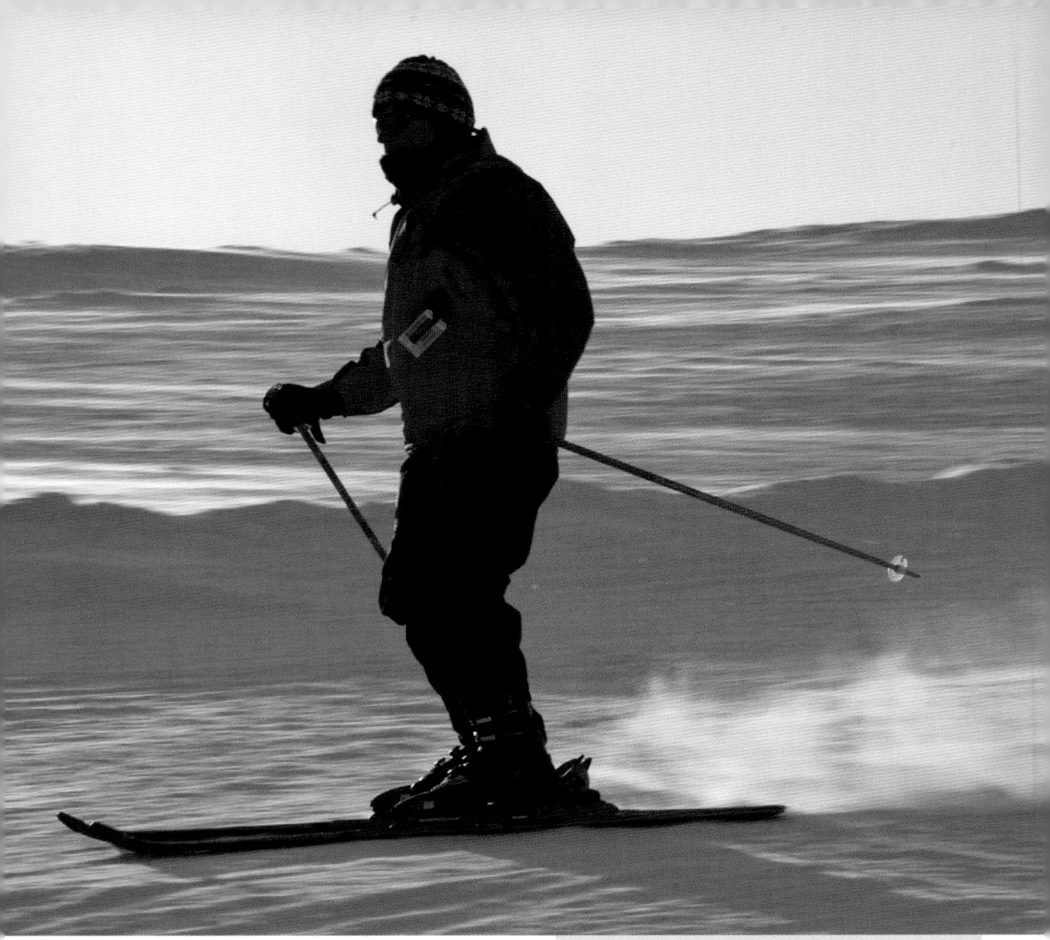

Skier, Ylläs, Finland
A subject moving across the frame requires the camera to make use of multiple focus points.
Fujifilm FinePix S3Pro, focal length 70mm, ISO 100, 1/125sec at f/13

FOCUS POINT SELECTION

The first autofocus systems were severely handicapped by being able to focus only on the centre of the frame. Current cameras are much more flexible, typically offering anything from nine focus points to 51 (a record currently shared by several high-end Nikons). Even 51 AF points don't cover the whole of the frame, but they go a long way towards ensuring that most subjects can be kept in focus. Like AF modes, options for focus point selection do vary between cameras, but again they usually boil down to single (or manual), continuous (or dynamic) and automatic.

Manual selection

This tends to go naturally with Single-shot AF; the available focus points are shown in the viewfinder and the user selects between them using the controller on the back of the camera. With a smaller number of focus points, selection is quicker, but when there are more to choose from it becomes more precise.

Continuous selection

This naturally aligns with Continuous AF, allowing the camera to switch automatically to different focus points if the subject moves within the frame (a single focus point would work if the subject were only moving directly towards or away from the camera). As a rule, the initial focus point still has to be selected manually; in some cameras, in some modes, it defaults to the centre point.

Automatic selection

Here the camera selects the initial focus point automatically, based on various rules programmed into it. These may include face-detection algorithms; if more than one face is detected the camera will generally prioritze the closest. The limitations are obvious, in that focusing on the nearest person is not necessarily what you want. Automatic focus point selection is very useful for casual shooting but can work against you when you want to be fully in control.

DEPTH OF FIELD

Focusing is not as cut and dried as 'in focus' or 'out of focus'. In many photos we can see a continuous transition from perfectly focused, through slightly soft, all the way to completely defocused. And, though the camera can focus precisely at just one distance, objects either side of that distance may still appear to be sharp. This is the essence of depth of field. This can be defined as the zone, extending both before and behind the point of focus, in which objects appear to be sharp in the final image.

Depth of field is a complex issue, and depends on several factors, including distance to the subject, the focal length of the lens and aperture. This last factor, aperture, is the one that causes many photographs to turn out differently from the image seen in the viewfinder before shooting. The SLR viewfinder shows the image with the lens at its maximum aperture (e.g. f/2.8), but if a smaller aperture (e.g. f/11) is set, the camera stops down to this to take the picture. Smaller apertures increase depth of field, so the final image no longer matches the viewfinder image.

FOCUS AND RELEASE PRIORITY

If the camera fails to acquire focus in Single-shot mode, it usually won't allow you to release the shutter; this is called focus priority. In Continuous AF, it's more likely that the camera will allow the shutter to be released even when perfect focus has not been acquired; this is called release priority. On some DSLRs you can change this behaviour (look in the Custom Settings Menu).

FOCUS LOCK

What do you do if the subject you want to focus on is outside the area covered by the focus points? Switching to manual focus would be one option; another is to use focus lock. Aim the camera so that the desired subject coincides with the selected focus point, half-press the shutter-release button to acquire focus and then keep it pressed to hold focus while you re-aim the camera to frame the picture as you want it. This works most easily in Single-shot AF mode.

Depth of field preview/review

Most DSLRs have a depth of field preview button, which stops the lens down to the taking aperture so you can preview the effect on depth of field. This is a time-honoured feature and I'd hate to be without it, but it's always been limited by the darkening of the viewfinder which goes with it. Unlike film SLRs, DSLRs also have a depth of field review option; zooming in on image playback allows a much clearer indication of what parts of the scene are or are not sharp. This is really valuable in landscape photography, for example, where depth of field is often crucial and there's usually a little more time to play with.

Depth of field is greater on smaller format sensors and less on larger ones, so full-frame cameras make it easier to isolate a subject using shallow depth of field, but may make you work a bit harder to achieve front-to-back sharpness in a landscape shot.

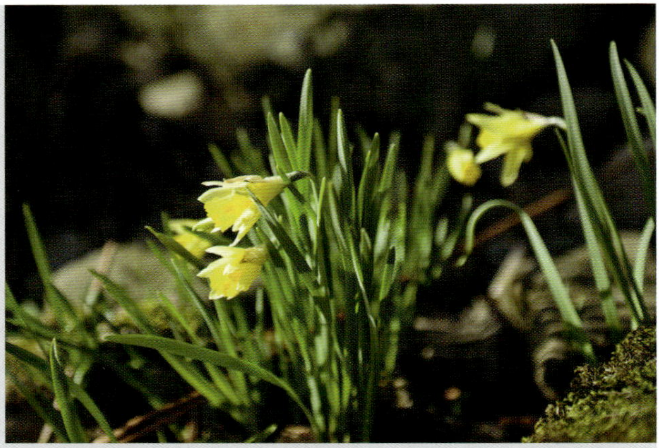

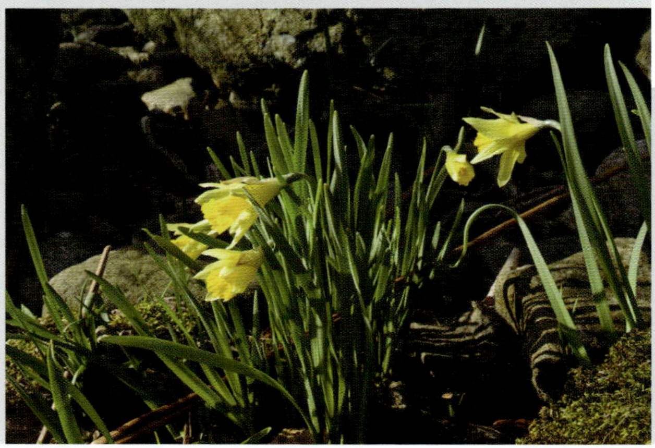

Beside Ullswater, Cumbria, UK
The top image at f/2.8, matches the viewfinder image; the bottom image, at f/22, looks significantly different.
Nikon D700, focal length 46mm, ISO 250, 1/1600sec at f/2.8/ 1/25sec at f/22

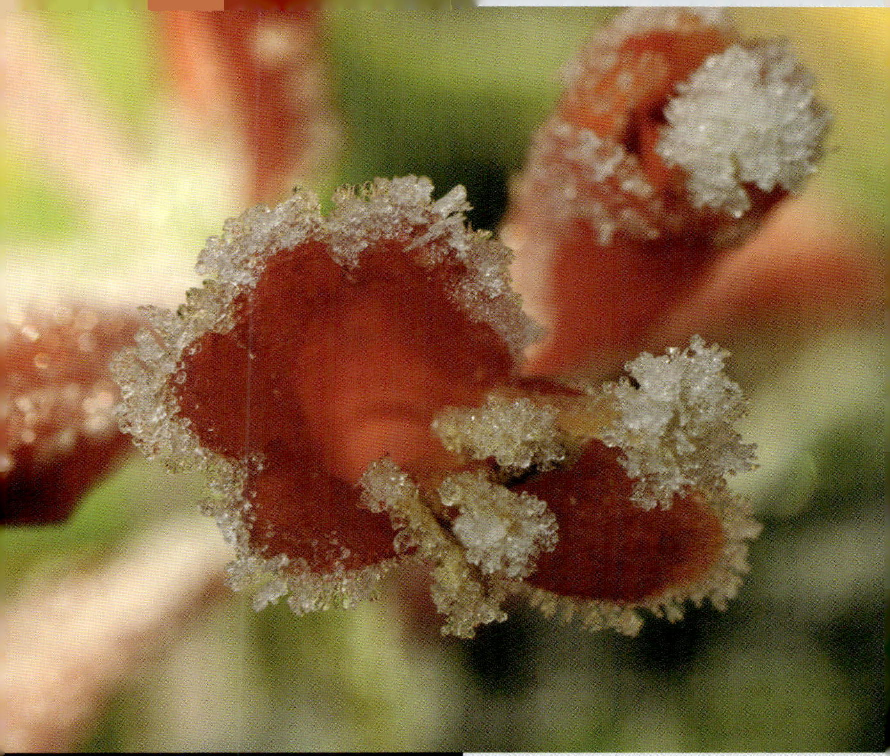

Frost on honeysuckle
In macro photography depth of field is minimal and precise focusing is essential.
Nikon D90, focal length 50mm, ISO 200, 1/30sec at f/9

LIVE VIEW FOCUSING

Because the reflex mirror is raised in Live View mode, focusing may operate differently. For details you definitely need to consult the camera manual, but here are a couple of things to look out for.

To focus in Live View, the camera needs to read the image from the sensor itself. This may make focusing slower than normal, but removes possible inaccuracies due to factors like a slight misalignment of the reflex mirror. Therefore Live View focusing may struggle to keep up with moving subjects, but should be unerringly

photography, where depth of field is absolutel minimal and there's therefore no margin for ever the slightest focusing error.

Live View focusing may also allow you to position the focus area anywhere within the frame, rather than limiting you to the usual focus points. Again, for certain compositions, this can

Flash

Flash is extremely useful, and any decent DSLR has highly advanced flash capabilities, but flash can't work miracles. All flash, especially the built-in units on most DSLRs, has massive limitations. Above all, flash is small and – however dazzling it may seem – it is weak.

Flash confuses people, none more so than those you see hopefully flashing away at stadium rock concerts and firework displays. The small size of a flash unit gives its light a strongly directional, hard-edged quality. Its weakness sets an ultimate limit on its useful range. Built-in units have an additional limitation in their fixed position.

RANGE AND POWER

The raw power of any flashgun is indicated by its guide number (GN). The effective GN varies with the ISO sensitivity – like any light source, you can extract more from it at higher ISO ratings. The GN relates aperture and distance; one of the things it can tell you is the maximum range of a flashgun for any given ISO and aperture.

FLASH RANGE

Without memorizing lots of figures, it is worth knowing the maximum range of your flash for certain conditions: for instance, at ISO 400 with your standard lens, wide open and at a more usual working aperture like f/8 or f/11.

Let's take a simple example. A small flashgun with a GN of 20 at ISO 200 can give decent illumination to a subject 10m (33ft) away at an aperture of f/2. At f/4 the distance halves to 5m (16.4ft), and so on. Take the ISO up to 1600, still at f/2, and the flash can potentially reach 56m (184ft), which might be enough for that stadium rock event; however, if you can shoot at f/2 and 1600 ISO I'm betting the stage lights will be more than enough and you'll get much more interesting results that way.

In any case, while quoted GNs will give an indication of the relative power of different units, you'll rarely need to do any actual calculations with them. The camera manual should give a table of the operating range of the built-in flash for various ISO and aperture values. A separate flashgun should also give such information in its instructions, and may even have figures etched on the unit itself. In any case, built-in flash and dedicated accessory units integrate well with the camera's metering system to deliver accurate exposure in most cases. Flash compensation and flash bracketing allow the flash levels to be fine-tuned.

USING FLASH

The uses of flash are many, but can be divided into two main areas: as the main light, and for fill-in illumination.

Flash as the main light

Using a built-in flash as the main lightsource cruelly exposes all its limitations – not only the limited range, but also the harsh frontal light, which makes portraits look like police mugshots. Even the cheapest accessory flashgun, plus an extension cable (or sync lead) opens up many new possibilities by shifting the flash off-camera. By adding a diffuser, or bouncing the flash off a reflector, wall or ceiling, the light can be spread and its harsh quality can be dissipated.

Fill-in flash

Fill-in flash is a different story. Arguably this is the real, if not the only, reason for having built-in flash on a DSLR. By throwing light back into the shadows it counteracts the harshness of direct sunlight and softens excessive contrast. This is especially useful in outdoor portraits and close-up work, and most DSLRs handle metering and exposure for fill-in flash very well.

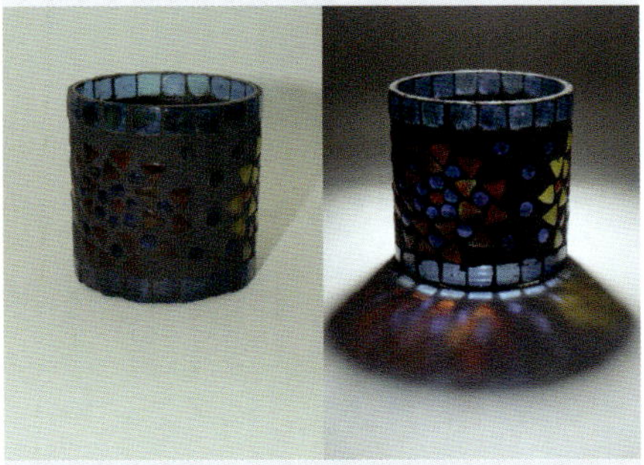

Flash comparison
On-camera flash produces a flat result with an ugly shadow (left). Using a single flash off-camera allows all sorts of possibilities to be explored (right).
Nikon D700, focal length 50mm, ISO 400, 1/60sec at f/9

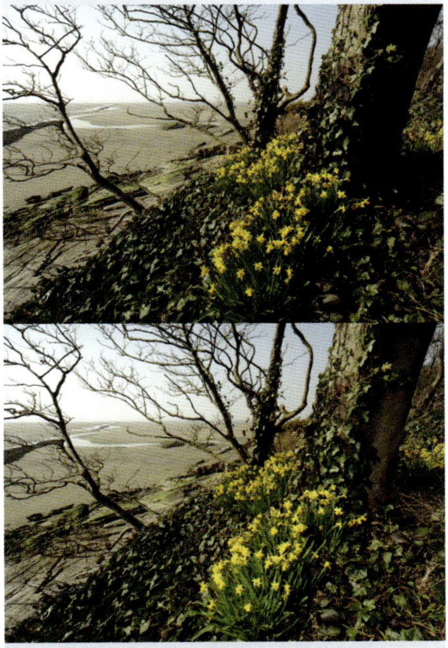

Jenny Brown's Point, Silverdale, Lancashire, UK
Two otherwise identical shots, one taken with and one without fill-in flash.
Nikon D700, focal length 16mm, ISO 200, 1/200sec at f/11

ON REFLECTION

As an alternative to fill-in flash, a reflector (which can be as simple as a sheet of white card) has much to recommend it, both because you can see the effect before you shoot and because – unlike a built-in flash – you can put the light just where you want it.

Drive mode

The basic drive mode – or release mode – options are Single and Continuous, and they're pretty self-explanatory. In Single release mode, press the button once and the camera takes one picture. In Continuous mode, it keeps firing as long as you keep the button pressed.

The maximum continuous firing rate varies from around 3 frames per second (fps) – slower in some older DSLRs – to the sizzling 9fps of the Nikon D3 (11fps in DX crop mode).

It's debatable whether such speeds really benefit the average photographer. Action photography still demands anticipation and fast reactions. Simply rattling off a continuous burst at 9fps doesn't guarantee you'll catch the 'decisive moment', but it does fill up memory cards and creates heaps of editing work. 3fps doesn't confer bragging rights but it can still get you some great shots. Even Nikon D3 owners can set its Continuous (low-speed) mode to 3fps, or indeed anywhere from 1 to 9fps. Many other DSLRs also have an adjustable speed setting.

Skier, Gålå, Norway
I sensed a fall was imminent, but it was hard to predict exactly when shooting continuously made sure I caught it.
Nikon D700, focal length 160mm, ISO 200, 1/400sec at f/4.5

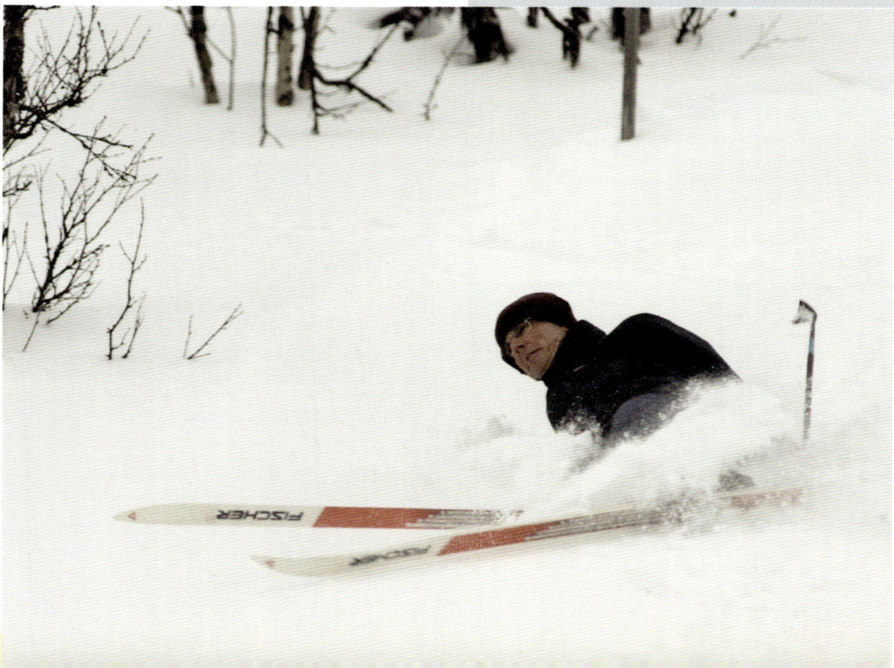

OTHER DRIVE OPTIONS

In addition to the basic options, the self-timer is not only useful for putting yourself in the picture, it's also one way of reducing vibration when you fire the shutter. A two-second delay is usually sufficient for this, and most DSLRs have some option (probably in the Setup or Shooting Menu) to vary the delay time.

Another option for reducing camera shake, found mostly on high-end DSLRs, is Mirror-up mode. This recognizes that the reflex mirror is a heftier affair than the shutter itself, and its operation is more likely to cause camera shake. Mirror-up mode requires a double press on the shutter button; the first one raises the mirror, the second fires the shutter.

LIVE VIEW

Live View is also a mirror-up mode, but works in a different way. In fact it seems to be different for each manufacturer (and some, like Fuji, don't yet offer Live View at all on their DSLRs). In Nikon's case, for example, the mirror flips back down briefly when the shutter is pressed, to allow exposure to be set. This is literally and metaphorically clunky but Live View is still relatively new on DSLRs and its implementation will improve. Canon offers a silent mode in its Live View options, which has obvious promise, but there's still some mirror noise at the start and end of operation; it's not a full-on 'stealth mode' just yet.

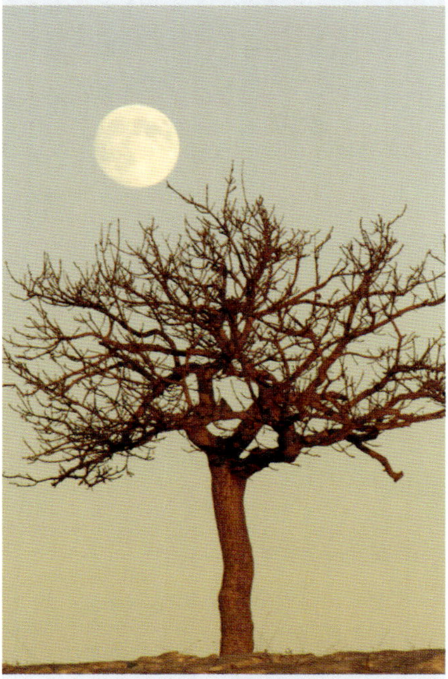

Moon and ash, Farleton Fell, Cumbria, UK
Using a 300mm lens, I used Mirror-up mode and a cable release to minimize any possible vibration.
Nikon D2x, focal length 300mm, ISO 125, 1/10sec at f/22

POINT OF VIEW

My regular fast-action fodder is cycling and mountain biking. At close range, the action happens pretty fast, but I'll often use Single-shot release mode, especially for mountain-biking where I want to shoot at a key spot such as a drop-off. I'll generally switch to Continuous mode for panning shots.

Accessories

The DSLR is a system camera, defined by its extendability. As well as external flashguns and reflectors (already mentioned) camera support is often essential for good pictures. Digital imaging may have reduced the need for some filters, but others remain extremely valuable.

CAMERA SUPPORT

Image stabilization is all very well; it might, for example, let you hand-hold successfully at 1/8sec instead of 1/30sec. However, many shots require still longer exposures and no one, not even a Zen master, can hand-hold a camera perfectly still for a second or more. Sooner or later we all need to employ some form of camera support.

There are many varieties, from the monopod to the homemade beanbag and various proprietary developments thereof. However, the original and best is the tripod. The tripod is not just an excellent way of holding the camera steady; it also has a more subtle advantage. It slows you down – yes, that really is an advantage. It makes you stop and think about position, angle and framing.

FILTERS

The DSLR's White Balance control effectively removes the need to use filters for colour correction, but some filters remain highly valuable. A UV or skylight filter cuts out excess blue light form the sky, and helps protect the lens against knocks and scratches.

The polarizing filter is still a great standby, especially for landscape photographers. It cuts down on reflections, intensifying the colours of many surfaces. It can also cut through atmospheric haze and make blue skies appear more dramatic and colourful. These effects are hard or impossible to replicate in digital post-processing.

The grey (more properly, neutral-density) graduated filter is also still sporadically useful for overcoming excessive differences in brightness between for example, land and sky. All-over neutral-density filters can also be useful when you want a super-slow shutter speed, to achieve creative blur.

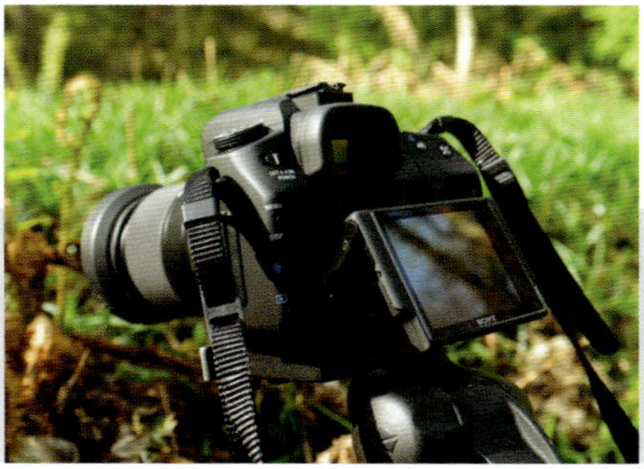

Low-level shooting
The fold-out screens of some newer DSLRs (like this Sony α350) can make life easier when using a tripod at low level.

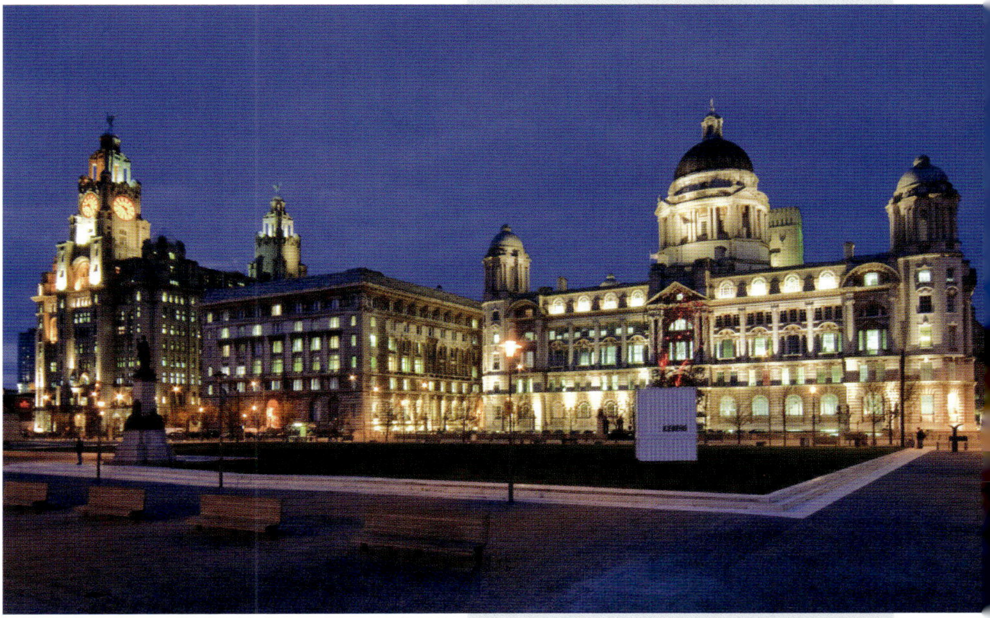

The Three Graces, Pier Head, Liverpool, UK
Sometimes there simply is no alternative to a tripod.
Nikon D2x, focal length 14mm, ISO 125, 8 seconds at f/11

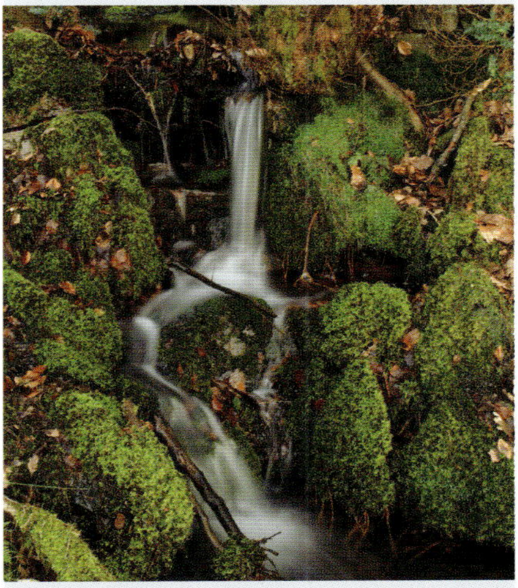

Quernmore valley, near Lancaster, UK
A neutral-density filter can help when a longer exposure is called for. Smoothing out the motion of a waterfall is a common example.
Nikon D700, focal length 40mm, ISO 100, 2.5secs at f/16

TRIPOD TIPS

Beware of tripods that are too light and flimsy to hold the camera properly; they may be easier to carry around but if they don't do the job, the effort's wasted anyway. Long lenses and/or high winds pose particular challenges for tripods.

Don't go to all the trouble of setting up a tripod and then waste it by vigorously jabbing the shutter release. Be gentle; ideally use the self-timer or, better still, a cable release (another invaluable accessory).

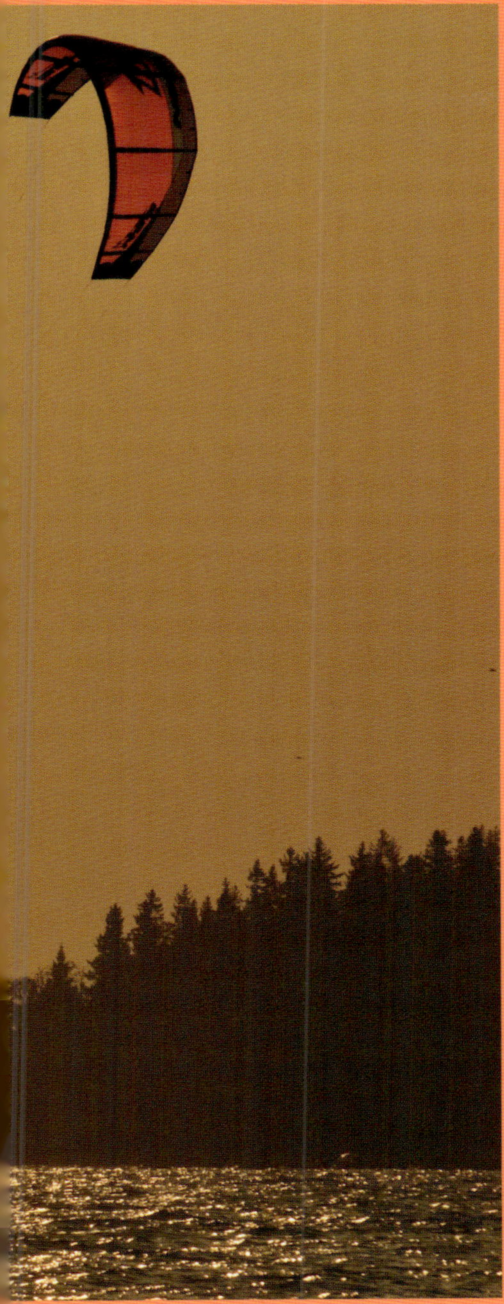

06:
YOUR DSLR IN THE FIELD

The digital revolution is sometimes accused of making photography too easy, but that's missing the point. It's a big world out there, full of photographic opportunities and challenges. Meeting those challenges has always been about much more than correct focus and exposure. Making focus and exposure more accurate liberates the photographer to concentrate on the real challenges of capturing a moment, a mood, an expression, a sense of place.

Kite surfer, Yyteri, Finland
Nikon D2x, focal length 200mm, ISO 200, 1/2000sec at f/11

Vision

The things that make a great picture are fundamentally the same, whether you shoot on film or digital. Great pictures tell a story, capture a moment or evoke a mood, independent of the technology used to make them.

Photography is not about cameras; photography is about vision. A better camera won't make you a better photographer, but it may make it easier to realize your vision. The first requirement is to be fully at home with whatever camera you have, to have a clear sense of its potential power as well as its limitations. I hope this book can help, but in the end there is no substitute for actually using your DSLR. Luck plays its part in photography, as in everything else, but as Arnold Palmer once said, 'It's a funny thing, the more I practice the luckier I get.'

Still, let's not get too hung up on this. When we say 'practice' we really just mean getting out there and taking pictures. And practice can be very productive – one of the beauties of digital is the instant feedback, which can really speed up the learning process.

POINT OF VIEW

I really don't consider rules when I'm taking pictures. Every scene and every subject is different, and trying to fit them all to the rule of thirds or some other formula tries to make them all the same. However, many of my photos will appear in keeping with this rule or that. Deliberately breaking the rule every time seems just as pointless as following it slavishly.

COMPOSITION AND FRAMING

A great example of practice makes perfect is in the area of composition. Personally, I much prefer to use the word 'framing'. This is partly because framing sounds closer to what photographers actually do, and partly because discussions of composition all too frequently turn into nothing more than a few simple prescriptive rules. I still cringe at the memory of the photo student who once said in front of a class, 'This is a good picture because it follows the rule of thirds.' Cart before horse, surely? Anyway, whether you believe in rules or not, the essence of framing is in the numerous decisions we make before every single shot: where to stand, where to point the camera, how wide a view to take, what to include and what to leave out.

Often we make these decisions without conscious thought, but setting out to be more aware of them has got to help; and the more you do it, the more intuitive it all gets. A great pianist doesn't spend countless hours practising scales so they can get better at playing scales; they do it so they can be better at making music.

I don't like rules of composition, but there are two general principles I aim to follow: know where the edges are, and see what the camera sees. You can't apply the rule of thirds, or any other rule, without reference to the edges of the frame. The edges define the picture. One

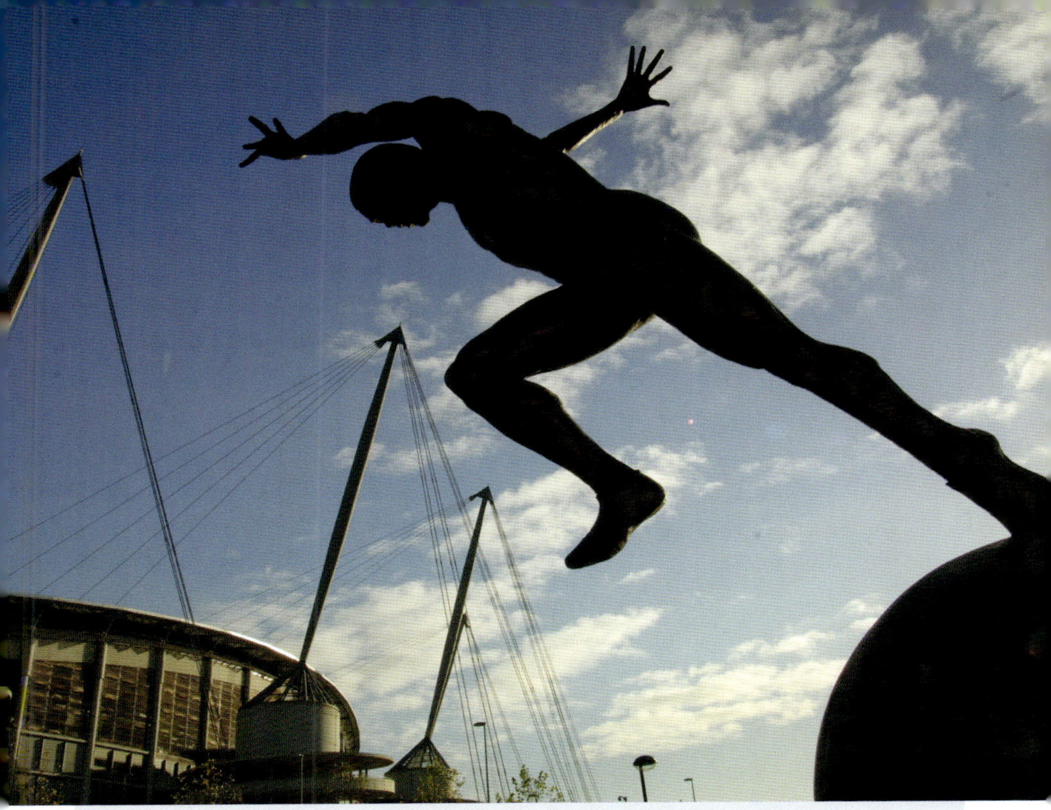

Running man, Sportcity, Manchester, UK
Forget rules, this was all about balance. Using a wide-angle lens, tiny shifts in position altered the framing dramatically. I soon found that the shot worked best if the runner and stadium did not quite overlap.
Nikon D2x, focal length 18mm, ISO 100, 1/100sec at f/14

simple exercise I've carried out many times (a bit like the pianist practising scales) is to observe the edges of the frame while slowly moving the camera or zooming the lens. It's great for awareness of the edges, and it's great for making you notice things other than the subject. This is important because the camera doesn't know what the subject is and it will record whatever is in the frame, whether you're interested in it or not. Part of the photographer's craft is to see what's there, both the stuff you're interested in and everything else.

As more and more DSLRs now have Live View, it's interesting to experiment with framing pictures using the rear screen instead of the viewfinder. I wouldn't recommend doing this all the time, but there are occasions (especially when using a tripod) when it's easy to do and it does make you look at the image in a different way.

Landscape

Photographing a landscape should be easy. It's always there. It doesn't fly away if you get too close, and it doesn't tend to offer blink-and-you've-missed-it moments. Yet landscape (both natural and man-made) is endlessly challenging to millions of photographers.

Part of the challenge is the very fact that it is always there, and all around us. Natural landscapes, in particular, are big, complex and often chaotic. The challenge of landscape photography is how to make some clear visual statement about that chaos. Landscape photography is not ultimately about what camera or lens you use: above all, it's about seeing. And this is where everything said on the preceding pages about framing comes home to roost.

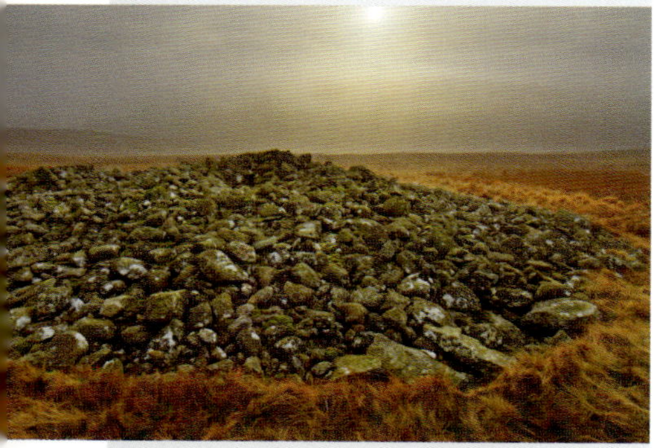

Ancient burial cairn, above Dudon valley, Lake District, UK
The light was suitably mysterious but the dynamic range was massive. This result was only achieved by combining several originals, with exposures spread over 7EV.
Nikon D2x, focal length 18mm, ISO 100, various shutter speeds, f/16

LANDSCAPE AND LIGHT

There is (allegedly) an ancient Chinese curse: May you live in interesting times. The landscape photographer's curse probably runs: May you shoot in interesting light. Or is it a blessing?

The way landscape appears to us is incredibly responsive to season and weather and, above all, to light. There's much talk of pictorial lighting and the magic hour. You might conclude that the landscape photographer's most important piece of kit is an alarm clock.

It's true, dawn and dusk are great times to take pictures. However, exciting light does not occur only at the ends of the day. A high sun can produce relatively flat light, but a few clouds – and their shadows – soon restore contrast. Great opportunities can occur on the 'worst' days. A shaft of sunlight piercing the clouds can be as dramatic as any dawn – and may demand that you react almost as quickly as the sports shooter. And in forests and canyons only a high sun may penetrate the depths.

For the DSLR user, interesting light means two things in particular: colour and dynamic range. The colour of natural light can vary enormously, from blue and cold in shadows on a sunny day to hot and red at sunrise and sunset. As a rule these changes are things we want to explore and celebrate in landscape photography. When the

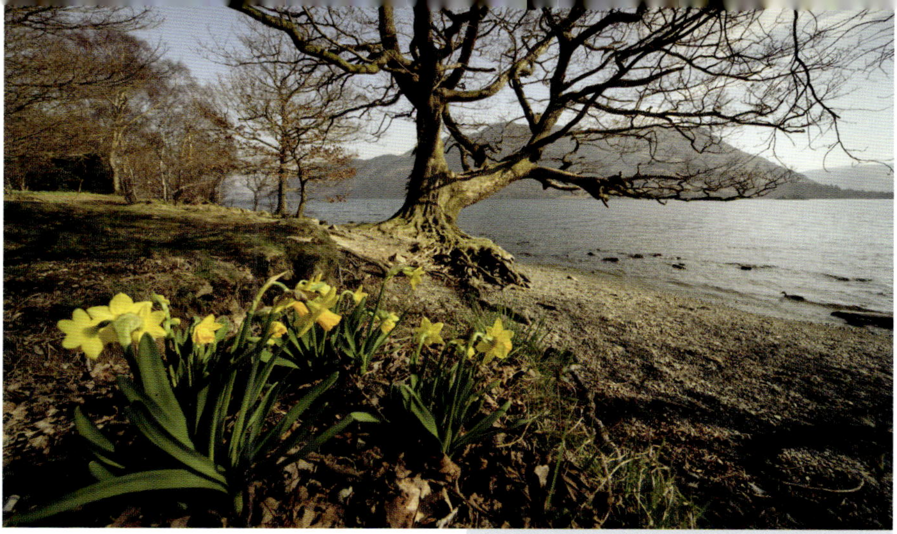

Daffodils by Ullswater, Cumbria, UK
I wanted everything in focus here, from the closest flower to the far side of the lake, which meant setting a small aperture and choosing the focus point carefully.
Nikon D700, focal length 12mm, ISO 250, 1/160sec at f/11

setting sun daubs the grey rocks red, we don't want them reverting to grey in the final picture – so beware of Auto White Balance!

Many inviting landscapes also display vast dynamic range – from a bright sky, perhaps with white clouds, to the deep shadows that give definition to the land. Some of the latest DSLRs have terrific dynamic range abilities, measured at up to 12 or 13EV in some cases, but exciting landscape images often present us with even wider ranges.

LANDSCAPE AND THE THIRD DIMENSION

The sheer scale of landscape invites the use of wide-angle lenses; the widest views are obtained on full-frame DSLRs. However, wide-angle lenses don't just introduce more width, they also expand the third dimension, depth. Depth enhances the sense of scale and brings in the foreground detail that makes the landscape come alive. Foregrounds put us in the landscape; they connect us to it. But they also mean more complexity, more to deal with in framing – and they demand close attention to depth of field.

LANDSCAPE MODE

Most DSLRs have a Landscape mode. It will set a small aperture for depth of field and (in JPEG shooting) will process the image for a punchy result, while employing some tonal controls to deal with high dynamic rage – all sound general strategies. But Landscape mode takes away the precise control over depth of field and can leave you at the mercy of unpredictable Auto White Balance. Aperture priority (or Manual) is a natural choice; Canon users can also investigate their A-DEP mode, which analyzes the distance to near and far objects to determine the required aperture and focus distance.

Action

In its broadest sense, action photography is any photography that deals with movement – which means most photography is action photography.

Even in landscape photography, there's often movement of some kind to contend with – breaking waves, waterfalls, foliage blowing in the wind – but above all, action photography suggests sports and wildlife.

The way that movement translates into a still image depends on several factors, notably the speed and direction of the movement and also the shutter speed (which clearly suggests using Shutter-priority mode). Speed of movement should be seen, not in terms of absolute speed, but its apparent speed across the camera's field of view. It can be harder to stop the movement of a cyclist close to the camera than a jet plane, which, though much faster, is naturally seen at a much greater (and safer!) distance.

To freeze the action completely obviously requires a high shutter speed, but the exact setting required depends on this question of the apparent speed. For a walker I might be happy with 1/125sec; for a mountain-biker on a climb, 1/250sec; but for the same biker on a fast downhill stretch I might choose 1/500sec or 1/1000sec. This is based on experience, but reviewing your images on the camera screen gives instant guidance.

Freezing the action is only one option, and doesn't always give the most dynamic impression. Consider a downhill skier on a gliding section – they may be doing 100kph, and you might need 1/4000sec to freeze their image, but it probably won't look terribly dynamic. This is a good case for the panning shot, which demands a much slower shutter speed. In other cases one might go slower still, aiming deliberately for a partly blurred image.

SPORTS MODE

Like other scene modes, Sports mode is a blunt instrument. It will aim to set a high shutter speed to freeze the action, but as the camera does not know what kind of action you're shooting it can easily set either a faster shutter speed than is really needed (thereby sacrificing potentially valuable depth of field); equally, sometimes it may not go fast enough. Shutter priority gives you direct control over the key parameter. Nor does sports mode make any allowance for alternative approaches like panning and deliberate blur.

SHOOTING MOVIES

At the time of writing, the ability to shoot movies has only appeared on a couple of DSLRs – namely the Nikon D90 and the Canon EOS 5D Mk II – but it's a racing certainty that movie capture will feature on many forthcoming DSLRs. It's questionable, however, whether this will be a big thing for most DSLR users or merely a pleasing diversion.

For some, including many photojournalists, being able to shoot both high-quality stills and movies on one camera is a big thing. When print

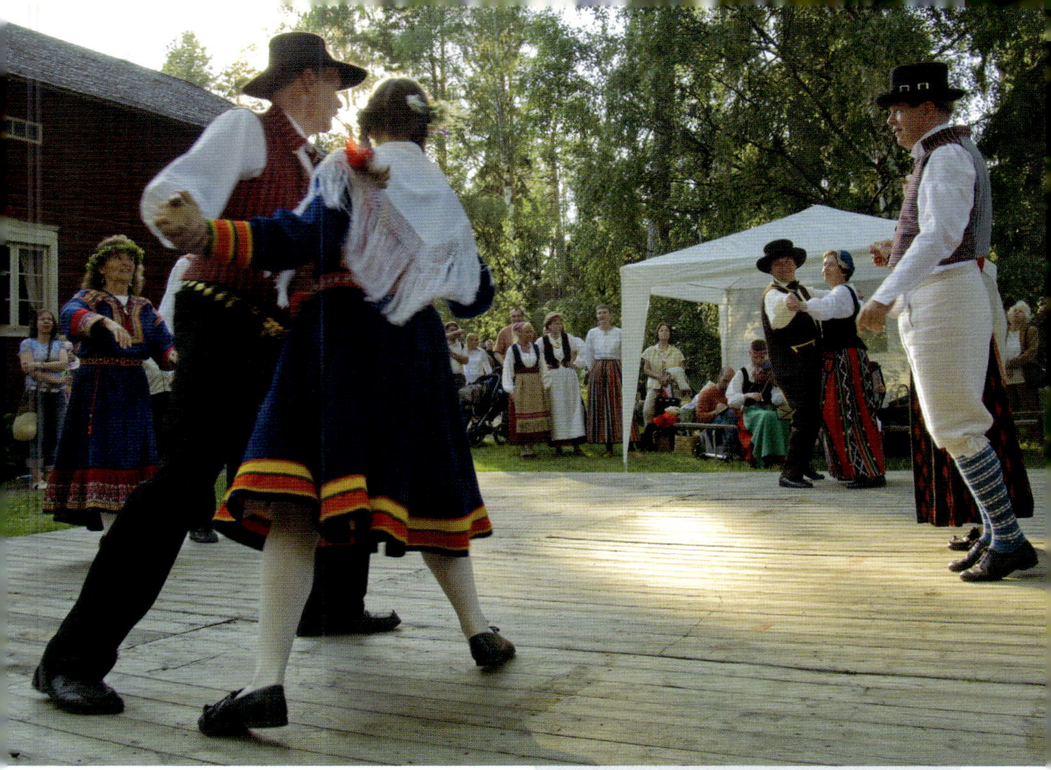

Midsummer Eve, Seurasaari, Helsinki, Finland
A moderate shutter speed means the nearest dancers show a little blur, but to me this seems to enhance the feeling of movement.
Nikon D2x, focal length 18mm, ISO 400, 1/125sec at f/6.3

was king, stills also ruled, but in the internet age video is equally in demand. And the HD output of the latest DSLRs (and camcorders) is a massive advance in quality from the blocky, jerky, discoloured material that's so much in evidence on YouTube and elsewhere.

However, there's no such thing as a free lunch. The design of the SLR is superbly evolved for shooting still images, but precisely for this reason, handling can be awkward for video use. Video on DSLRs is an offshoot of Live View and this means you can't use the viewfinder, only the rear screen. DSLRs are not designed to be held this way; it's awkward enough shooting hand-held stills in Live View (and why bother?); for video it's really tricky to focus and zoom smoothly. Unless you actually want wobbly pictures, a tripod is essential. This very real limitation may disappear if the mirrorless DSLR (see p20) really takes over; being able to shoot video via an electronic viewfinder would restore most of the SLR's handling qualities.

SLRs do have some plus points for video use. Their large sensors give very clean images, especially in low light, and they offer access to a huge range of lenses and other accessories. In particular it's possible to use ultra-wide lenses that can't be matched by camcorders. They can also produce much shallower depth of field, and for this reason alone a number of video-makers have seized on DSLRs for at least some of their work.

Portrait

By one estimate, 80 billion photographs are taken annually. Most of them are pictures of people. Arguably, this is the heart of photography, and DSLRs are pretty darn good at it.

Good portrait photography depends as much on people skills as on photographic technique. Many portrait photographers have built distinguished careers on the basis of very simple technique; – the great Jane Bown worked with a 40-year-old camera (obviously not a DSLR), one or two prime lenses and available light.

Available light has many advantages over flash: it's more comfortable for the subject and lets the photographer see what they're getting. Outdoors, direct sunlight can be harsh, but can be moderated using fill-in flash or a reflector. Great portraits can also be made on overcast days, when the whole sky acts like a giant studio 'softbox'.

Processing settings for portraits generally favour softer results, with moderate contrast and saturation, but there's always an alternative, perhaps going for a harder-edged, punchier look when it seems to suit the subject.

POINT OF VIEW

If there's one scene mode I would consider using, it is Portrait, but I'm more likely to use the built-in flash for fill-in when light levels are high (but usually prefer a reflector). In low light I'd rather use off-camera flash or bounce flash, or ramp the ISO up to 6400 and stick with the available light.

PORTRAIT MODE

Portrait mode generally aims for a wide-ish aperture to throw the background out of focus, processes JPEG images with moderate contrast and saturation, and automatically uses flash when light levels are low. On some DSLRs it will also exploit face detection technology to aid focusing. For anyone who isn't completely sure of their photographic technique, this level of automation certainly sets you free to concentrate on interacting with the subject and catching interesting postures or expressions.

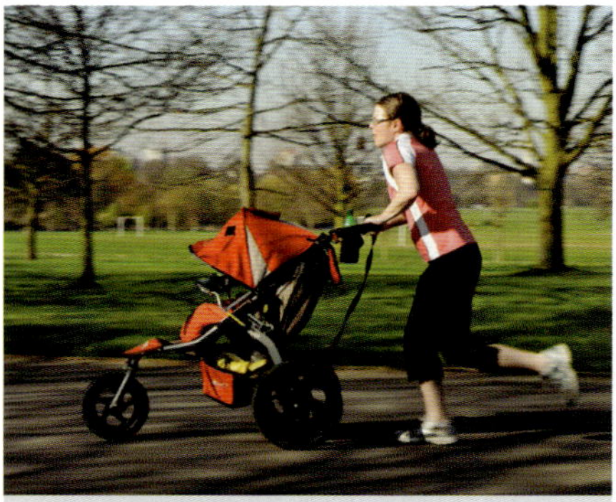

Regent's Park, London, UK
A portrait can also be an action shot, and vice versa.
Nikon D700, focal length 70mm, ISO 200, 1/80sec at f/13

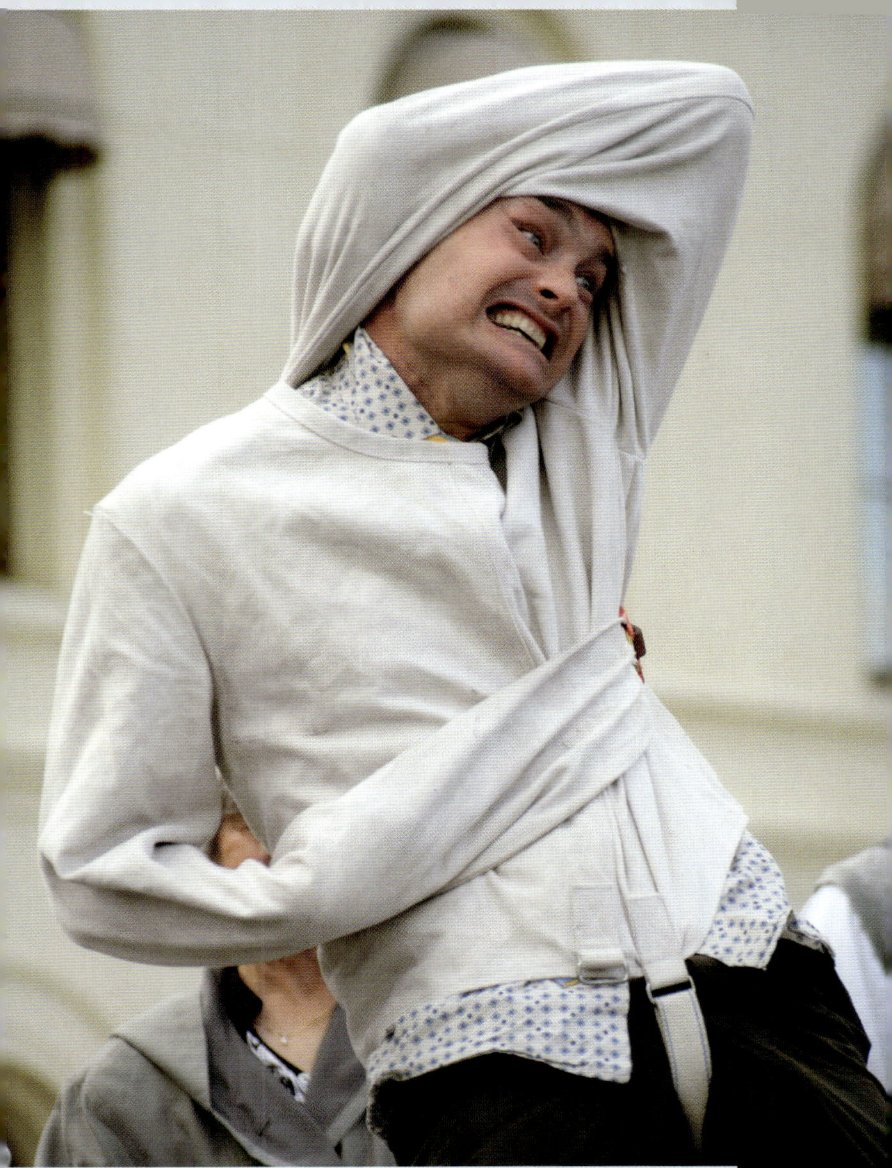

Street performer, Oslo, Norway
With the audience surrounding the performer, it was hard to get a completely 'clean' shot but a small aperture and a low viewpoint both helped.
Nikon D2x, focal length 180mm, ISO 200, 1/200sec at f/5.6

Macro

The SLR is the close-up camera par excellence. Reflex viewing is practically essential at close distances. However, straight out of the box with a kit lens, most DSLRs are not quite ready for serious close-up work. This is down to the limitations of the lens and, more seriously, of the built-in flash.

MACRO LENSES

A true macro lens can provide life-size (1:1) reproduction, and will also double as a good all-round lens. Yet, true macro lenses are not cheap, and are invariably prime lenses, rather than zooms. Surprisingly, the cheapest macro lenses I could find were not from one of the independents but from the camera makers, with Olympus appearing first and Canon also just ahead of Sigma.

Fortunately, several cheaper lenses achieve 1:2 reproduction, and you can do a lot with that. There are also many accessories including close-up attachment lenses, which screw in like filters, and extension tubes (aka extension rings), which attach between camera and lens. These give an economical entry into macro photography.

MACRO

Macro photography is traditionally defined as recording objects at life-size or larger. This means filling the frame with an object equal to the size of the sensor (24x16mm on an APS-format camera), such as postage stamps or small coins. Many lenses claim 'macro' capability when their limit is half- or quarter- life-size (denoted 1:2 or 1:4).

CLOSE-UP FLASH

As with portraits, close-ups expose the failings of the built-in flash. The light is ugly at best, and at really close range the subject may be cast into shadow by the lens. Off-camera flash really comes into its own in this situation. At short working distances, high power is not required; a single inexpensive flashgun, a sync lead, and probably a reflector, will take you a long way. Dedicated macro flash units fit around the lens, using either a ring-light or twin flash heads to achieve even illumination.

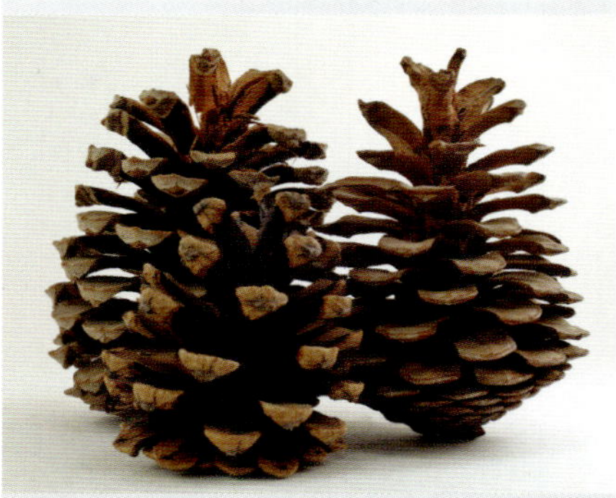

Fir cones
This shot was taken using a single flashgun, fired repeatedly from different directions – a technique sometimes called 'painting with light'.
Nikon D700, focal length 50mm, ISO: 100, 20secs at f/22

CLOSE-UP MODE

Close-up mode struggles to achieve a compromise between a small aperture for depth of field (always shallow at close distances) and a high shutter speed (to freeze any movement of camera or subject). It's also likely to pop up the flash automatically. This may be fine for fill-in at moderate distances, but hopeless as main light; the closer the subject, the worse it gets. This mode may be serviceable for modest close-ups but doesn't really work for true macro shots.

Beech leaves
Both the lighting and the shallow depth help to separate the leaves from the background. The main areas of the leaves are at much the same distance and all in focus, but the curled edges quickly lose sharpness.
Nikon D300, focal length 50mm, ISO 200, 1/13sec at f/11

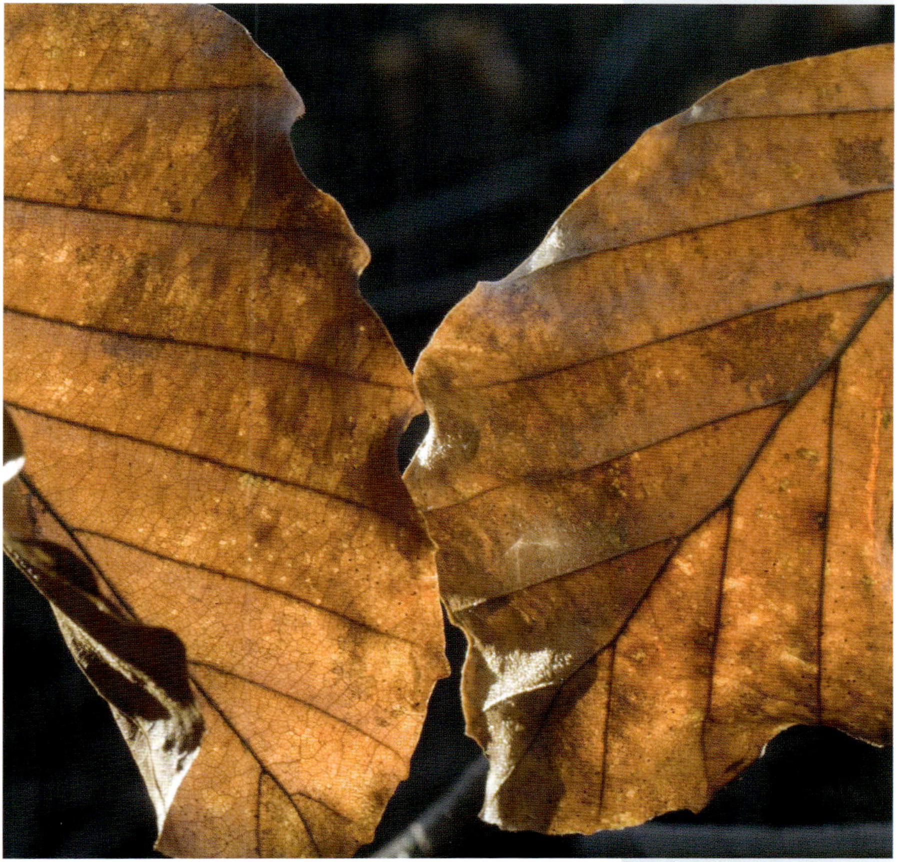

Lenses

The majority of DSLRs are sold with a midrange zoom lens – typically around 18–70mm – as a 'kit' deal. The focal-length range makes these pretty versatile, but they're only the starting point.

Nothing exemplifies the DSLR's 'system camera' status better than the vast range of lenses available, from 10mm or so to at least 800mm, plus specialist types like macro lenses (see p130), tilt/shift lenses opposite, fisheye lenses and so on. Where the camera-maker's own lens range is limited, look to the independents (principally Sigma, Tamron and Tokina).

Of course focal length isn't the only distinguishing feature. The main manufacturers may offer several lenses with similar focal length range but very different prices. Modern computer-aided design means there are very few really bad lenses out there any more, but there are still notable differences in both build quality and optical performance. Kit lenses are almost invariably built with competitive pricing in mind, usually with extensive use of plastics in the lens body (though, unlike compacts, rarely in the optical elements themselves).

FORMAT COVERAGE

Nikon, Canon and Sony produce both full-frame and APS-format cameras (see p35). Many lenses, like Nikon's DX and Sigma's DC series, are now made specifically for the smaller format and do not cover the full sensor area of the full-frame (FX) camera. DX lenses can be fitted to FX cameras but the image area is reduced, losing much of the benefit of having a larger sensor.

LENS SPEED

Some lenses do focus very rapidly, but the word 'fast' applied to lenses means that they have a wide maximum aperture, e.g. f/1.4 to f/1.8 for some prime lenses and f/2.8 for longer prime lenses and some zooms.

Fast lenses give a brighter viewfinder image, greater flexibility in low light, and allow faster shutter speeds to be used (which was how they

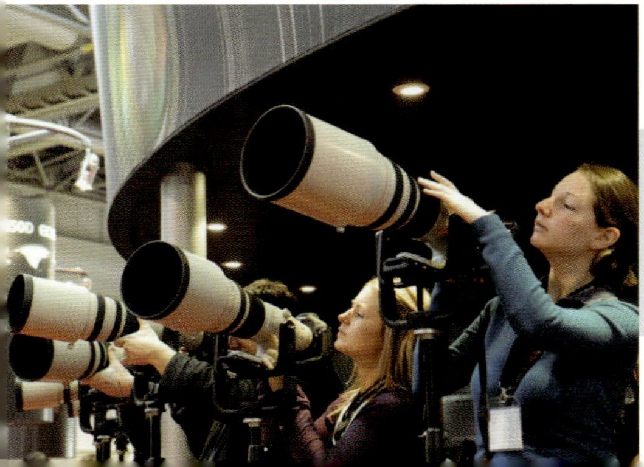

Trying Canon lenses, National Exhibition Centre, Birmingham, UK
Nikon D700, focal length 70mm, ISO 3200, 1/50sec at f/5.6

got the name in the first place). A wide aperture also gives shallow depth of field, which is great for isolating the subject from the background. This combination of fast shutter speed and minimal depth of field is characteristic of sports and wildlife images, but can also be exploited in portraiture and for emphasizing details in a landscape. Downsides of the fast lens include cost, size and weight; the laws of optics dictate that they need larger glass elements than slower lenses of the same focal length.

PERSPECTIVE CONTROL LENSES

Perspective control (or 'tilt and shift') lenses bring some of the flexibility of the view camera to the DSLR. One key application is in photographing architecture. With normal lenses it's often necessary to tilt the camera upwards, resulting in converging verticals (buildings appearing to lean back or even to one side). Using the shift function of the PC lens, the camera back can remain vertical, which means that vertical lines in the subject remain vertical in the image. The tilt function also enables depth of field to be controlled in ways that are not possible with other lenses. The perspective correction can, to some extent, be replicated in Photoshop (as in the photo on the right), but depth of field effects cannot.

PC lenses are expensive and ill-suited to casual snapping; in fact, they virtually demand to be used on a tripod. Canon currently produces four PC lenses and Nikon has three (which can also be used on Fujifilm DSLRs). Options for other makes are more limited but include the Ukrainian Arax 80mm lens (in most fittings), using an adaptor or seeking out older lenses.

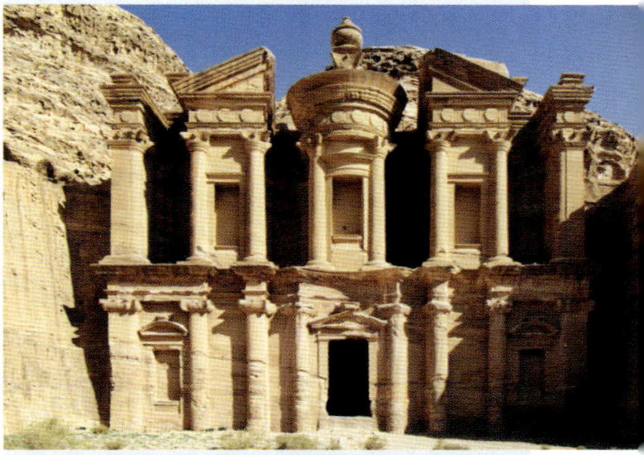

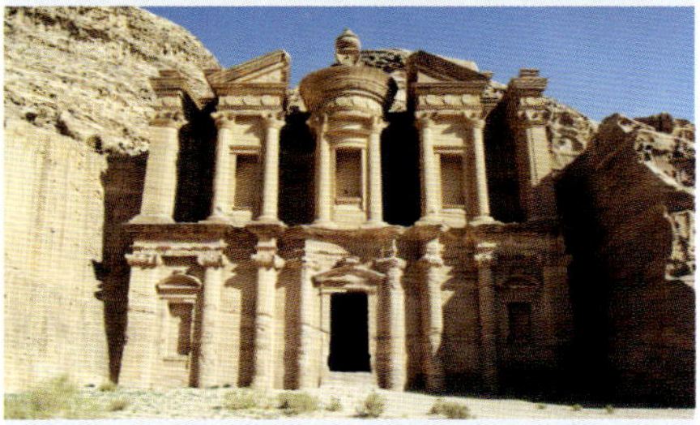

The Monastery, Petra, Jordan
An image with corrected perspective (top) and the uncorrected version (below).
Nikon D2X, focal length 18mm, ISO 250, 1/200sec at f/14

SUPERZOOMS

Lenses with a very wide range, such as an 18–200mm, have the obvious advantage of covering all the focal lengths you may need in one package. Apart from lightness and convenience, there's an additional advantage – if you never change lenses you won't have any problems with dust entering the camera. On the other hand, superzooms are slow (maximum aperture at longer focal lengths may be f/5.6 or worse) and there are always optical compromises. There may, for example, be some tendency to distortion ('barrel' or 'pin-cushion').

Managing and editing in the field

Digital cameras, especially the latest DSLRs with their fantastic rear screens, certainly make it easy, and very tempting, to review your images as you go along. But should you? Or, perhaps a better question, to what extent?

Let's think about some downsides first. First, those big, bright, beautiful screens consume power; using them too freely can drain the camera battery. The camera may be able to take a thousand shots or more on a single charge, but only under ideal conditions, which don't include lots of screen time. Imagine the frustration when the battery suddenly dies just as a perfect sunset is coming to the boil, leaving you with an expensive brick sitting on top of your tripod. Of course, one lesson is to acquire at least one spare battery, and to keep all your batteries charged and ready. But there are still limits, especially on long excursions. A one-second glance at the histogram is often all you need; this minimizes battery drain and maximizes valuable shooting time.

Second, time spent looking at the camera back is time that's *not* spent observing the real landscape or action in front of you – and this, it seems to me, is the real reason for being out there in the first place. There's a particularly obvious risk in areas like news or sports photography: missing a key moment because you were absorbed in reviewing your previous shots.

Third, it can be really hard to see the screen properly in bright conditions. There are clip-on screen shades available, but you can mimic the effect with a simple cardboard tube, or even go back to the old-time photographer's black cloth!

Of course, there are upsides, too. I've already enthused about the value of the histogram in confirming that exposure is correct. Image review (with a zoom function) is also invaluable in determining whether depth of field really covers everything you want to cover, whether your portrait subject blinked, and lots more.

In action shooting, image review makes it clear whether you've caught the moment or not. If you're shooting a sporting event you can't ask a competitor to do that bit again, but you may be able to decide if you want to retry a particular angle when they come round for the next lap. If you're working with co-operative subjects, the option to repeat the action does exist. Above all, perhaps, image review can really help you hone your timing and anticipation.

Image review can play a great role in helping all of us improve our photography, by giving immediate feedback on timing, exposure, framing and many other issues. And in this regard the screens on the latest DSLRs really are streets ahead of their predecessors.

BACKUP IN THE FIELD

As you accumulate more and more images, especially on long trips or expeditions, the stakes get higher. Dropping a memory card down a crevasse, having your bag stolen, or suffering a data corruption problem can lose hundreds or even thousands of precious images. Backing up is easy enough if you have regular access to a laptop or a portable device such as an iPod (with camera connector) but if you're trekking or backpacking it's more stuff to carry and more batteries and chargers to worry about too.

In the wilds, your options may be pretty limited, though at least theft is generally less of an issue than in cities. A few cameras have dual card slots: Nikon's D3 and D3X have dual Compact Flash slots while Canon's EOS-1Ds Mk III has slots for Compact Flash and Secure Digital cards. One option available through the menus is to use the second slot for backup.

Failing that, one final suggestion is to spread the risk. Rather than accumulating all your images on a single large-capacity card, use several smaller ones. That way, if you lose a card or the data is corrupted, you haven't lost everything. On the other hand, swapping cards is exactly the time when the risk of dropping or losing them is greatest. Take great care and treat removed cards as one of your most precious possessions.

CAMERA CARE AND PROTECTION

However well made, all DSLRs are full of highly complex electronic and optical technology, which is potentially vulnerable to damage. A few straightforward precautions in handling and care minimize the risks. Skylight filters and lens caps protect delicate lenses; keep the monitor cover in place too. Think about your surroundings and any specific hazards they may present.

Carrying

It's always advisable to keep the camera in some sort of case when not in use. For the basic camera and lens combination, nothing beats a simple drop-in pouch which can be worn on a waist belt. Excellent examples, with good protective padding, come from makers like Camera Care Systems and LowePro. For multi-lens outfits, shoulder bags allow rapid access but for heavier loads and/or longer distances, a backpack-type bag is much better for your spine (which is even more irreplaceable than the camera!).

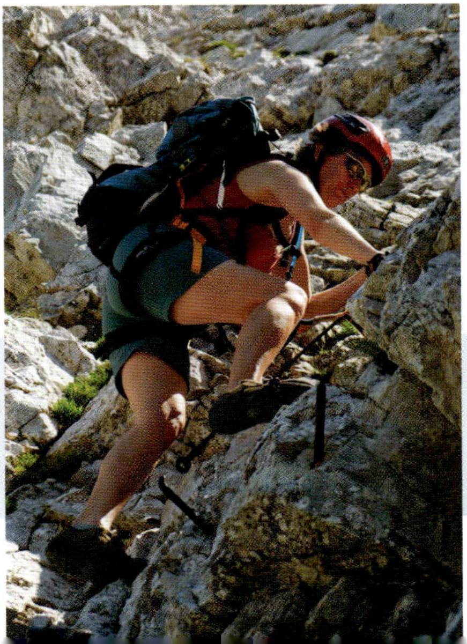

Via Ferrata in Slovenia
Definitely a situation where the camera needs to be secure yet readily accessible.
Nikon D2x, focal length 102mm, ISO 100, 1/250 sec at f/7.1

Water protection

Pro DSLRs have advanced weatherproofing, but other models may be less well protected; consult the maker's manual for detail. A microfibre cloth is handy to wipe off any accidental splashes. The built-in flash is usually a weak point, so avoid using it in the rain. A hotshoe cover probably came with the camera: use it.

Salt water is doubly hostile to electronic components than fresh, so take extra care to avoid contact. If this does occur, clean immediately with a cloth dampened with fresh water (ideally de-ionised water).

When shooting in wet conditions, protect the camera with a waterproof cover. A simple plastic bag with a hole for the lens will serve the purpose, but there are various purpose-made rain-guards and waterproof cases on the market. Kata Rain Covers combine good protection with access to camera controls. Aquapac make excellent submersible cases but at present they only accommodate smaller DSLRs.

Using an Aquapac SLR case in the rain
Rain spots on the front glass must be wiped off regularly.
Nikon D2x, focal length 18mm, ISO 200, 1/50sec at f/5.6

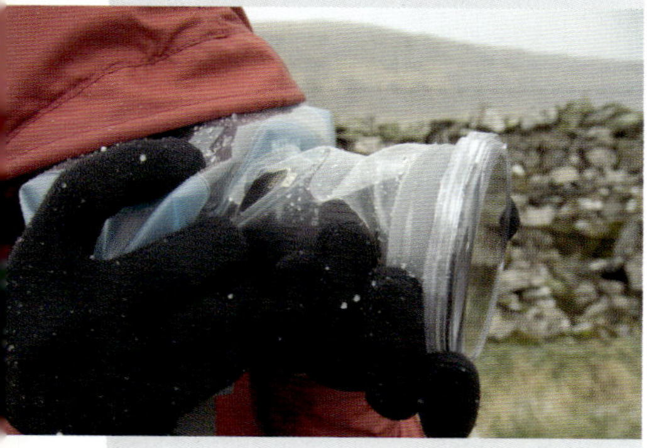

Dust protection

Dust particles inside the camera can result in spotty pictures and may damage the shutter mechanism. Take care when changing lenses and above all keep your back to the wind. In really bad conditions (sandstorms!) avoid changing lenses at all.

Exterior cleaning

Regular cleaning is a sensible precaution. Remove dust and dirt with a blower, then wipe with a soft, dry cloth. Lenses require extra care; again, use a blower to remove loose material. Remove fingerprints and other marks using a dedicated lens cleaner and soft cloth, preferably one of optical grade. Use similar care on the viewfinder eyepiece and the playback monitor.

Cleaning the sensor

Strictly speaking, it's the low-pass filter (see p37) that may need cleaning, not the sensor itself. Dust on the filter shows as dark spots in the image.

Most current DSLRs have a self-cleaning facility which vibrates the filter to shift the dust – but it doesn't miraculously vanish altogether. As far as possible, keep it from entering in the first place.

Stubborn spots may remain on the low-pass filter and as a last resort you can clean it manually. Several companies produce dedicated sensor cleaning swabs and, better still, complete kits like the Visible Dust system, which include illuminated magnifiers so you can see the problem clearly. Take very careful note of instructions, both for the cleaning kit and the camera itself. If you mess up and damage the low-pass filter your warranty may be void and replacement is horribly expensive. Dust spots can be removed from images in post-processing (see p150).

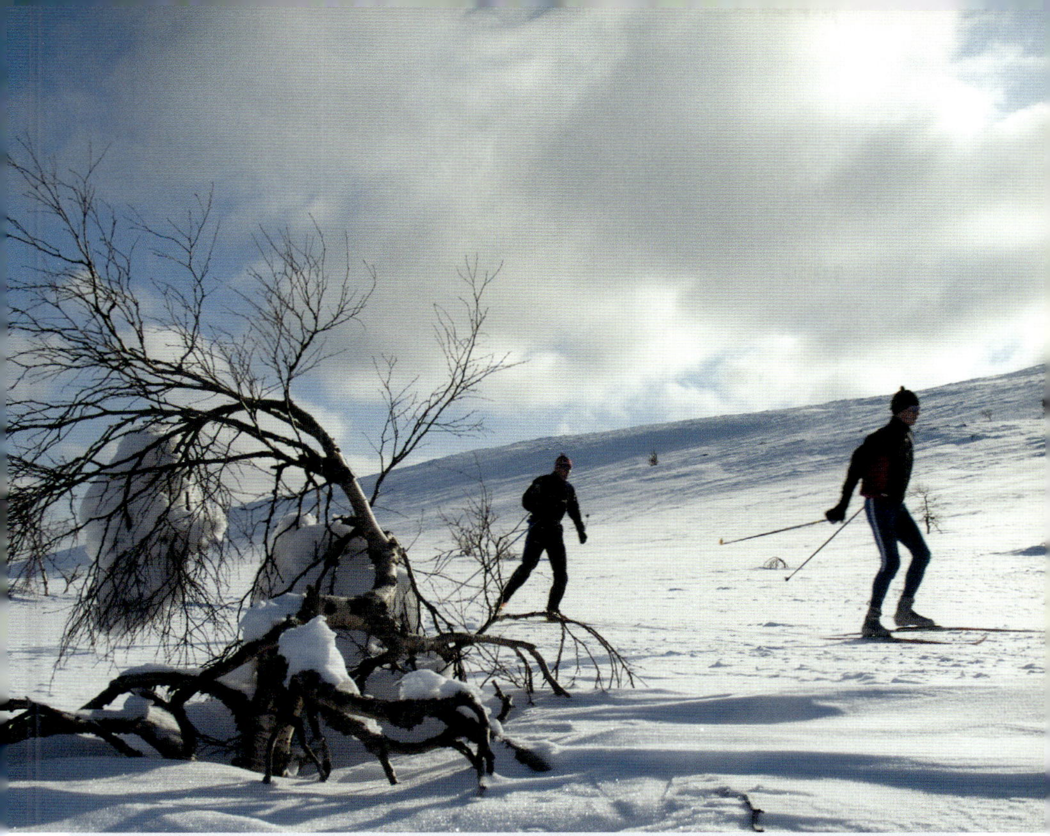

Cross-country skiers, Ylläs, Finland
Don't miss out on great shots because it's a bit chilly: the estimated temperature here was -15°C (5°F) but the camera never missed a beat.
Fujifilm FinePix S3 Pro, focal length 18mm, ISO 100, 1/125sec at f/11

Heat and cold

The manufacturer will specify an operating temperature range for your DSLR, typically around 0–40°C (32–104°F). This primarily means that the camera is not guaranteed to perform normally outside this range. At lower temperatures, keep the camera in an insulated case or under outer clothing (but not too near your skin). As the temperature drops, battery life may be severely reduced, LCD displays may become erratic and ultimately the camera may give up. Pro DSLRs have greater thermal mass and beefier batteries and should keep going for longer. Allow the camera to warm up gently afterwards and no permanent harm should result.

Extremes of heat and humidity are more likely to lead to long-term damage. Rapid transfers from cool environments to hot and humid ones can lead to internal condensation. This is hard to rectify; forestall it by packing camera and lens(es) in airtight containers with sachets of silica gel. Allow the equipment to reach ambient temperature before unpacking.

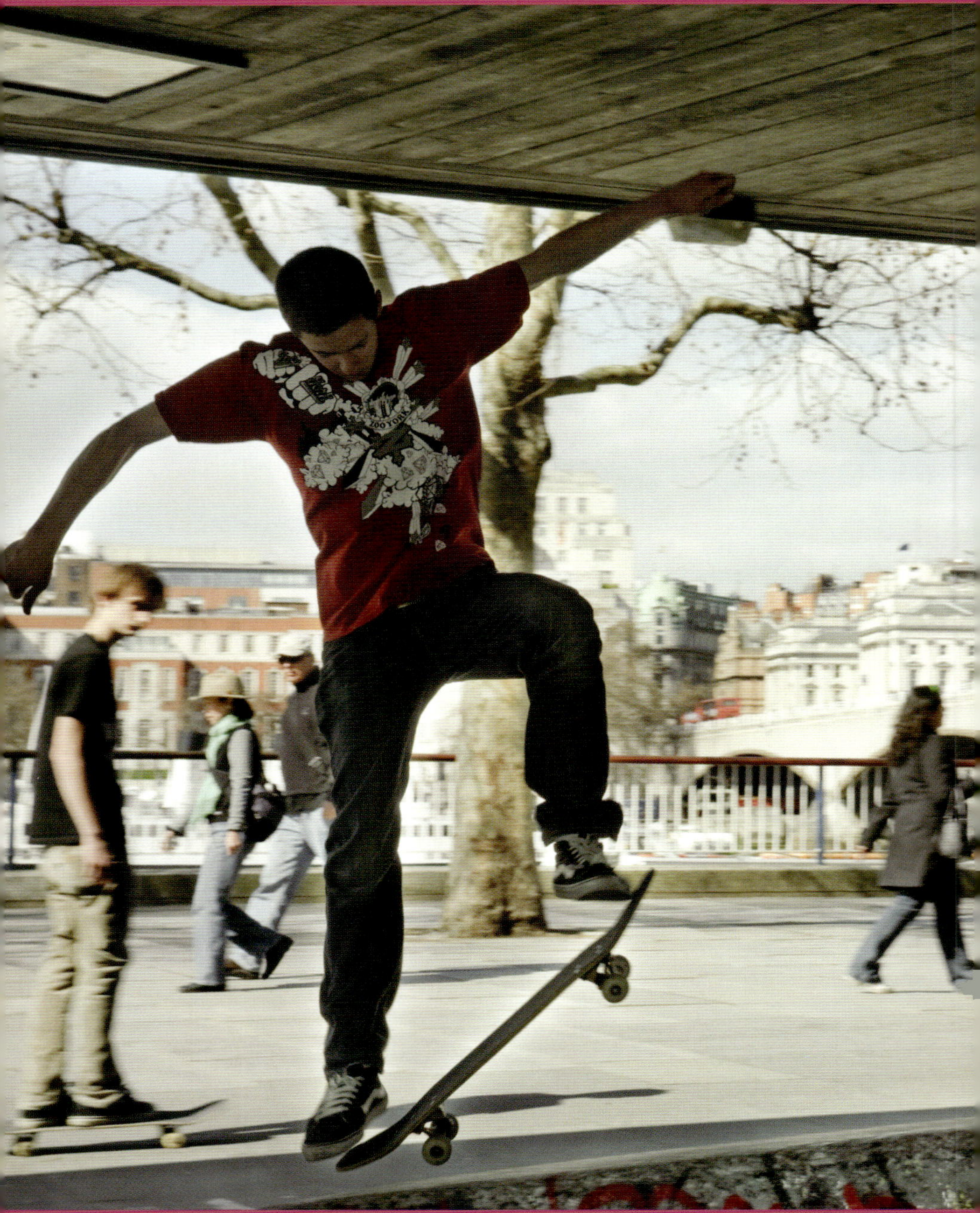
ZOO YORK

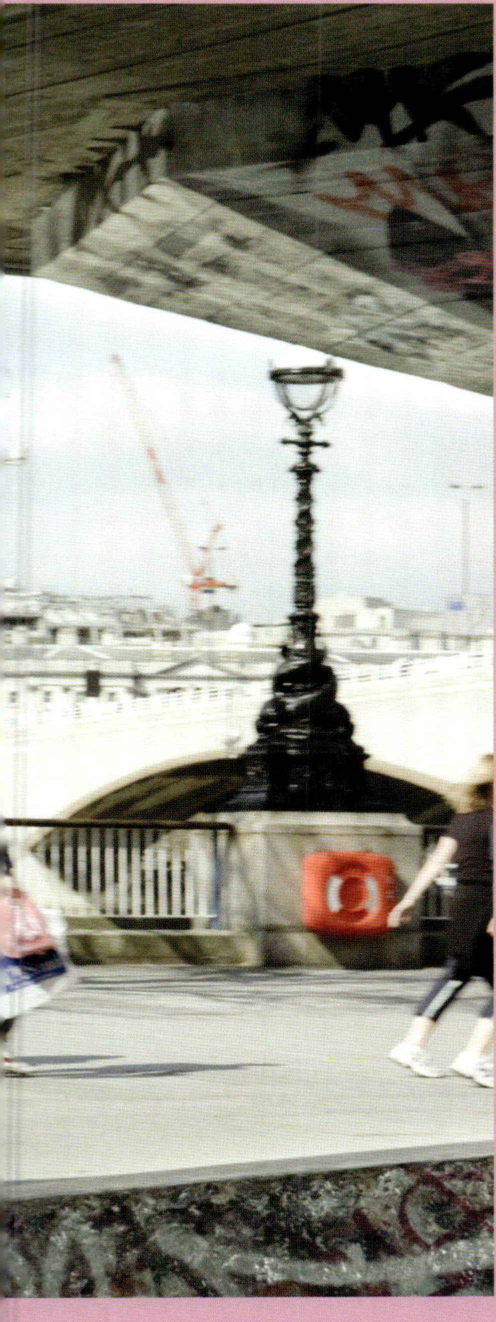

07:
THE DIGITAL DESKTOP

Workflow is like a tripod. What you do before shooting, what you do while shooting, and what you do afterwards are all interconnected. In this chapter we'll look more closely at the third leg of the tripod – what you do with your pictures after shooting.

Skateboarder, South Bank, London, UK
Nikon D700, focal length 70mm, ISO 200, 1/125sec at f/11

Workflow stages

In Chapter Six we observed that some workflow processes can, to a degree, take place in the field. Most, however, take place either on a desktop system or on its mobile equivalent, a laptop computer with a broadband connection and/or an extra mobile hard drive. There are five basic stages to consider: downloading, backing up, cataloguing, storage and editing.

Unfortunately, as previously mentioned, 'editing' is ambiguous. It may mean weeding out rejects, marking the best images, and so on, but it may also mean processing images in 'editing' applications like Photoshop – straightening, cropping, enhancing tones and colours, removing dust spots and much more besides. From here on I'll call this image-processing, and use the word 'edit' only in the first sense. Outside these pages it is widely used in both senses, though it's usually clear from the context which is meant. Although I've identified five distinct stages, this does not mean you're faced with five completely separate operations every time you return from a shoot, still less that you need five different software packages to do it all. In fact, it is often possible to perform all five operations from within one single application program – we'll call this an integrated workflow, as distinct from a modular workflow, which uses two or more bits of software at different stages. In any case, it's worth thinking about each one individually, just to make sure that all the bases are covered. If you shoot RAW, then arguably there's a sixth stage, RAW conversion, but we'll consider this as part of image processing (at least for now).

DOWNLOADING

Getting the images from the camera into the computer – a technique called 'ingesting' – is a fundamental element of digital workflow. The physical connection may be made in several different ways (see p58); equally, there are different approaches to managing the download, either using a separate download manager or an integrated element of a wider software package.

BACKING UP

I make no apologies for repeating myself on this subject. If you don't back up your images you will eventually live to regret it. Like everything else, backup needs to be seen in the broader context of your workflow. If you shoot JPEG and get settings right in-camera, so that little later processing is required, then backing up as you download is easy and logical. If you shoot RAW and/or process images extensively, then you need to think about backing up the processed versions instead (or ideally, doing both).

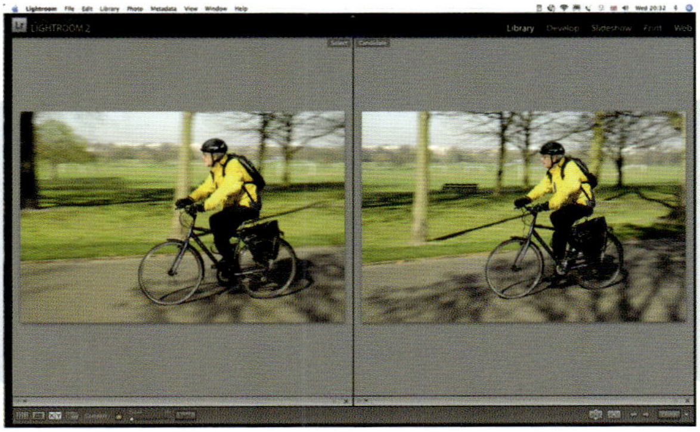

Cyclist, Regent's Park, London, UK
Directly comparing two similar shots often eliminates one of them.
Nikon D700, focal length 70mm, ISO 200, 1/125sec at f/11

CATALOGUING

In the early stages, when you've amassed only small numbers of images, cataloguing seems like an unnecessary chore. But this is exactly the time to start, rather than leaving it to the day when you suddenly realize it's taken half an hour to find a particular shot. It's never too soon to start thinking about when and how you may want to find images in the future.

STORAGE

The primary storage medium is nearly always the internal hard drive of your computer. Yet this may not be ideal; having plenty of free space on your hard drive speeds up most operations, especially intensive ones like image processing. If the computer has an expansion bay, a second internal drive is an inexpensive solution and allows speedy access to images. For external drives, FireWire is faster than USB; 7200rpm drives are also preferable to slower ones.

For backup storage, speed is less critical but an external hard drive is usually the most convenient solution. CDs and DVDs are equally safe but less convenient. Online storage is another increasingly viable option, though 'free' services lack the sort of capacity needed to cope with the number and size of images an active DSLR user can generate.

EDITING

The best way to edit is by shooting thoughtfully in the first place. The fact that you can shoot hundreds, if not thousands, of images without reloading makes some people trigger-happy. But trigger-happy is one step away from sloppy; taking care when you shoot doesn't just reduce the editing burden, it produces better results, and it's a lot more satisfying. Still, we all make a few mistakes, we all shoot action sequences where one shot's clearly the best, and we all take the 'insurance' shot only to find a better angle or better light a few minutes later. There's no escape from editing.

MOVIES

If you shoot movies on your DSLR as well as stills, you'll need to deal with them differently. You can keep track of them using the same software you use to catalogue your photos, but the editing process, which creates a real movie from a collection of clips, possibly shot out of sequence, is very different. Any recent Mac system will give you iMovie, a companion to iPhoto and similarly easy to use. The Windows equivalent is Windows Movie Maker, which should be found on any system running Windows XP or Vista.

Modular workflow

There are several reasons to favour a modular workflow. For some people, it feels more natural to keep the general work of organizing an image collection separate from the processing and enhancement of individual photos.

If you shoot good JPEGs, you may need to spend little time on the processing; the fact that it's done in a separate software package won't matter. Dedicated RAW shooters may also opt for a modular workflow because a particular RAW converter gives the best results for their DSLR and/or their style of photography. The key elements of a modular workflow are the browser or digital asset management (DAM) software and the image-processing software; for RAW shooters they may also include a separate *RAW converter*.

DIGITAL ASSET MANAGEMENT

Back in the days when I shot on film, I had filing cabinets full of slides. They were largely filed geographically, so that, for instance, all my images of Lancaster (my home town) were in one place. Eventually I'd amassed so many images of this very photogenic city that I subdivided the collection by smaller areas (city centre, riverside, castle precincts, and so on). This involved a lot of physical reshuffling of slides but meant that I could quickly locate images of a specific location, like the castle. Yet, because any one slide can only exist in one place, this

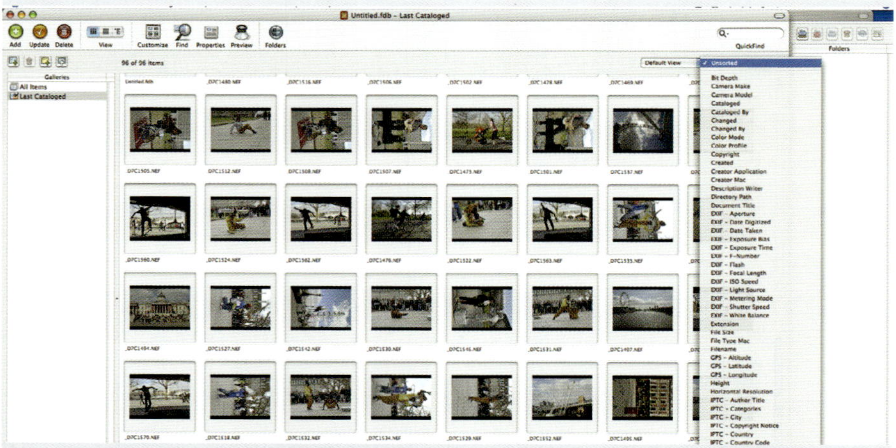

Extensis Portfolio allows images to be sorted by any criterion from a long list (not all of it is visible here!).

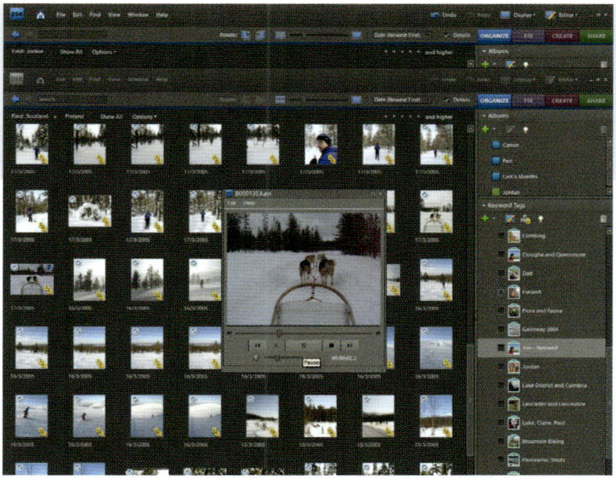

Movie playing in Photoshop Elements 7

system was no help in locating thematic images: people cycling, or snow scenes, for example. I tried to maintain a database to help me keep track of these images, but never quite kept up with it. Even when I'd located relevant entries in the database, I still had to move to the physical storage to pick out the actual slides.

With digital images, database and physical storage have merged. The actual image itself still only exists in one place, but you can find it and see it in different ways: I can instantly see all my castle images, or all my cycling images, or all my snow images. Cataloguing and retrieval is the central function of all DAM software, but it does much more besides, as we'll see below. Big hitters in this category include Adobe Bridge, Extensis Portfolio and Microsoft Expression Media (formerly iView MediaPro). Many other apps include DAM capabilities, but because they also include image processing, they come under the heading of integrated workflow. Examples include Picasa, iPhoto, Aperture, Lightroom and possibly Photoshop Elements. Most DAM apps now allow movies to be catalogued and in some cases viewed: Portfolio, Expression Media and the Windows version of Photoshop Elements all play movies directly while Bridge displays a still frame and uses an external player such as QuickTime.

Download management

Most of the camera makers supply a standalone download manager, such as Nikon Transfer or Canon EOS Utility. Once installed from the CD supplied with the camera, it will start up automatically when you connect the camera or insert a memory card. However, most people will find it more natural to integrate the download process with the rest of their image management. If you decide you don't want to use the maker's software, uninstall it or disable automatic launching using the application preferences.

Backup options

In most download managers and DAM apps it's straightforward to set things up so that photos are automatically backed up to a second location as they're downloaded.

This looks like a good idea, but if you download first and then edit, you're only editing the primary set of files, leaving the backup set still clogged with the rejects. You can partly avoid this by using the download manager to select which files to download. In other words, do at least a preliminary edit before downloading and backing up.

If you shoot RAW and/or process images extensively, then you need to think about backing up the processed versions instead (or ideally, doing both). Backup can be managed as part of your photographic workflow or integrated into general system backup using software such as Apple's Time Machine. External hard drives often come with backup software such as Retrospect Express.

Catalogue approaches

Cataloguing is the central function of browser/ DAM software. Different applications do it in different ways, but then photographers also have different needs. However, we can see some common ground. DAM apps offer most or all of the following methods for organizing, sorting and finding images:

Rating

Assigning star ratings (usually 1–5) to images is self-explanatory. Ratings can be assigned to a selected image or images simply by pressing the appropriate numeric key. Subsequently, you can sort images (a whole library, or a subset such as a particular album) according to rating. Personally, I only use ratings for short-term needs, like making selections on the initial edit or when choosing a batch of images for submission to a client; my ratings are temporary, not permanent.

Collections/Albums/Galleries

The terms may vary but the idea is basically the same. Each image is assigned to one or more collections – for instance, an image of a cyclist in Helsinki won't only live in the Finland collection, but can also be assigned to Cities, Transport, Bikes, People, Summer, and so on.

Most DAM apps allow you to create hierarchical collections; for example Europe > Finland > Helsinki. Adding an image to Helsinki then means that it shows up when I view the Europe collection (though I'm not sure how often I'd actually want to view all my Europe images – thousands of them – en masse). Similarly, my Bikes collection is subdivided into Mountain Bikes and Road.

Tags/Keywords

Using verbal tags allows a greater depth of organization, and greater flexibility in finding images. Using keywords to find images is fairly intuitive and will feel familiar to anyone who's used to doing Google searches on the Web. The advantage over using collections is that you can use multiple keywords for a search, so that I could search for Bike + Helsinki, for example, without having to scan multiple collections. If you want to sell images online, keywording is vital: keyword searching is how buyers find images.

Of course keyword searches only work if you've added keywords to the images in the first place. This can be a time-consuming and

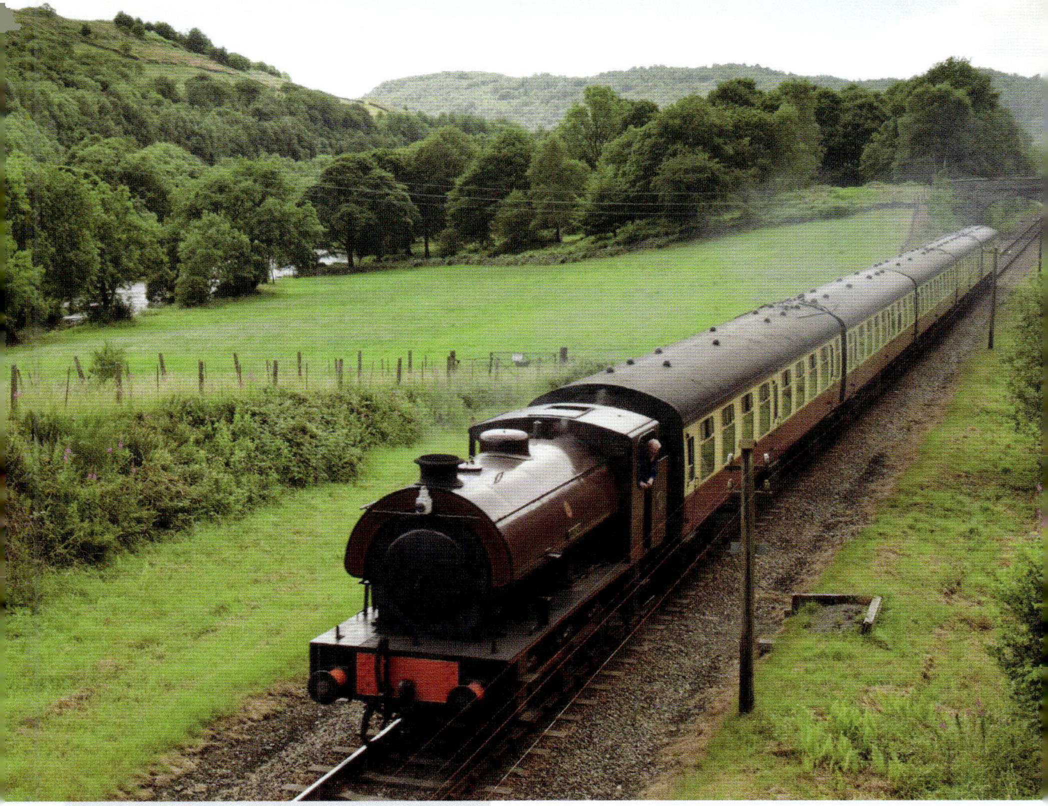

Train on the Lakeside & Haverthwaite Railway, Cumbria, UK
This shot has sold repeatedly through online library Alamy, a result that owes more to subject matter and effective keywording than any special photographic quality.
Nikon D2x focal length 34mm, ISO 100, 1/80sec at f/10

tedious task, but good DAM software helps to simplify and accelerate the process. Most apps allow existing keywords and tags to be added to batches of images simply by dragging and dropping; you only need to type when you want to add new keywords. Many apps also allow the creation of keyword sets, which can be applied quickly to images with similar content.

POINT OF VIEW

Keywording is not my idea of fun, and I mostly use filters and collections to find images. However, because I sell images online, they need to have accurate and comprehensive keywords. For me, by far the best (or least tedious) approach is to add keywords to each batch of images as part of the download process.

Here are the keywords for the image of a steam train, which have enabled buyers to find it on several occasions: Travel, Europe, Britain, UK, England, Cumbria, Lakeland, Lake, District, heritage, conserve, protect, national, park, landscape, scenic, environment, summer, fell, hill, view, vista, valley, season, beauty, great, outdoors, rail, railway, railroad, train, carriage, tank, engine.

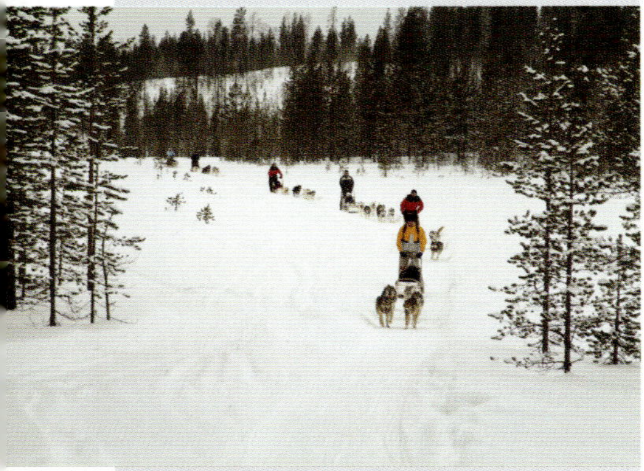

Dog-teams, Ylläs, Finland
This shot is found in several collections: Finland, Arctic, Winter, Outdoor Pursuits, Animals, and so on.
Fujifilm FinePix S3 Pro, focal length 70mm, ISO 100, 1/125sec at f/8

Filters

Filters allow you to sort images by criteria that already exist in the metadata. Filtering by date is an obvious example; in fact most apps do this by default. In many DAM apps you can also sort by criteria such as the camera or lens used. This is very useful for me when writing books like this. If I want to see photos taken with a 300mm lens, I can do so in a couple of clicks. Sorting by camera could also be useful where more than one person share a computer but use different cameras.

METADATA

Metadata is data about data. Even a simple word-processing document has metadata, recording things such as when it was created and when it was last changed. Digital cameras record masses of metadata, including the date and time of the shot the camera, lens and settings used, and in some cases extras like GPS data. They normally use the exchangeable image file format (EXIF), which is readable by any decent imaging application. Additional data (e.g. white balance/colour temperature) may not be so readily visible but is used by many apps, especially RAW converters. IPTC metadata (developed by the International Press Telecommunications Council) is widely used to record image tags, keywords, etc. It's been somewhat overtaken by the Extensible Metadata Platform (XMP), developed by Adobe; now the two are almost interchangeable. All professional DAM software can read and export EXIF, XMP and IPTC metadata.

TRY BEFORE YOU BUY

Much of the software we'll discuss is either free (Picasa) or already on your system (iPhoto on the Mac, or whatever the maker of your DSLR provides). The rest is usually available on a trial basis, typically limited to 30 days. The obvious advantage of trial software is that you can get a feel for a product and how it might fit into your workflow before committing your hard-earned cash. The downside is that you can spend a lot of time evaluating different products and end up more confused than enlightened. It helps to be clear about what you want from the software before you start. Read independent reviews and comparisons too; this should narrow down the field.

diting

diting is not just about sifting out the duds nd the duplicates; it's also about identifying he cream of the crop. These are the shots we'll efinitely do something with, whether it's loading hem on Flickr, making a fine print, or offering hem for sale through a professional library. ny decent browser makes editing easy. For stance, you can view similar images side-by-side to make a direct comparison, and zoom in any image for a critical look. While a preliminary edit (e.g. before download) may identify outright duds, the main edit should look more critically at images. It's often tempting to cling on to images that are slightly soft (e.g. because of focusing errors or camera shake), but in reality they have no future for fine prints. If they're solely destined for web use there's more margin for error.

The Organizer module in Photoshop Elements 7

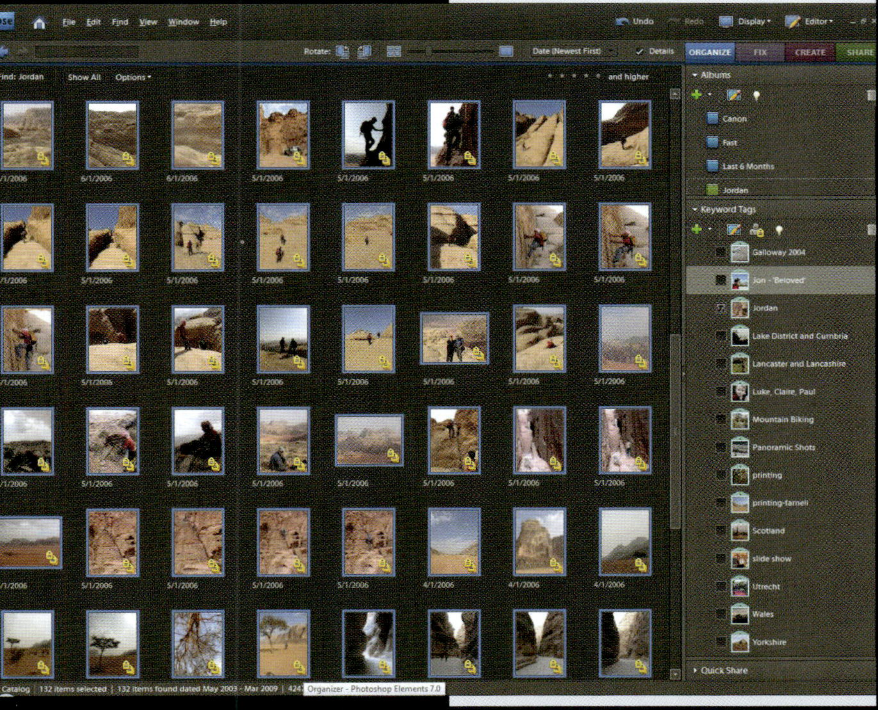

RAW CONVERSION

All the camera makers produce dedicated RAW conversion software, including Canon Digital Photo Professional 3.5, Nikon Capture NX2, and Sony Image Data Converter SR 2.0. It's often supplied with the camera, so you've already paid for it (not so Nikon Capture NX2, so black marks to Nikon). It's designed specifically for that maker's cameras, so you'd expect it to deliver excellent results, but own-brand software sometimes has a quirky interface or slow operation.

The daddy of independent products is of course Adobe Camera RAW, which is integrated into Adobe Photoshop, Photoshop Elements and Lightroom. It handles RAW files from just about every DSLR out there, and many other cameras besides. Many other apps can at least view and open RAW files, though control of the conversion process may be limited, which surely defeats the object of shooting RAW. An example is Apple's iPhoto, unbeatable for simplicity and ease of use but a very basic RAW converter.

Third-party RAW converters include Capture One 4 (also a Pro version). This has long been the first choice of many professionals but it's quite expensive and the latest version has attracted lots of criticism. Other well-regarded options include Bibble Pro and DXO Optics Pro.

It would take a whole book to compare all the different RAW converters for interface, speed, and nature of the results. Yet they all perform broadly similar functions. Lets take Adobe Camera RAW (ACR) as an example. ACR opens automatically when you double-click on a RAW file in Bridge or select Open in Photoshop or Photoshop Elements. The interface is straightforward, with a preview image, histogram, and a series of slider controls. Most of these are self-explanatory and the effect is seen immediately as both the histogram and the preview are updated automatically. Work through the controls from top to bottom, setting White Balance and Tint first, then Exposure, and so on. Once you're satisfied with the results, apply the settings to other images as a batch, or save as a preset for future use.

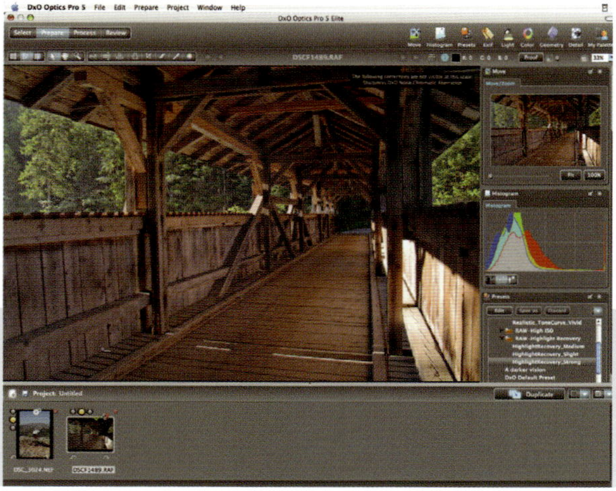

DXO Optics Pro
Not a household name but a very capable RAW converter.

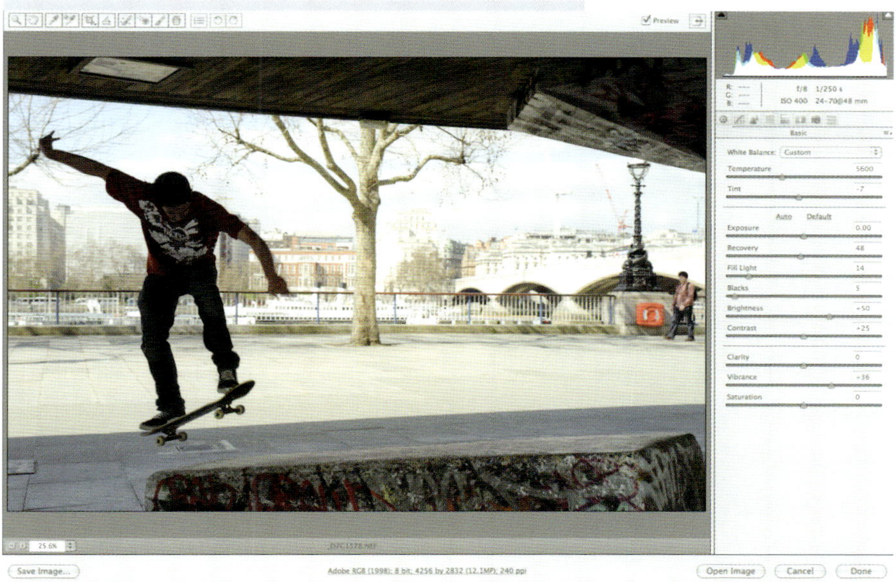

Adobe Camera RAW 5
Using Adobe Camera RAW 5, with the Basic Development tab open.

Some of the tools are self-explanatory, others less so. Recovery aims to bring out any latent detail in the highlights while Fill Light does the same for the shadows. Clarity increases localized contrast. Vibrance is akin to Saturation, but while Saturation affects all colours equally, Vibrance has greater effect on colours that start out less saturated. (I use Vibrance all the time, Saturation quite rarely.)

There are numerous other controls and in the latest version (ACR 5) some additional tools allow selective adjustments to localized areas of the image. These include Graduated Filters and Adjustment Brushes, which allow adjustments such as Exposure, Clarity and Vibrance to be applied only where they are needed. While Graduated Filters can mimic the effect of a filter in front of the camera lens, they're much more flexible than that. You can apply multiple Graduated Filters for subtle control, including the ability to, for example, lighten one bottom corner while also darkening the sky. Another invaluable tool is the Spot Removal brush.

IN-CAMERA RAW PROCESSING

The ability to create JPEG images from RAW files in-camera is relatively new. I'd almost always prefer to tackle RAW conversion on the computer, but I can see in-camera conversion having its uses when I've shot a RAW image but want to make it available immediately for printing or for a client to view.

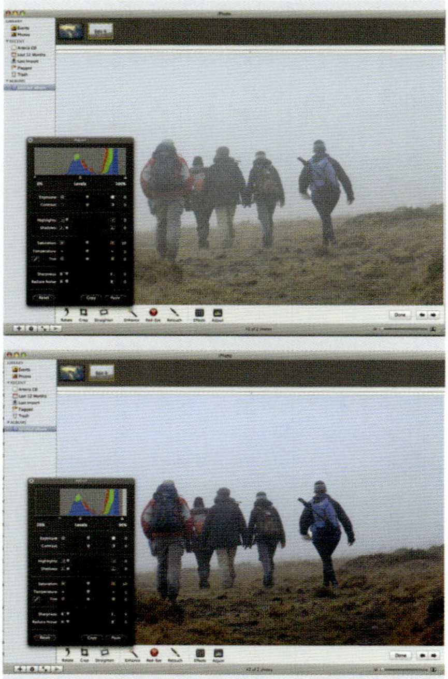

The Levels control in iPhoto

IMAGE PROCESSING

For working on files converted from RAW, as well as JPEGs shot in camera, there's an equally wide choice of software. Many basic tasks are broadly the same across the board, including cropping, rotating and resizing images. Even the simplest apps have tools for getting rid of blemishes like red-eye and dust spots. The processing stage is also the time to look at sharpening any images which may need it, but ideally this should be done last and really only when exporting images for a purpose; the amount of sharpening needed for display on the Web is very different from what's needed for a large print.

Processing basics: Levels and Curves

These are the fundamental adjustment tools in most imaging apps; anything that doesn't have these should be regarded as strictly entry-level. (iPhoto has Levels, but not Curves, so it's halfway there.)

Levels

If you've familiarized yourself with the camera's histogram, then using the Levels tool should be an easy step. Conversely, experimenting with Levels is a great way to see the histogram in action and grasp how it really works.

You can usually view a summary histogram which combines all three colour channels, or view and edit the channels individually. One of the prime uses of Levels is in controlling the end points of the histogram. In the first example (left, top) the photo as shot is quite flat and the histogram (left, below) shows that the tones only spread over about half the full range. By moving the left and right sliders the tones are spread out across the full width of the histogram. Moving the midpoint slider shifts pixels to left or right, affecting the overall brightness.

Levels (and Curves) dialogs often also include eyedropper tools. Apps like *Photoshop* have eyedroppers for setting black and white points; this is basically another way of defining the limits of the histogram. Even iPhoto has a single eyedropper; click with this on an area that should be neutral in colour and it can remove colour-casts, but use with caution – in example 2 (opposite page, left) clicking on the shadows did indeed remove the blue 'cast' there but also introduced a strong orange cast to the highlights.

Curves

The Curves dialog allows even more control over the image. Pulling part of the curve down darkens tones around that value; pulling it up lightens them. Making part of the curve steeper increases contrast in that tonal region: increase steepness in the midsection to increase mid-tone contrast, for example. This has the result of making other parts of the curve flatter, so it inevitably reduces contrast there.

In the example (now using Photoshop) Curves has been used instead of Levels (below, top right). This increases contrast in the middle tones but does not move the ends of the scale towards pure black and pure white. In the second example, (below, bottom right) purely for illustration purposes, I brightened the red channel while leaving the other two untouched, shifting the overall colour balance towards red.

NOTE

Converting an image to 16-bit will make no immediate difference to what you see on screen, but can make a big difference to the end product.

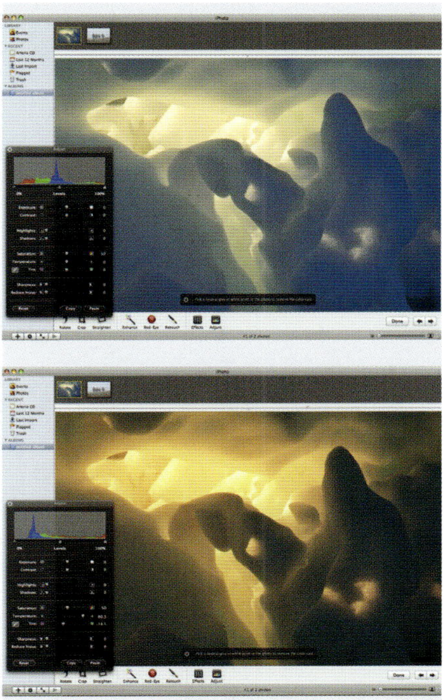

Eyedropper
This does not always give the desired result.

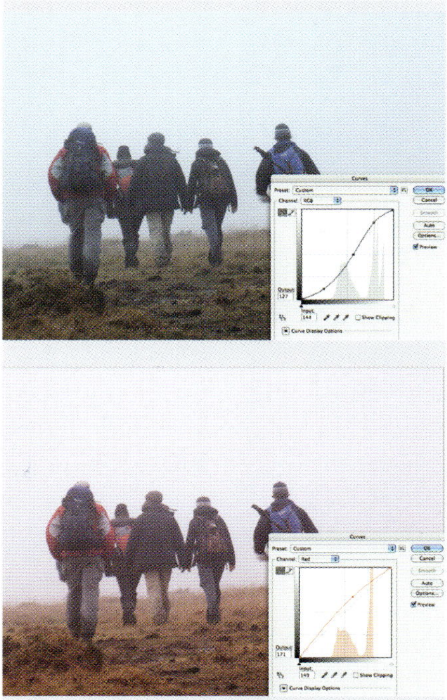

Using Curves in Photoshop

Editing in 16-bit

It's already been noted (p45) that 16-bit image files give much more room for manoeuvre at the processing stage than 8-bit. This really applies RAW images will be recorded by the camera as 12- or 14-bit data and converted to 16-bit during processing. Even images shot as 8-bit JPEG will benefit from being converted to 16-bit before extensive adjustment that affects tonal values – Levels, Curves, Hue, Saturation and so on. Photoshop Elements can handle most adjustments on 16-bit images but some of its features only work in 8-bit.

Selective adjustments

Photoshop is an incredibly powerful tool, and even most professional photographers use only a fraction of its potential. There are numerous books, magazines and websites dedicated purely to this one program. In our limited space I'd like to offer just one illustration of what it can do. This is a technique I use quite frequently when I want to make controlled adjustments to areas of an image, or to merge multiple versions (usually bracketed exposures). There are several other ways to limit effects to just part of an images, including selection tools like the Marquee and Magic Wand and darkroom-like tools such as Dodge and Burn. However, using Layer Masks is much more flexible as you can redefine the area that's affected at any stage.

Note that the example on page 153 is deliberately crude so that the method is clear, though the result is less than ideal; I've also added a colour cast to the highlight image to make the effect even more obvious. (The originals – Images A & B – were shot with a Nikon D3x, but even its 13-stop dynamic range couldn't cope with the difference between the cave interior and the daylit scene outside). Doing this for real, I'd probably use a third image for better results in certain areas like the edge of the cave-mouth.

Image C

The lighter image is dragged over the darker one as a new layer. At first it completely hides the dark layer underneath. I then added a Layer Mask and painted crudely on it in black. This 'unmasks' the image beneath.

Image D

I then work on the mask a bit more, using Brush and Eraser tools. Remember, all this work is done on the layer mask – none of it affects the actual image data in either layer, just hides or reveals it. This result is still crude and obviously artificial but then it's meant to be: for an example where you can't see the join, look at p124.

NOTE

Photoshop Elements has Layers, but doesn't support Layer Masks. You could roughly mimic this operation by using the Eraser on the front layer, but if you erase too much you can't just paint it back in again; with Layer Masks you can.

High Dynamic Range

Recent versions of Photoshop have High Dynamic Range (HDR) abilities and there are also dedicated HDR software apps which can automate the merging of bracketed exposures.

A

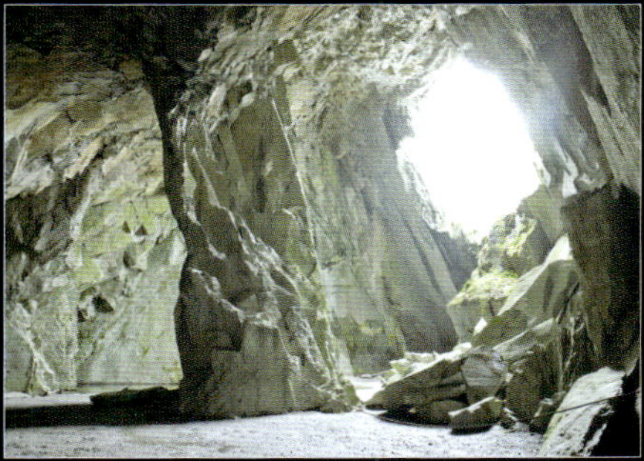

Cathedral Quarry, Little Langdale, Lake District, UK
Local adjustments with layer masks.
Nikon D3X, focal length 24mm, ISO 400, f/11, shutter speed varies

B

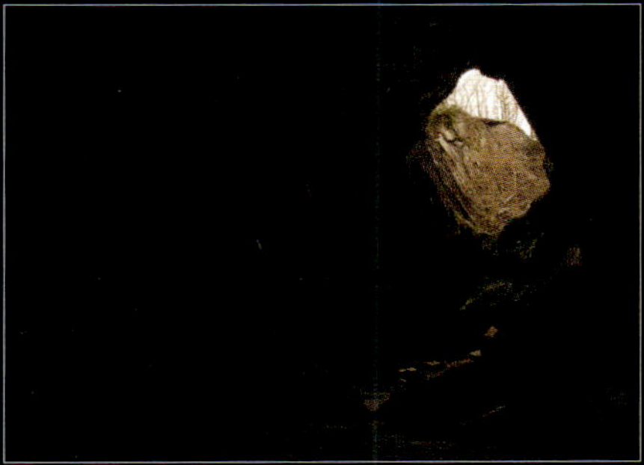

C

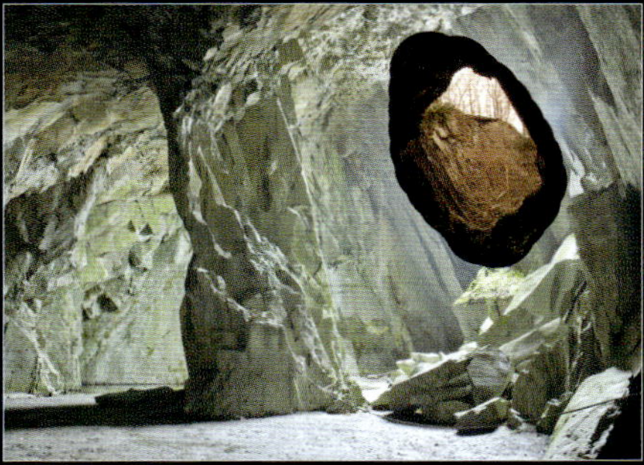

D

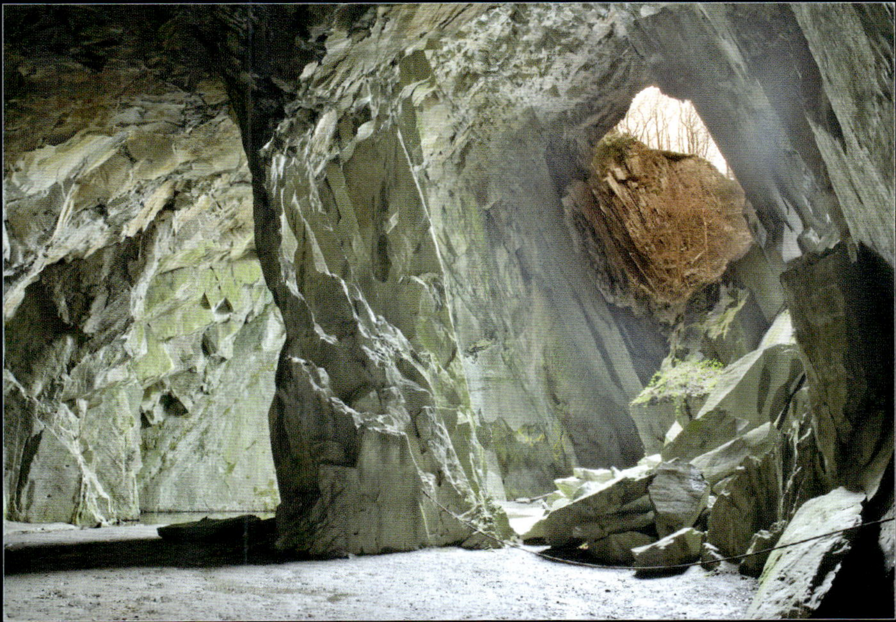

Integrated workflow

The idea of combining all the stages of a workflow into one single software package has an obvious attraction, and there is now a range of integrated workflow applications suitable for all users from entry-level to professional.

Apple's Aperture and Adobe Lightroom are important applications that have become the bedrock of many workflows (mine included), but they're not quite as revolutionary as was claimed when they were launched in 2005–6. Apple already had iPhoto and Adobe had Photoshop Elements, both of which unite organizing and processing. Elements in particular is a remarkably powerful package, with access to the same underlying Adobe Camera RAW engine that's used by Photoshop and Lightroom, and many of the same powerful image-processing tools as Photoshop itself. iPhoto and the more recent Picasa might be called entry-level products, but can still do everything that many users will require. iPhoto has more power than might initially be apparent from its user-friendly interface. Photoshop Elements is a step up, more of a mid-range product, fully meeting the needs of most enthusiasts and surprisingly capable at a semi-professional level. Aperture and Lightroom are the heavyweights.

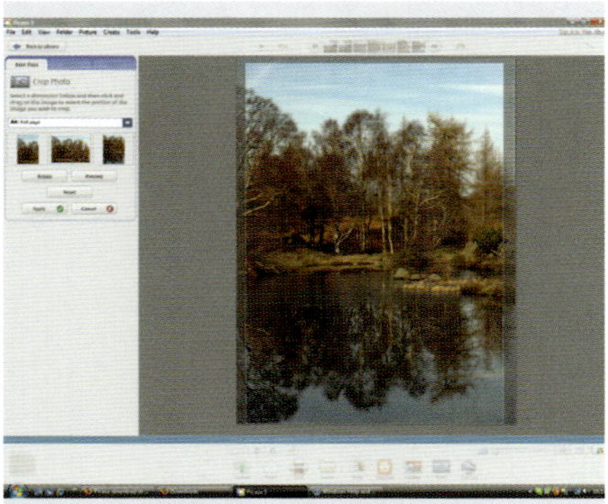

Cropping an image in Picasa

PICASA

Google's Picasa runs on Windows (XP/Vista) and Linux but only made it to the Mac more recently (Intel Macs only), no doubt because iPhoto already covers a very similar range of functions. By default, when first launched, Picasa scans your entire system for image files. It does not move them but indexes them where they are (though you can move photos around in Picasa). Like several other apps, Picasa uses Albums as the basis of its cataloguing. One photo can be included in multiple Albums. You can also use Tags, similar to Keywords. The image-processing tools are also fairly basic, and clearly aimed at users of compacts rather than DSLRs, but if you're canny about shooting JPEGs with your DSLR, and use in-camera processing where required, you might not need them anyway.

Surprisingly for a Google product, Picasa's cataloguing is quite limited. Its strengths are the ease with which you can email selected photos or upload them to Web albums. It also allows geotagging: location information can be attached to photos taken on DSLRs with a GPS attachment such as Nikon's GP-1. Picasa links tagged photos to their location in Google Earth or Google Maps.

iPHOTO

iPhoto is only available on the Mac, as part of Apple's iLife suite, and comes pre-loaded on new Macs. Unlike Picasa, you have to tell it to import existing images. However, like Picasa, it can automatically import new photos whenever a camera or memory card is connected. iPhoto uses Events, rather than Albums, for basic cataloguing. Events are automatically created according to the date of imported photos, but you can create your own Events and add photos to them just like Albums/ Collections in other apps. iPhoto '09 also organizes images by Faces and Places. Faces uses the latest face-detection algorithms to match faces that appear to be the same person. Places uses GPS information in a similar way to Picasa, and also integrates with Google Maps. iPhoto is more elegant and powerful than Picasa, and its image-processing tools are much more sophisticated.

iPhoto also makes it easy to send pictures by email, to create books and other products (see p167) and to upload to Facebook and Flickr. You can create sophisticated web pages using Apple's MobileMe service, but this requires a subscription. (Picasa offers free Web Albums.)

ADOBE PHOTOSHOP ELEMENTS

Photoshop Elements is a powerful program that offers much of the power of Photoshop itself – at least, most of the key features for DSLR users – for about an eighth of the price. Elements has full support for RAW files and uses the same Camera RAW engine as Photoshop and Lightroom, so it can work with RAW files from just about every DSLR in existence. It also works – within limits – with 16-bit images. The key Levels dialog is essentially the same as in Photoshop itself, though the Curves dialog is somewhat different. Elements also has support for Layers (see p152), though not Layer Masks.

All these features are accessed in Full Edit mode. For the novice user, Elements also has Quick Edit and Guided Edit modes, which offer simplified editing tools more on the lines of iPhoto and Picasa. Photoshop Elements 7 on Windows has an inbuilt Organizer module; although the Mac (v6) doesn't. Therefore Elements fosters integrated workflow on Windows but not on Mac, though it's still a very capable image-processing program.

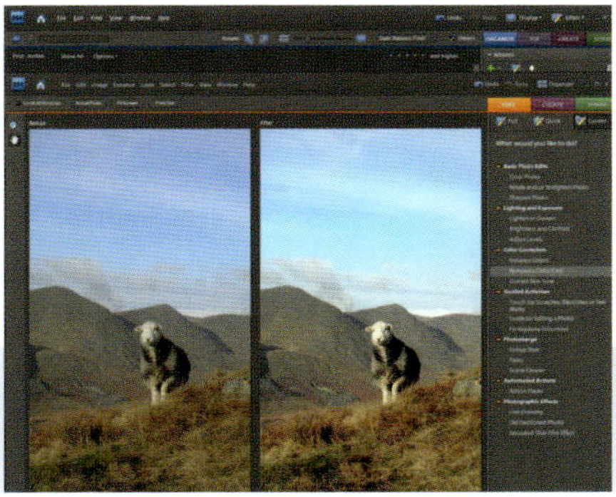

Guided Edit mode in Photoshop Elements

LIGHTROOM AND APERTURE

Lightroom and Aperture appeared at around the same time and have many features in common. Both are dedicated mainly to working with RAW images. That's not to say that they can't handle other formats, but their benefits are perhaps less clear-cut when doing so. Both combine powerful cataloguing features with image-processing power to cover most, if not all, workflow stages. And both make much of their non-destructive editing (by our own rules, we should call it non-destructive image-processing).

In fact, all RAW conversion software is non-destructive; the original RAW file remains intact and unaltered. However, other RAW converters expect you to create a new file (usually TIFF or JPEG) based on the conversion settings applied (as in the example on p149). Lightroom and Aperture do it a bit differently. In both apps, your main image library is your RAW files. When you use the app as a browser, you see preview images; as with any browser, you can view these as thumbnails, as full-screen images, or zoom in to view them at pixel level. In Browser mode, you can also assign photos to collections, add star ratings, flag them as picks or rejects, and add keywords. But at any time you can switch seamlessly to Develop mode to make adjustments to the RAW image. However, these do not create a new file; changes are reflected in the preview images. You can also turn images into a slideshow or send them to your desktop printer without ever leaving Lightroom/Aperture.

Sometimes, however, you do need to create JPEG or TIFF files (or occasionally other formats) to email, upload to the web, send to a printer or publisher, and so on. For this you use the Export command.

Adobe Lightroom

It's now officially called Adobe Photoshop Lightroom, but everyone just calls it Lightroom, or simply LR. LR has five modules, including Print, Slideshow and Web, but the meat of the app is in the Library and Develop modules.

On importing images, you can choose where to save them and also whether to back up to a separate location. You can also change file-naming, apply develop presets (a time-saving shortcut for further adjustments), and add keywords at this stage.

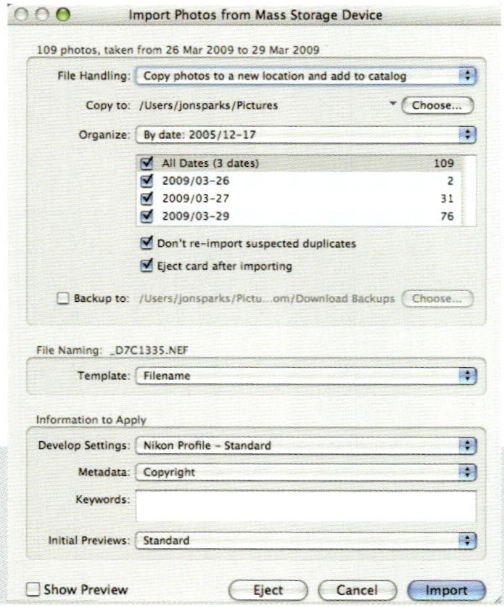

Import dialog in Lightroom
The next step might be to add some keywords.

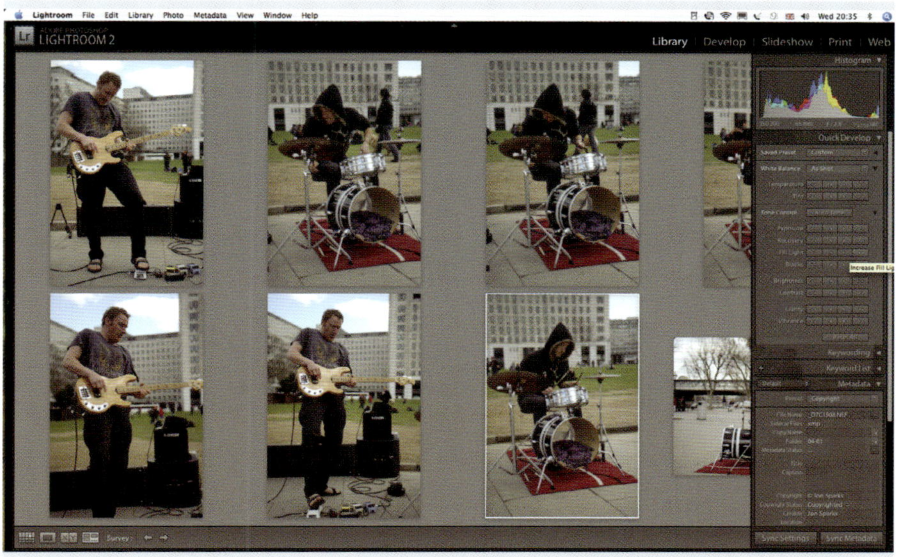

Image comparison
Comparing a series of images, with the Quick Develop tab being used for preliminary adjustments.

Lightroom's Library module is a fairly full-featured DAM program in its own right, and is powerful enough for most users. It allows for the creation of Collections and Smart Collections (based on a wide range of criteria; new images meeting these criteria are automatically added to the appropriate Smart Collections). You can also use ratings, colour labels and filters.

Images within the Grid view can be sorted by various criteria or moved around manually. Compare two images using the – yes – Compare view; compare three or more using Survey; and use the Loupe to see an individual image full-screen or zoomed to 100 per cent. Switching between these views (with just a single keystroke) makes assessment and editing of new images extremely easy. There's also a Quick Develop panel, accessible within the Library module, which allows a range of adjustments to be applied for speedy judgement of a photo's potential.

For more in-depth adjustment, we go to the Develop module. The primary controls here are the same as in Camera RAW, allowing extensive enhancement to RAW files (and other formats too). Lightroom 2 has all the new tools from the latest version of ACR, including Graduated Filters and Adjustment Brushes and Spot Removal. I used to have to open many images in Photoshop to make localized adjustments; now I need to do so much less often. Some images do still need the extra power of Photoshop, like the example on p152.

Having made adjustments, global and local, to one image, it's then possible to synchronize or copy and paste the settings to apply them to a batch of images. This is a huge time-saver – not least when applied to the Spot Removal brush! Lightroom also allows you to create multiple versions of an image. The master RAW file is still untouched; versions are simply different sets of adjustments, each with their own preview image. I've used this extensively for images with high dynamic range, making multiple versions – one is optimized for the highlights and one for the shadows, with sometimes a third for the mid-tones. When exported, these images can be combined in Photoshop, using Layer Masks as outlined on p152.

Apple Aperture

Like iPhoto, Aperture is only available for the Mac, though the context is somewhat different; whereas the Mac has a relatively small market share in the consumer computer sphere, it is much more dominant among professional photographers and other creative trades. Almost every feature in Lightroom has an equivalent in Aperture, and vice versa. This is not to suggest that Apple is copying Adobe, or the other way around; both products have evolved to meet the same sorts of needs and for the same sorts of users, i.e. professional photographers. The interface is different and many features have different names; Aperture uses Projects and Albums instead of Collections, and Adjust instead of Develop. There are other, more subtle differences in the way it works, too. One that's fairly obvious is Aperture's rather slinky Loupe tool, which neatly mimics a magnifier hovered over a section of an image; it can also be set to show 50%, 200% and higher magnifications, something that Lightroom does not offer.

THE THIRD WAY?

Currently, Mac users have a choice between Aperture and Lightroom, while Windows users only have the latter. You might want to keep an eye on an open-source software project, along similar lines, called BlueMarine (see http://bluemarine.tidalwave.it/home.html). It's still in development (and welcomes input from photographers) and does not claim to be suitable for general use as yet.

There's also LightZone, which has much in common with Aperture and Lightroom, though it's not as strong on the cataloguing side. It does, however, have powerful RAW conversion tools and a lot of interesting one-click adjustment presets. For Linux users, who can't use Aperture or Lightroom, it's especially worth a look.

POINT OF VIEW

Lightroom changed my life. It's that simple. As I shoot RAW most of the time, and need to produce everything from basic JPEGs for email to high-quality files for professional publication, it gave me – for the first time – a workflow that made sense. But why Lightroom and not Aperture?

Aperture initially seemed to run only on the most powerful Macs. Lightroom also first appeared as a free beta version, and installed itself at the heart of my workflow even before the full version arrived. The fact that I've continued to use it does not mean that I think it's better than Aperture. If I was starting from scratch now I'd look seriously at both and I'd advise any Mac owner to do the same. Sorry, Windows-gazers, you don't have the choice.

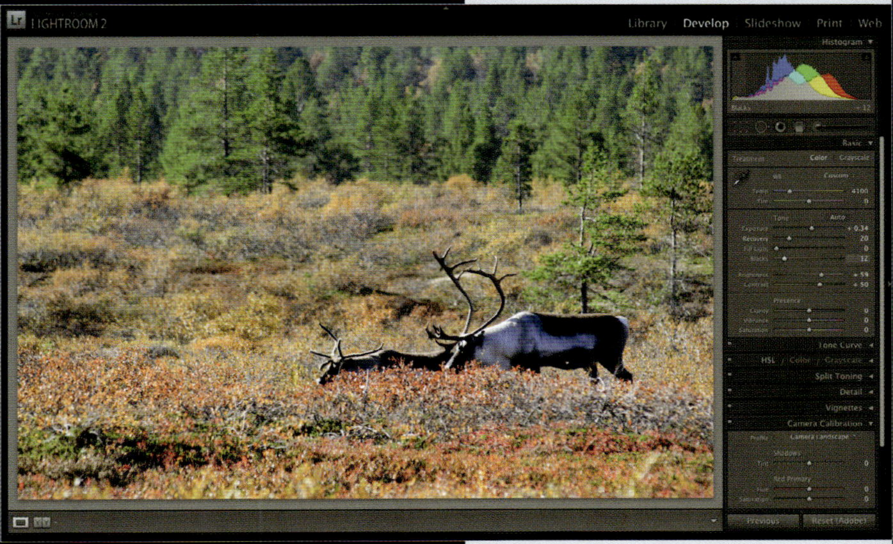

The Develop module in Lightroom

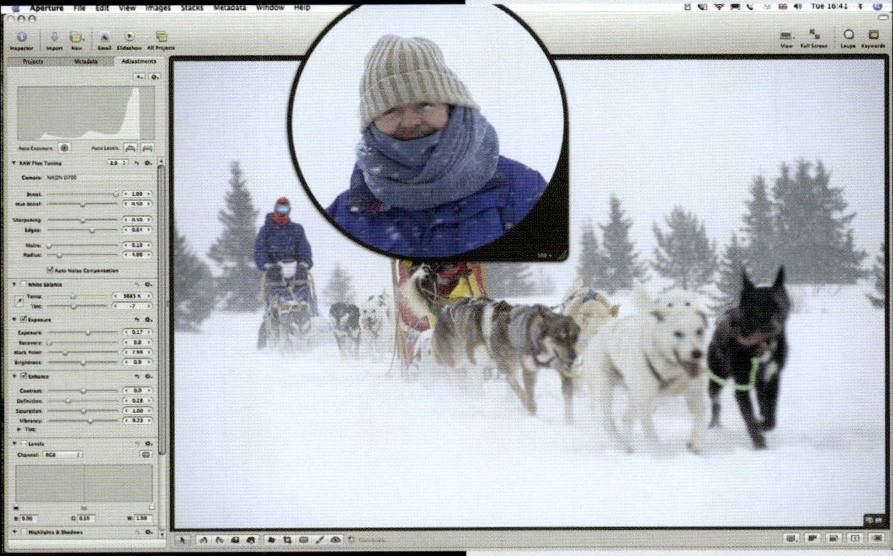

Aperture's Loupe tool
This tool is highly customizable.

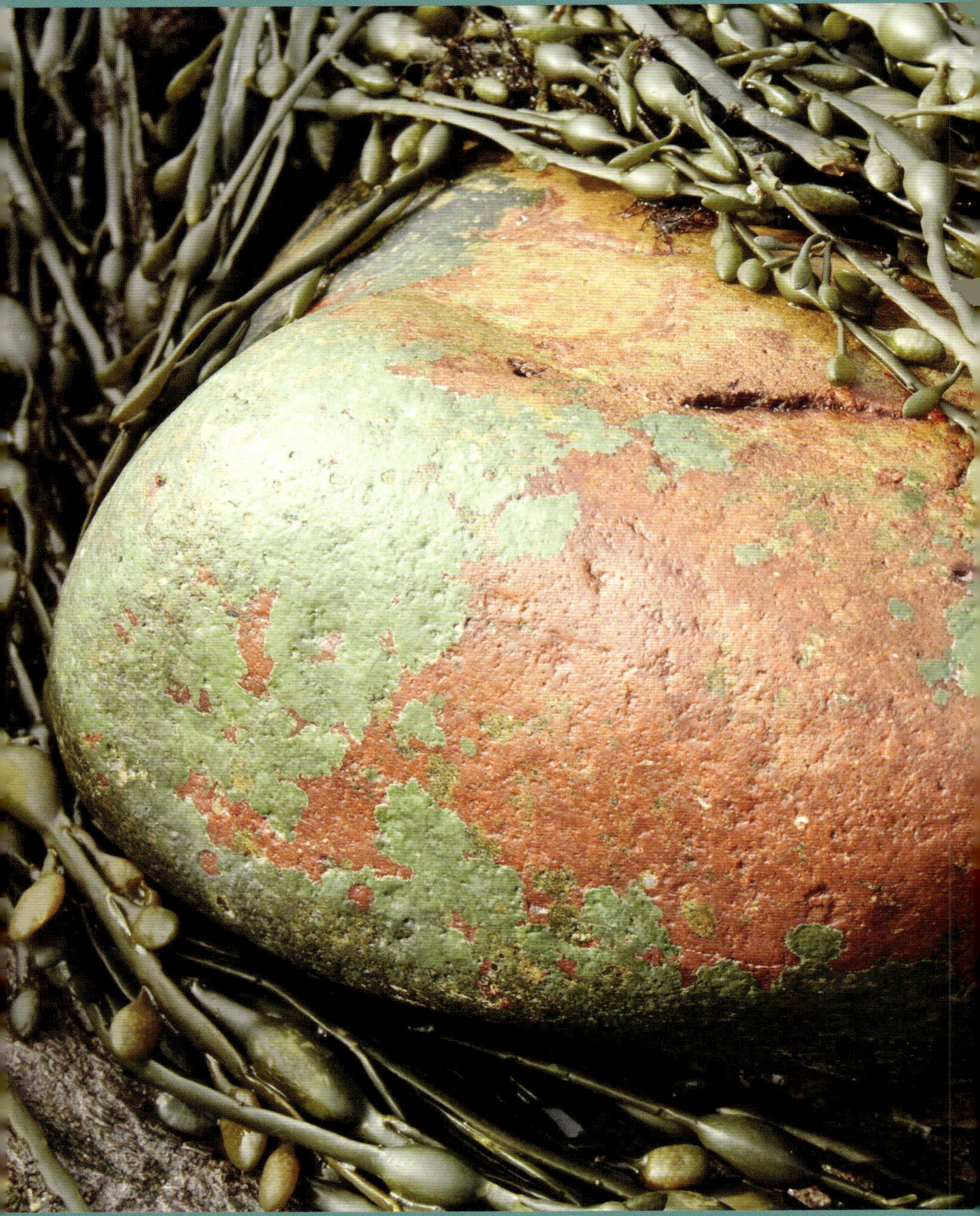

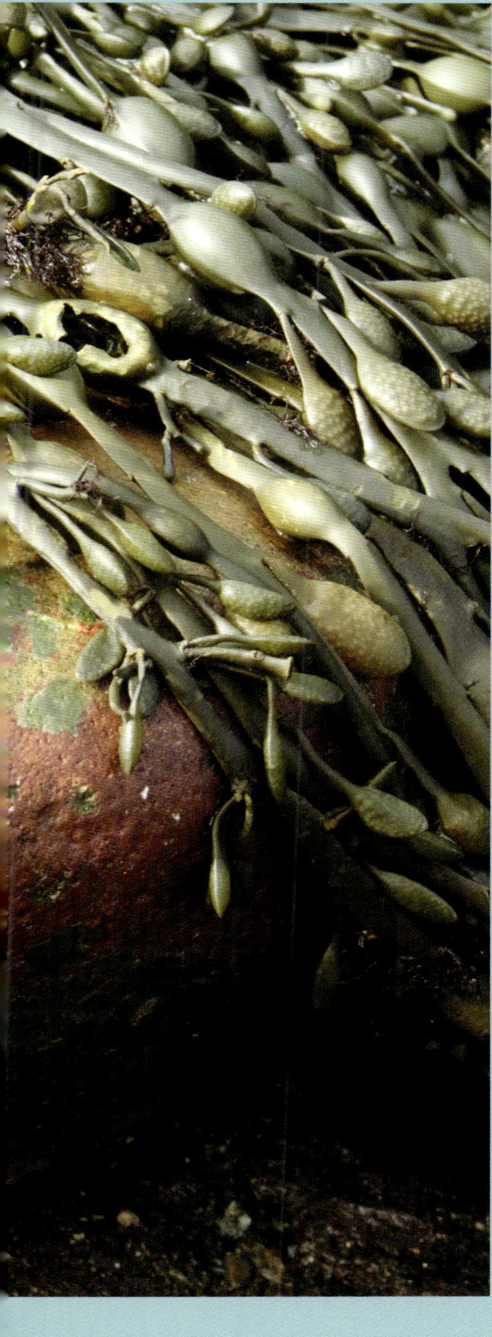

08: SAVING AND SHARING

So far we've really only discussed pictures seen on your own screen, either on the camera back or on a laptop or desktop computer. But the digital revolution doesn't just change how we shoot and process our pictures – it also offers far more channels than ever before for getting those images in front of other people. Some of these are new ways to approach traditional media such as prints and books, while there's also a whole raft of new media that never existed before.

Stone and wrack, Niarbyl, Isle of Man, UK
Nikon D2x, focal length 50mm, ISO 320, 1/50sec at f/10

Printing

For many people, 'photograph' is synonymous with 'print' – it still doesn't seem real until they can hold it in their hands. This may be partly a generational phenomenon and those who've grown up with digital may have a different perspective. What should be clear is that it is no longer necessary to print every shot just to tell whether we like it or not.

Cost and sustainability are factors that should make us think before we print. In short, print when you have a good reason to print. Printing more selectively might also make us think more about the quality of those prints.

Anyway, hard copy is not dead; in fact, it's diversified. However, equivalents to the traditional photographic print remain central. Printing your photos at home used to be the preserve of a relatively small band of darkroom enthusiasts. Now it's far more accessible. The main options for home printing are inkjet and dye-sublimation printers. Colour laser printers that can produce photo-quality output are relatively expensive to buy but cheap to run. They can make sense for high volumes, but not for the enthusiast.

INKJET PRINTING

Entry-level inkjet printers are almost ridiculously cheap now. The cynics say that companies are virtually giving their printers away on the basis that they'll make their profit on the sale of consumables (ink and paper).

PRINTER CALIBRATION

Translating a mosaic of RGB pixels on a screen into dots of CMYK ink on paper is a complex process. One is seen by transmitted light, the other by reflected light. The gamut of the screen will never match the gamut of the print. Still, within these ultimate limitations, there are ways to ensure that the printed image matches the screen image as closely as possible. The key to this is printer calibration.

There's little point in attempting to calibrate the printer unless the monitor is calibrated first (see p62). Unfortunately, printer calibration can get even more complex. You probably only use one monitor, but you may use different brands of ink and – even more likely – different brands and/or grades of paper. For instance, I regularly use everyday paper for printing letters, invoices

POINT OF VIEW

I side with the cynics on the issue of consumables, and for this very reason I buy my ink and paper from third-party sources, not from the printer manufacturer.

PRINT RESOLUTION

'ou may well wonder why you need a printer hat operates at some outrageous resolution like 440 or 2880dpi when everyone tells you to repare your images at 300dpi.

The easy way to understand this is by ecognizing that the 'dots' in the printer esolution are not the same as the 'dots' in the mage resolution. In fact, strictly speaking we houldn't use dpi to describe the image at all; ve should use ppi – pixels per inch – instead. Remember, each pixel in the image is defined by evels of red, blue and green, and even in an 8-bit mage (which is nearly always what gets printed) here are 16.7 million possible combinations. o replicate this the printer needs to lay down ninute dots of cyan, magenta, yellow and black nk, and it's immediately obvious that it would need at least four ink dots for each image pixel. However, because the grid of image pixels isn't necessarily scaled exactly in correspondence with the grid of ink dots, results are even better if he printer has an even finer grid.

Three hundred dpi is a common standard in commercial printing for books, magazines and so on, but there's no self-evident reason why it should be enforced across the board for inkje printing as well. There's a superficially convincin argument that we might get marginally bette quality by printing at 288dpi, as this divide exactly into the 1440 or 2880dpi output of man inkjets. In practice there's no real evidence tha we can see any difference. But then in practic few of us can readily distinguish between print made at 240dpi and 300dpi.

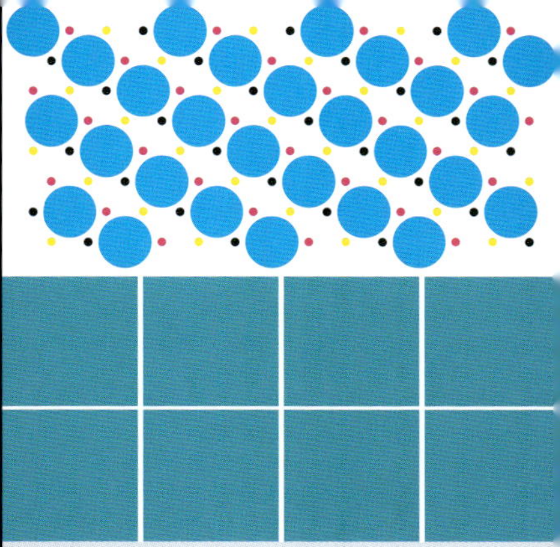

Pixels and ink dots
Diagram showing schematically how dots of ink (top) might represent a few image pixels (bottom).

MAXIMUM PRINT SIZES FROM TYPICAL DSLR IMAGES, WITHOUT INTERPOLATION, AT DIFFERENT RESOLUTIONS

	Pixel dimensions	Print at 240 dpi	Print at 288 dpi	Print at 300 dpi	
Nikon D70 (6Mp)	3008 x 2000	12.5 x 8.3 31.8 x 21.2	10.4 x 6.9 26.5 x 17.6	10.0 x 6.7 25.5 x 16.9	inches cm
Nikon D700 (12Mp)	4256 x 2832	17.7 x 11.8 45 x 30	14.8 x 9.8 37.5 x 25	14.2 x 9.4 36 x 24	inches cm

and so on; a superior coated paper for 'contact sheets' (clients use these for reference when I send images on disk); and heavyweight photo paper for fine prints. I'm not concerned about printing photos on the basic paper, but want to ensure that results are as good as possible on both the 'contact' paper and the 'fine print' paper. Some photographers who do a lot of printing may want to use several different paper types for fine prints – matt or gloss, smooth or textured, for example. Because each paper absorbs ink slightly differently, a separate printer profile is required for each.

As printers, even the same model, also vary, anyone seeking the ultimate quality will need to print off a standardized test image and measure the results with a colorimeter (or, realistically, have it done by a profiling service). However, for most users, this is slightly excessive as ready-made (or 'canned') profiles are usually available. If you confine yourself to the printer manufacturer's own inks and papers, canned profiles should already be on your system (having been loaded from the printer installation CD). Profiles for third-party papers should be available from the maker's website, along with instructions for installing them on your system.

These all assume you're using the printer manufacturer's own inks. Independent ink suppliers are less good at offering canned profiles, but this may be less of a problem, as ink behaviour does not vary as widely as papers do.

To benefit from printer profiling, there's one further step – you need to turn off colour management by the printer. This may sound

Printer dialog in Photoshop Elements 6
There's a long list of colour profiles to choose from, including profiles for monitors, scanners, and other printers, which are irrelevant for this task.

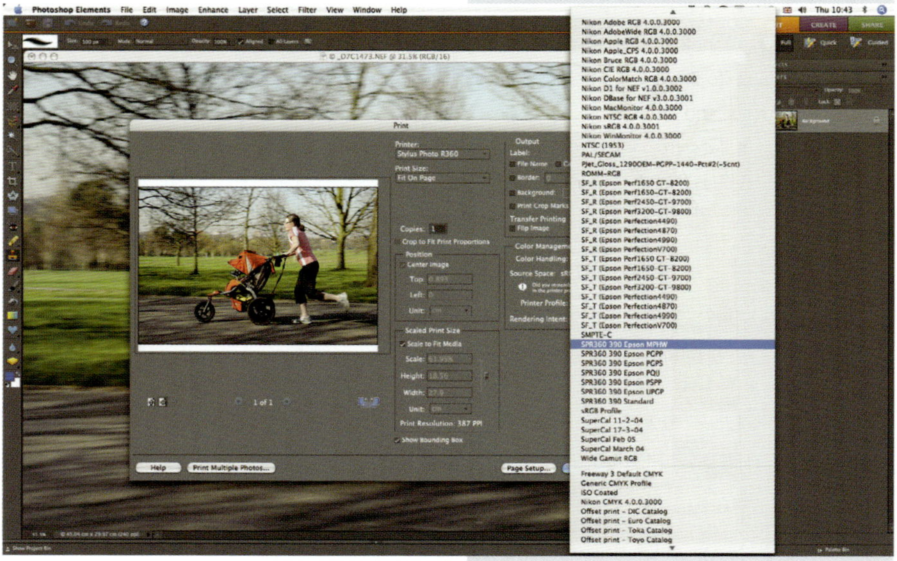

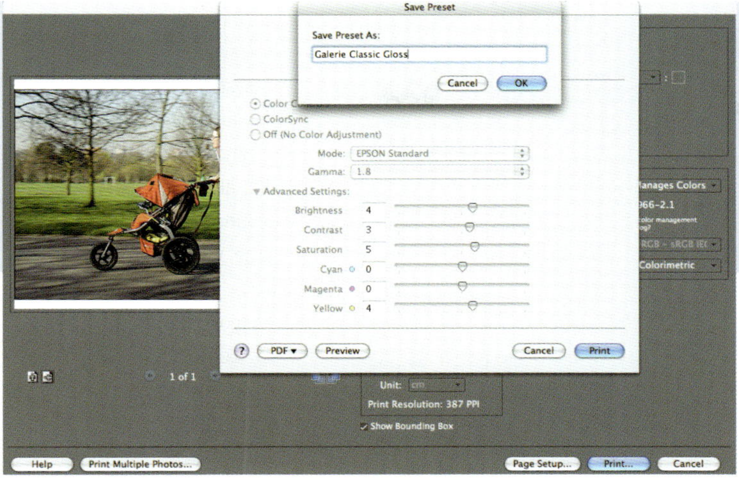

Dialog from an Epson printer Adjusted settings can be saved as a preset.

perverse, but it actually allows your imaging software (e.g. Photoshop) to do the colour management. More basic imaging apps don't offer this level of colour management and require a different approach (see Keeping it simple, below).

If there's one conclusion to be drawn from all this, it must be to find what works and stick with it. Chopping and changing papers and inks promises endless trouble and will almost certainly prove to be a false economy.

Keeping it simple

The use of printer profiles in printing is limited to the more advanced imaging apps. Photoshop and Photoshop Elements has it, of course. iPhoto doesn't, instead relying on the Mac's built-in colour management software, ColorSync, and using a limited repertoire of canned profiles. This can give good results with standard ink/paper combinations, but makes no provision for using different types of paper. If you're going to print from apps such as Picasa or iPhoto, it makes even more sense to stick with a small repertoire of paper types. If initial results are disappointing, don't mess with the colour or brightness of the image itself but instead investigate adjustments that should be available in the printer's own software; these vary widely between printers. When a good result is achieved, save those settings as a preset.

POINT OF VIEW

Three hundred dpi has become a bit of a 'magic number'. I still regularly ask people (some of whom should know better) what size images they want and get the answer, '300dpi'. But 300dpi is a measure of resolution only, not size. One of these days I'll succumb to temptation and send postage-stamp sized images – 'but they're 300dpi'.

DYE-SUBLIMATION PRINTERS

Dye-sublimation technology can produce prints with a look and feel similar to traditional photographic prints and is now found in numerous home printers claiming to offer 'lab-quality' output, usually direct from the memory card (though most can also be connected to a computer). These are clearly aimed more at the compact camera user than the DSLR devotee, and most are limited to 6x4in (15x10cm) prints; a few stretch to 7x5in (18x12cm). These are not money-saving devices, being cheap to buy but relatively expensive to run; some brands of ink cartridge can be refilled at places like Cartridge World, reducing the environmental cost, too. It's cheaper – often much cheaper – to get prints produced on the high street or by an online supplier. (In the UK, a *Which?* report found that the cheapest price per print was 17p; the first online source I looked at (Jessops) offered prints of the same size for 5p). These devices are also less versatile than inkjet printers – you can't print letters or posters, for example.

Don't even think about printer calibration with any of these devices, but make sure you shoot in sRGB colour space.

COMMERCIAL PRINTING

As the above suggests, commercial printing can often be cheaper than doing it yourself and frequently produces equal or better quality. Services range from cheap and cheerful automated booths in high street photo stores and supermarkets, right up to professional labs using fully colour-managed workflows and even personal supervision of your prints. Such labs often supply printer profiles to help match your images to their output; in Photoshop you can 'soft proof' the image by matching screen colours as closely as possible to the printer output.

The biggest growth has been in online ordering. The purchase of a camera or of imaging software usually brings an invitation to sign up for a site or 'community' which includes prints and other physical output among its services. There are lots of independent services too, probably the best-known worldwide being Snapfish (www3.snapfish.com).

You can speed up the process of ordering prints from a photo booth using Digital Print Order Format. This is a widely supported standard that allows images to be selected for printing directly from the camera. A menu item called something like Print set (DPOF) allows you to choose images and specify the number of copies, size, borders and so on. It does not work with RAW images but many DSLRs now allow JPEG copies to be created from images originally shot as RAW. DPOF also works with home dye-sub and many inkjet printers.

Connecting the camera direct to a printer is facilitated by PictBridge, an industry standard which is supported by current DSLRs and a wide range of printers.

Printing your shots straight from the camera or card has all the appeal of instant gratification and is certainly very tempting when away from base – especially, perhaps, if you have no way of viewing images except the camera's own screen – but there are too many variables for comfort if you're at all concerned about quality. I'd certainly want to print one or two test shots before committing to a larger order.

OTHER OUTPUT

The possibilities for hard-copy output from your images are not limited to conventional prints on paper. High street and online outlets offer greetings cards, calendars, mouse mats, table mats, mugs, cushions, T-shirts and lots more.

Photo books

There's still something special about a well-printed photo book, and it's now possible to get books produced in any quantity you want, right down to a single copy. Most of the online photo-printing services like Snapfish and PhotoBox offer this option. iPhoto and Aperture allow books to be created and ordered directly within the application, and the quality of the Apple photo-books has been generally commended. Lulu (www.lulu.com) allows users not only to print their own books but to offer them for sale, with copies being printed on demand. Blurb (www.blurb.com) specializes in photo-books, with US prices starting at $12.95 for a 40-page 7x7in (18x18cm) softcover. The quality of some of these products now is such that professional photographers are starting to use them as an alternative to the traditional portfolio.

WARNING

High-street print kiosks and other consumer-oriented print outlets will be set up to work with photos in sRGB colour space. If your DSLR is set to use Adobe RGB, results may be disappointing.

Creating books
Books an be compiled and ordered directly from iPhoto.

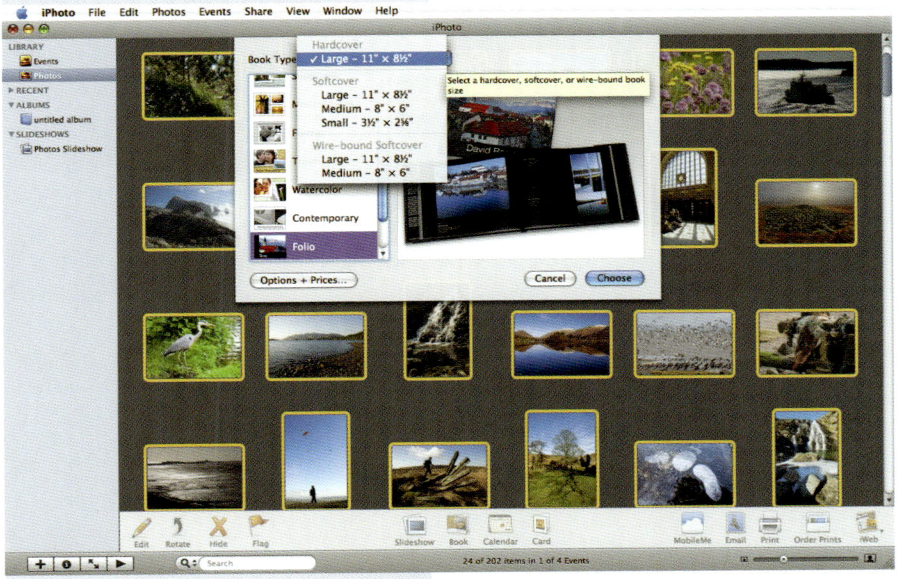

Sharing in the virtual world

As I mentioned at the start of this chapter, digital images are generally first seen on screen. Many images can have a lasting presence without ever taking hard-copy form, from your own computer to a TV screen, and of course the Worldwide Web.

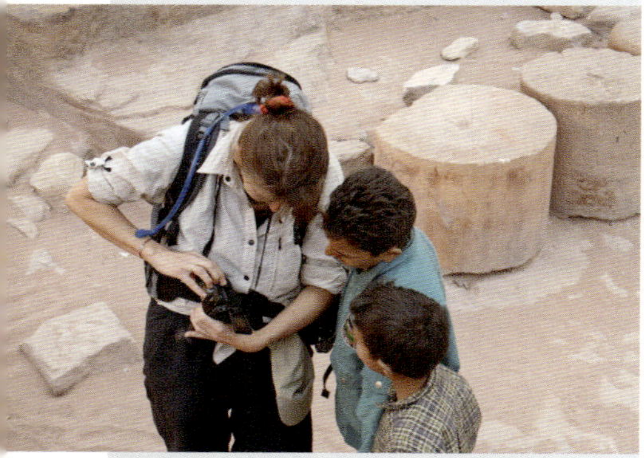

Visitor with local boys, Petra, Jordan
Though limited by its small size, the camera screen allows instant sharing, which often brings people together.
Nikon D2x, focal length 50mm, ISO 100, 1/25sec at f/7.1

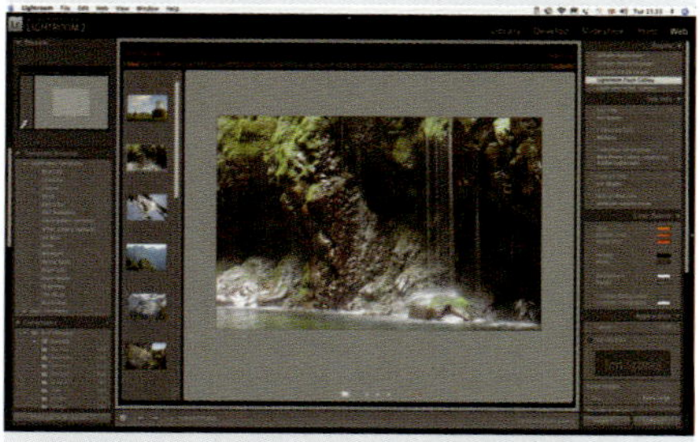

Building a web gallery direct from Lightroom
This needs to be loaded to a pre-existing internet account.

IMAGES ON THE WEB

The Internet allows images to be distributed in many ways, from the familiar email attachment to a full-blown website. Most imaging apps now have features enabling you to quickly save photos in the best format for web use; in iPhoto, for example, you can attach a photo to an email with two mouse clicks.

Sharing websites

There are now many sites and online communities which allow users to post their own photos, view other people's, comment on them and share experience and ideas. The best-known example is undoubtedly Flickr (www.flickr.com). Some apps, notably iPhoto, let you upload photos directly to a Flickr account. There are smaller and more defined communities associated with most of the main photo magazines, with the main camera brands (e.g. my Picturetown for Nikon users), and with many software providers. A fairly new example here is www.photoshop.com.

Personal web galleries

Creating web galleries has never been easier. Almost all imaging software now has tools to turn a selected set of images into a gallery ready for upload in a few minutes. There's no longer

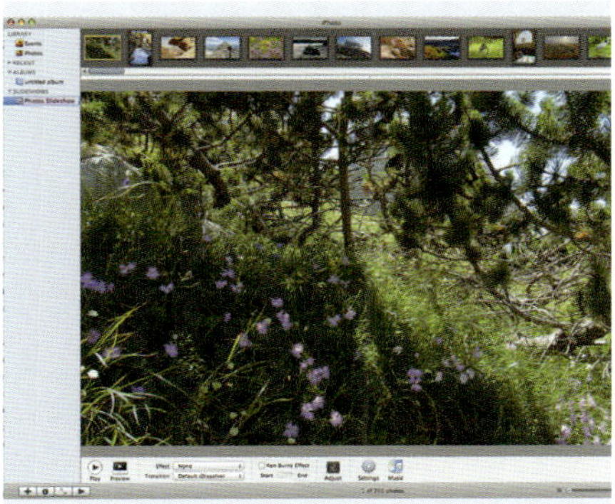

Setting up a slideshow in iPhoto

any need for most of us to be bothered with HTML coding or even to use separate website-building software. If you don't already have a domain name and server space, some apps even include some free space.

Other options

The possibilities continue to expand. Most imaging apps make it easy to create slideshows complete with slick transitions, titles, and soundtrack. As usual, iPhoto takes the palm for ease of use; Lightroom also has a good slideshow module. As well as viewing on your own computer, slideshows can be burned to a CD or DVD for export, viewed on a TV set (they can look stunning on an HDTV), and so on.

Another option is the digital photo frame, which displays the photo or photos on a memory card or, in some cases, via a wireless connection. Simply loading a memory card straight from the camera has obvious pitfalls; although in-camera editing and processing can surmount these, it is better to create a set of images specifically for the purpose.

PROTECTING YOUR RIGHTS

Sharing and communities are great things but some people take unfair advantage. There are many examples of people stealing images and passing them off as their own and/or using them for commercial gain. Creators, including photographers, should have their work acknowledged and respected. If it has commercial value, the creator should benefit. Why should someone else make a profit from your images instead of you?

Your images are your creation and this is legally recognized by copyright law. In the UK and most other countries, copyright exists automatically in every photograph you make. You don't have to register it, and you don't have to be a professional photographer. In some countries, like the USA, copyright registration may give additional protection.

If you make a free and informed choice to give your work away, licensing schemes such as Creative Commons (http://creativecommons.org) help you to set limits on what can be done with it.

Here are a few suggestions for protecting yourself against the worst of the ripoffs:

- Don't post photos to community/sharing sites without checking the terms and conditions.
- Always consider watermarking images that are going to be seen on the Web.
- Don't upload full-size images. If it's 800 pixels wide it can still be stolen for use elsewhere on the Web but isn't much use in print.
- Don't enter photo competitions that require you to assign copyright.
- Don't enter photo competitions that give the organizers free use of all entries, not just the winners.

Glossary

Accessory shoe
See Hotshoe.

Aperture
The lens opening, which admits light. Relative aperture sizes are expressed in f-numbers (*see* f-number).

Artefact
Visible flaws in the image, arising from incorrect processing of sensor data.

Bracketing
Taking a series of shots in which just one parameter (e.g. exposure) is varied.

Buffer
Onboard memory that holds images until they can be written to the memory card.

Burst
A number of frames shot in quick succession; the maximum burst size is limited by buffer capacity.

CCD (Charge-Coupled Device)
A common type of digital image sensor.

Clipping
Absence of detail in highlight and/or shadow areas of the image, leaving them as blank white or black.

CMOS (Complementary Metal Oxide Semiconductor)
A common type of digital image sensor.

Colour temperature
The colour of light, expressed in degrees Kelvin (K).

CPU (Central Processing Unit)
Onboard computer that controls the camera – also found in many lenses.

Crop factor
See Focal-length multiplication factor.

dpi (dots per inch)
A measure of resolution, strictly applicable only to printers (*see* pp1).

Dynamic range
The range of brightness from shadows to highlights within which the camera can record detail.

Exposure
Used in several senses but principally refers to the amount of light hitting the image sensor, and to systems of measuring this. *See also* Overexposure, Underexposure.

Ev (Exposure value)
A unit of exposure. One Ev is equivalent to one 'stop' in traditional photographic parlance.

f-number
Lens aperture expressed as a fraction of focal length; f/2 is a wide aperture and f/16 is narrow.

Fast (lens)
Lens with a wide maximum aperture, e.g. f/1.8.

Fill-in flash
Flash used alongside daylight, to brighten shadow areas.

Filter
A piece of glass or plastic placed in front of, within or behind the lens to modify light.

FireWire
A data transfer standard, used to connect to a computer.

Firmware
Software that controls the camera: upgrades can be transferred to the camera via memory card.

Focal-length multiplication factor
Sensors smaller than a frame of 35mm film multiply the effective focal length of all lenses.

fps (frames per second)
The number of photographs that can be taken in a second.

Highlights
The brightest areas of the scene and/or image.

Histogram
Graph representing the distribution of tones in an image, from pure black to pure white.

ISO (International Standards Organization)
The sensitivity of digital sensors is quoted as ISO-equivalent.

JPEG (Joint Photographic Experts Group)
A compressed image file standard.

LCD
Liquid crystal display; flat screen like a DSLR's rear monitor.

Macro
Describes close focusing ability of a lens. A true macro lens has a reproduction ratio of 1:1 or better.

Megapixel
One million pixels.

Memory card
A removable storage device.

Noise
Image interference seen as random variations in pixel brightness and/or colour.

Overexposure
When too much light reaches the sensor, resulting in a too bright image, often with clipped highlights.

Pixel (Picture element)
Individual coloured dots making up a digital image. One million pixels = one megapixel.

ppi (pixels per inch)
A measure of image resolution.

Raw
Image file format that records sensor data as is, for subsequent processing on computer.

Reproduction ratio
The ratio between the real size of an object and the size of its image on the sensor.

Resolution
Amount of detail recorded for a given dimension, e.g. 300ppi is a measure of image resolution.

RGB (Red Green Blue)
Digital cameras record colour in terms of brightness levels of the three primary colours.

Sensor
The light-sensitive chip at the heart of every digital camera.

Shutter
The mechanism which opens and closes to expose the sensor to light.

Speedlight/Speedlite
A flashgun.

Spotmetering
A metering method which measures light reflected by a small portion of the scene.

Telephoto lens
A lens with a long focal length and narrow angle of view.

TIFF (Tagged Image File Format)
A file format supported by virtually all image-editing applications.

Underexposure
When insufficient light reaches the sensor, resulting in a too dark image, often with clipped shadows.

USB (Universal Serial Bus)
A data transfer standard, used to connect to a computer.

Viewfinder
An optical system used for framing the image; on a DSLR camera it shows the view through the lens.

White balance
A function allowing for different colour temperatures so that images may be recorded with correct colour balance.

Wideangle lens
A lens with a short focal length and a wide angle of view.

Zoom
A lens with variable focal length that gives a range of viewing angles. Optical zoom describes the genuine zoom ability of a lens; digital zoom is the cropping of an image to simulate the same result.

DSLR features and terminology

	Nikon	Canon	Fujifilm	Olympus	Panasonic	Pentax	Samsung	Sigma	Sony
Lens mount	Nikon F	Canon EF/EF-S	Nikon F	Four Thirds	Micro Four Thirds	Pentax KA	Pentax KA	Sigma SA	Sony
RAW file designation	.NEF	.CR2	.RAF	.ORF	RAW	.PEF/.DNG	.DNG	RAW	.ARW
Metering pattern (plus centreweighted and spot)	Matrix	Evaluative	Matrix	Multi-pattern	Intelligent Multiple	Multi-segment	Multi	Evaluative	Multi-segment
Exposure mode groups	Exposure Modes Scene Modes	Creative Zone Basic Zone	Exposure Modes	Shooting Modes Scene Modes	Exposure Modes Scene Modes	Exposure Modes Picture Modes, Scene Modes	Exposure Modes User Mode	Exposure Modes	Exposure Modes Scene Selection
Menu headings (typical: may vary between models from same maker)	Playback Setup Shooting Custom Settings Retouch My Menu/ Recent Settings	Shooting Playback Setup Custom Functions My Menu	Shooting Setup Playback	Record Play Custom Menu	Record Custom Menu Setup My Menu Playback	Record Playback Setup Custom Functions	Capture Custom Setup Playback	Record Playback Setup Custom Functions	Record Custom Play Setup
Tonal controls	Active D-Lighting	Highlight Tone Priority	Expanded Dynamic Range	Shadow Adjustment Technology		Dynamic Range Enlargement	Picture Wizard		D-range Optimizer
Picture controls	Picture Controls	Picture Styles	Film Simulation Modes	Picture Mode, Art Filter	Film Mode	Custom Image Function, Digital Filter	Image Presets	Picture Effects Mode	Creative Styles/ Creative Mode
Vibration reduction	Vibration Reduction (in lens)	Image Stabilization (in lens)	Vibration Reduction (in lens)	Image Stabilization (in body)	(in body)	Shake Reduction (in body)	Optical Anti-Shake (in body)		Super Steady Shot (In body)

Useful websites

CAMERA MAKERS

Canon
www.canon.co.uk
www.canon.com

Fujifilm
www.fujifilm.co.uk/consumer/digital
www.fujifilm.com

Nikon
www.nikon.co.uk
www.nikon.com
www.nikonusa.com

Olympus
www.olympus.co.uk/cameras
www.olympusamerica.com

Panasonic
www.panasonic.net/avc/lumix

Pentax
www.pentaximaging.com/slr

Samsung
www.samsungcamera.co.uk
www.samsungcamera.com

Sigma
www.sigma-sd14.com

Sony
www.sony.co.uk/hub/dslr
www.sony.com

LENSES AND ACCESSORIES

Aquapac waterproof cases
www.aquapac.net

Sigma
Independent lenses and flash units
www.sigma-imaging-uk.com
www.sigmaphoto.com

Tamron
www.tamron.com/lenses

Tokina
www.tokinalens.com

SOFTWARE

(See camera-makers' sites for own-brand software.)

Adobe: Photoshop, Photoshop Elements, Lightroom
www.adobe.com

Apple: Aperture and iPhoto
www.apple.com

Bibble Labs: Bibble Pro
http://bibblelabs.com

DXO: DXO Optics Pro
www.dxo.com

Extensis: Portfolio
www.extensis.com

Google: Picasa
www.picasa.google.co.uk
www.picasa.google.com

Microsoft: Expression Media
www.microsoft.com/expression

Phase One: Capture One 4/Pro
www.phaseone.com/4

Light Crafts: LightZone
www.lightcrafts.com

GENERAL SITES

Digital Photography Review
Independent news and reviews.
www.dpreview.com

DXO Mark
RAW image quality guide.
www.dxomark.com

Cambridge in Colour
Helpful tutorials.
www.cambridgeincolour.com

Jon Sparks
Landscape and outdoor pursuits photography.
www.jon-sparks.co.uk

Photographers' Institute Press
A wide range of photography books, *Black & White Photography* magazine, *Outdoor Photography* magazine.
www.pipress.com

Index

Captions to photographs are indicated by page numbers in **bold**.

Contact us for a complete catalogue, or visit our website:

Ammonite Press, Castle Place, 166 High Street, Lewes,
East Sussex, BN7 1XU, United Kingdom
Tel: 01273 488005 Fax: 01273 402866
www.ae-publications.com